Best wishes *[signature]*

A History of
Caludon Castle

THE LORDS OF THE MANOR OF CALUDON

George Demidowicz

Stephen Johnson

The coat of arms of John Edward Clarke OBE including the motto
'CALUDON MEUS INSTINCTUS' – Caludon My Inspiration

A History of
Caludon Castle

THE LORDS OF THE MANOR OF CALUDON

Publisher
John Edward Clarke OBE

Author and Editor
George Demidowicz

Co-author
Stephen Johnson

Published by Century Public Relations

2013

Published by
CENTURY PUBLIC RELATIONS
Coventry, United Kingdom

© John Edward Clarke OBE, 2013

ISBN 978-0-992-78540-6

Designed by Viccari Wheele Ltd
Printed by Printondemand-Worldwide.com, United Kingdom

Contents

List of Figures with credits, vii

Dedication, ix

Foreword, xi

Acknowledgements, xiii

Introduction, 1

Caludon Castle Poem, 6-7

CHAPTER 1
*The Origins of Caludon Castle and Manor of Caludon
~ the Earls of Chester and the Segraves c.1200-1359*..........*9*

CHAPTER 2
Caludon and the Mowbrays 1359 - c.1494........................*35*

CHAPTER 3
The Berkeleys at Caludon c.1494-1631............................*59*

CHAPTER 4
Life at Caludon with the Berkeleys 1592-1605..................*95*

CHAPTER 5
*The Morgan and Preston Lordships and
their Tenants 1631-1685*...*109*

CHAPTER 6
The Clifford Lordship and their Tenants 1685-1822........*131*

CHAPTER 7
From Manor to Municipal Park 1822-2013.....................*153*

CHAPTER 8
Caludon Castle ~ the Buildings..*189*

APPENDIX
Caludon and the Legend of St George.............................*205*

Bibliography..*207*

Index..*212*

List of Figures

Frontispiece: The coat of arms of John Edward Clarke OBE
Foreword: The Lord Clifford of Chudleigh

Fig 1   Photo of the ruins from the east side of the
         moat 2013 (GD)..2
Fig 2   A plan of Caludon with neighbouring
         ancient parishes (GD) 5
Fig 3   Pen and ink and watercolour of the castle
         ruins by Robert Overy 1982.........................8
Fig 4   A location plan of Caludon:
         Caludon in Coventry and the park
         in its surrounding streets (GD)...................11
Fig 5   Pedigree of the Earls of Chester (GD) 12
Fig 6   Contour plan of Caludon area with present streets
         overlaid (GD)..13
Fig 7   Segrave coat of arms....................................14
Fig 8   Segrave pedigree (GD) 15
Fig 9   Plan of the early medieval landscape
         of Caludon (GD)...17
Fig 10   Photo of the upper moat in
         Caludon Park 2013 (GD).............................18
Fig 11   Photo from the south end of the park over the
         upper and lower moats 2013 (GD)...............19
Fig 12   Seal of John de Segrave 1300-1301 26
Fig 13   Caludon Castle licence to crenellate 1305 (UHA)......27
Fig 14   Caludon Castle licence to crenellate
         with seal 1305 (UHA)..................................27
Fig 15   Photo looking from the dam across the former pool
         during flooding 2007 (JC) 29
Fig 16   Mowbray coat of arms..................................35
Fig 17   Mowbray pedigree (GD) 36
Fig 18   The Caludon feodary or survey 1353 (BL)................38
Fig 19   Map of Caludon Park and demesne
         showing field names (GD)...........................43
Fig 20   Photo of the Mowbray and Bolingbroke tournament
         plaque at Gosford Green (MW) 46
Fig 21   The Mowbray and Bolingbroke tournament
         at Gosford Green 48
Fig 22   Portrait of John Mowbray 2nd Duke of Norfolk
         (1392-1432)..50
Fig 23   Berkeley coat of arms 59
Fig 24   Berkeley pedigree (GD) 60-61
Fig 25   North east view of Berkeley Castle published by
         Samuel Lysons, May 1 1802, from A Collection of
         Gloucestershire Antiquities 68
Fig 26   Bird's eye view of Caludon Castle from south east
         c.1550-1570 by Pete Urmston 70

Fig 27   Seal of Lord Henry Berkeley 73
Fig 28   Whitefriars monastery 2011 (GD) 77
Fig 29   Bird's eye view of Caludon Castle from the
         north-west c.1550-1570 by Pete Urmston 78
Fig 30   Bird's eye view of Caludon Castle from the
         north east c.1550-1570 by Pete Urmston...................79
Fig 31   Title page of A Midsummer's Night Dream by
         William Shakespeare from the first quarto 1600 80
Fig 32   Photo of location of destroyed Berkeley tomb
         chests in the Drapers' Chapel, old Coventry
         Cathedral 2013 (GD) 81
Fig 33   Engraving by Wenceslaus Hollar of Berkeley
         tomb chests in St Michael's church, now old
         Coventry Cathedral 1656.............................82
Fig 34   Photo of the temporarily flooded former pool
         looking towards the ruins 2007 (JC) 84
Fig 35   Photo of the Berkeley monument in Berkeley
         church 2011 (GH) 87
Fig 36   Photo of the Berkeley monument –
         close up of recumbent figures of Henry and
         Katherine 2011 (GH) 89
Fig 37   Photo of inscription tablet to the Berkeley
         monument 2011 (GH)..................................90
Fig 38   Extract from Berkeley accounts of Caludon Castle
         Jan 1594/5 (BCA)..99
Fig 39   A contemporary engraving of musicians from the
         title page of Giardino Novo belissimo... Primo libro,
         published in 1605.......................................104
Fig 40   Photo of the Lachrimae Consort playing in
         Walsgrave church 2007 (JC)......................105
Fig 41   Extract from Berkeley accounts of Caludon Castle
         showing payment to John Dowland and his Consort
         Jan 1598/9 (BCA)......................................106
Fig 42   Morgan coat of arms...................................109
Fig 43   Morgan-Preston pedigree (GD) 110
Fig 44   Preston coat of arms...................................112
Fig 45   1666 deed with signatures of Richard Hayward and
         Timothy Gibbard (UHA) 117
Fig 46   Gibbard pedigree (GD)...............................119
Fig 47   Inventory of Timothy Gibbard 1670 (TNA).............121
Fig 48   Survey of Caludon 1668 (WRO) 123
Fig 49   Survey of Caludon, after 1670 (UHA) 124-25
Fig 50   Hayward pedigree (GD) 127
Fig 51   Clifford coat of arms...................................131

Fig 52   Clifford pedigree (GD) 132

Fig 53   Portrait of Hugh 2nd Lord Clifford
          (1663-1730) (UHA) 133

Fig 54   Portrait of Anne 2nd Lady Clifford
          (c.1669-1734) (UHA) 133

Fig 55   Survey of Caludon 1731 (CA& LS) 134

Fig 56   Goddard pedigree (GD) 135

Fig 57   Extract from a land tax roll for Caludon
          1748 (UHA) 137

Fig 58   Extract from Henry Beighton's map of
          Knightlow Hundred 1730 138

Fig 59   Photo of the site of Caludon Castle Farmhouse
          2013 (GD)...138

Fig 60   Photo of the site of Caludon Castle farm
          buildings (GD)...139

Fig 61   Watercolour of north side of castle ruin
          c.1800 (A&H BCL) 140

Fig 62   Watercolour of south side of castle ruin
          c.1800 (A&H BCL) 141

Fig 63   Engraving of south side of castle ruin published by
          George Eld c.1820? (BL).......................................142

Fig 64   Portrait of Charles 6th Lord Clifford
          (1759-1831)(UHA)..142

Fig 65   Advertisement for sale of Caludon estate,
          Coventry Mercury, 7 Nov 1814 (CA & LS)..............144

Fig 66   Extract from sale particulars relating to Caludon
          (Callowden) Farm 1815 (UHA)..............................145

Fig 67   Title page from the sale particulars for the
          Caludon estate 1815 (UHA) 146

Fig 68   Extract from a plan of Caludon estate,
          sale particulars 1815 (UHA) 147

Fig 69   Detail from sale particulars plan showing
          Caludon Farm and moat 1815 (UHA) 147

Fig 70   Summary document for the sale of the
          Caludon estate 1822 (UHA) 148

Fig 71   Brown and Garrard pedigree (GD) 149

Fig 72   Plan of the Caludon estate in the second quarter
          of the 19th century showing the tripartite division
          after the 1822 sale (GD)..153

Fig 73   Deed of sale of Caludon manor 1846 (WRO)..........156

Fig 74   Extract from OS 1:2500 map 1887 158

Fig 75   Detail from OS 1:2500 map 1887 showing
          garden on moat 159

Fig 76   Engraving of south side of ruined wall,
          published by Elizabeth Hodges 1895......................161

Fig 77   Earliest photo of Caludon Castle ruins, c.1880-1890?
          Lowe's newspapers cuttings (CA) 162

Fig 78   Pen and ink drawing of Caludon Castle ruins and farm
          in background by SJB 1897 (source unknown, initials
          unidentified) 163

Fig 79   Extract from OS 1:2500 map 1906 164

Fig 80   Photo of site of Caludon Lodge 2013 (GH)............165

Fig 81   Photo of Caludon Cottages 2013 (GH)....................166

Fig 82   Photo of north side of ruined wall 1936
          (source unknown) 167

Fig 83   Postcard of ruins from north side showing boundary
          hedge and crenellated garden wall, 1930s?..............167

Fig 84   Extract from OS 6-inch map 1925 168

Fig 85   Extract from OS 1:2500 map 1913 170

Fig 86   Extract from OS 1:2500 map 1925 171

Fig 87   Extract from OS 1:2500 map 1938 172

Fig 88   Photograph of garden and south side of ruined
          wall 1930 (CA) 175

Fig 89   Vertical photo 15 Jan 1946 (NMR).........................176

Fig 90   Vertical photo 10 May 1946 (NMR)........................177

Fig 91   Photo of boys on bikes in front of the castle ruins
          1950s (courtesy of Dr Robert Nash) 179

Fig 92   Sketch Plan of Caludon Farm by Brian D Fox, 1981
          (private collection)..180

Fig 93   Photo of 'Cromwell's Barn' (JC) 181

Fig 94   Photo of the ruined wall and Caludon Farm
          (source unknown) 181

Fig 95   Photo of Caludon School 2013 (GH)......................182

Fig 96   Pen and ink of Caludon Castle ruins c.1950s
          (CA & LS) 183

Fig 97   Photo of the dam from pool bed 2013 (GH) 183

Fig 98   Oblique aerial photo of Caludon Castle
          and park 2001 (NMR)..184

Fig 99   Photo of Caludon Castle plaque in the park (2013) ..185

Fig 100   Photo of the new park gates 2013 (GH)...................185

Fig 101   Photo of the ruined wall from south 2013 (GD) 190

Fig 102   Photo of the ruined wall from north 2011 (JC) 191

Fig 103   Photo of Caludon moat 2013 (GD)..........................192

Fig 104   Drawing of the north elevation of ruined wall (MF) ..193

Fig 105   Drawing of the south elevation of ruined wall (MF)..194

Fig 106   Plan of resistivity survey 1986 (MF) 195

Fig 107   Plan of resistivity survey by Northamptonshire
          Archaeology 2008 196

Fig 108   Six-phase plan of the development of Caludon (GD)..199

Fig 109   Photo of Caludon Farmhouse from north (n.d.)
          (source unknown) 202

Fig 110   St George and the Dragon as depicted on the new
          interpretation board 206

Figures courtesy of:

A&H BCL ...Archives and Heritage, Birmingham Central Library

BL ....British Library

CA& LS ......Coventry Archives and Local Studies, now the
                History Centre at the Herbert

Cov CC........Coventry City Council

GD...............George Demidowicz

GH ....Gary Haigh

JC ....John Clarke

MF..............Myk Flitcroft

MW ....Martin Whelan

NMR ....National Monuments Record, Swindon

TNA ....The National Archives, Kew

WRO ....Warwick County Record Office

UHA............Ugbrooke House, Devon

Dedication

To my beloved parents Jack and Jean.

To my dear wife Celeste and children Samantha, Charlotte and James.
To my brother Jim.

*All of whom have encouraged and supported me to bring the 800 year old history of
Caludon to life, for the interest and enjoyment of others for many years to come.*

Caludon Meus Instinctus.
Caludon My Inspiration

Foreword

The Lord Clifford of Chudleigh

Wandering through the mezzanine of Ugbrooke House, the residence known as the current 'Family Seat', I travel towards the muniment room through areas full of fascinating maps, plans, of places abroad and in Great Britain, gathered together by many of my ancestors both at times of conflict and periods of construction. Passing through another door I see racked 'pipes' (as containers of legal documents once were called) the Stewart Seals upon letters patent granted to the First Lord Clifford of the present line, and above these parchments of legal entitlement the sacred boxes containing the Family Tree.

It is incredulous to consider the history of each person, each leaf or route line of that increasingly spindly tree where the branches of the family have stretched to so many parts of the world, let alone to so many counties within this island of Great Britain.

Looking at this 'tree' I recognise that, like my ancestors, it is my responsibility to ensure that the three generations created since it was last presented by the College of Arms must be added for posterity, for the sake of history affixed by this 'tree', with ever expanding 'branches' and proud 'head' of Thomas Clifford, Lord Treasurer to Charles II and the initial 'C' of his Cabal Ministry. His successor in title, Hugh, had married Anne Preston, who brought Caludon and other Warwickshire estates with her as part of the marriage settlement. Caludon had tumbled from family to family, throughout the centuries; from Segrave to Mowbray, from that name to Berkeley, then Morgan, Preston, and to my own family which cosseted the estate for some 200 years before death duties and distance induced its sale in the nineteenth century.

And where is all this detail? Where is some of the knowledge to be found in this book? In the final room in the mezzanine; the muniment room. Here one is immersed in letters of not just persona, family significance, but also of national importance and of fascination to such experienced historians as George Demidowicz and Stephen Johnson who have helped research and write this book with its dedicated Publisher John Edward Clarke OBE.

Just as it is the responsibility of the guardian of such archives to share such knowledge, for knowledge is the portent of nobility, it gives me great pleasure to know that John Clarke has taken on the mantle as an avid historian to not only preserve and protect but also to celebrate the Lordship of the Manor of Caludon investing his enthusiasm for local history for the heritage of this part of the Midlands to present and preserve, for future generations the history of Caludon, formerly in Warwickshire, but now in Coventry.

Whilst John Clarke and his family act as loyal custodians of the historical legacy that has embraced the Manor of Caludon for more than 800 years, no politician will be able to eradicate that sense, that value of heritage, which ensures the everlasting existence of British Spirit.

The Lord Clifford of Chudleigh
Ugbrooke Park

Acknowledgements

I am eternally grateful to a number of loyal and passionate 'Caludonians' without whom this book would not have been possible. I am forever in debt to the publication's two researchers and writers George Demidowicz and Stephen Johnson, whose complementary skills have helped me to create the first ever official history of Caludon Castle and its Manor. George is a highly experienced and respected historian of national repute with a number of books and academic papers to his name and Stephen is an acknowledged expert in manorial history of many years experience.

The Lord Clifford of Chudleigh, whose family were once owners of the Lordship of Caludon and its Manor, has been extremely supportive allowing access to his archives in the muniments room at Ugbrooke Park where historic documents relating to Caludon from the 1220s are stored. Access to these documents have been integral to the research for the book.

A special thank you also to Myk Flitcroft whose dissertation on Caludon Castle for his MA was the first ever academic research about the castle site.

Indeed I have been blessed in the publication of this book not only with the support of experienced academics and historians but also creative professionals who have demonstrated a passion beyond their brief. I include the book's designers Steve Wheele and Peter Viccari of Viccari Wheele and also Rob Wheele in charge of production, who have all treated this book as their own.

Pete Urmston, a highly respected architectural illustrator, has expertly recreated Caludon Castle as it may have looked c.1550-1570 making full use of the results of the 2008 resistivity survey together with contemporary architecture of the period to produce the first ever illustrations of the complete castle, its park and mere.

Geoffrey Barrett, a passionate historian and one of the country's top legal experts on English manors, is now a key member of the unofficial Caludon 'inner cabinet' and has become a good friend as well as wise counsel offering his experience and advice about the Lordship of the Manor of Caludon.

Thank you also to Gary Haigh for his personal support and photography, including a memorable visit to Berkeley Castle where he took excellent photographs of the impressive effigies of Lord Henry and Lady Katherine Berkeley which appear in the pages of this book.

The writing of any history is inevitably dependent on access to libraries and archives and I am grateful for the help and co-operation of the staff in the following repositories: Archives and Local History in the Herbert Art Gallery and Museum (now The History Centre), The Clifford Archive at Ugbrooke House, Devon, Warwickshire County Record Office, Archives and Heritage, Birmingham Central Library, Gloucestershire County Record Office, The National Monuments Record, Swindon,

The National Archive, Kew and the British Library. The last stages of the book coincided with the first round of cuts in public expenditure following the banking collapse of 2007, which sadly fell on heritage services such as museums, archives and conservation and archaeology. My writers and I are acutely aware of the difficulties that depleted staff resources and budgets have caused to such services. Without these this book could not have been written.

Other private individuals have given freely of their information on Caludon, from memoirs, correspondence and photographs. Such material is invaluable in supplementing the official records.

The list of people and organisations who have given their support and encouragement over many years to help me publish 'A History of Caludon Castle' is too long to go into detail. However, I hope that the fact they are acknowledged in the list below should be regarded as a sincere personal thank you that their contribution to the book, however large or small, is valued and greatly appreciated.

Last but not least I would like to thank my family for all their interest, support and love during my forty-five year journey to finally publish the book. From my parents' early encouragement of my interest in local history and in particular the castle during my early school days, to more recently the support of my wife Celeste and children Samantha, Charlotte and James who have not only supported my passion to publish the history of Caludon but have actively been involved in every aspect of the publication of this book – the family firm united in the cause of creating at long last the first ever record of the 800 year history of Caludon.

Acknowledgements

The Lord Clifford of Chudleigh
George Demidowicz
Stephen Johnson
Myk Flitcroft
Geoffrey Barrett
Steve Wheele
Peter Viccari
Rob Wheele
Pete Urmston
Helen Turnbull
Gary Haigh
David Smith – Berkeley Castle
Brian Battey
Mike Ashley

Robert Smith, OStJ Manorial Society
* of Great Britain*
Michele Marr, Head Teacher Caludon
* Castle School*
Ces Edwards – Coventry City Council
Dave Lewis – Coventry City Council
English Heritage
Charlotte Tucker – Birmingham
* Central Library*
NMR National Monuments Record
British Library
The History Centre, Coventry
Warwickshire Record Office
Martin Whelan

Frank Olley
David Webb
The late Alec Flynn
Pete Chambers
Ernest Woodbridge
Richard Nelmes
John Burge
Gill Jones
Derek Priest

Friends of Caludon Park:
Faye Abbott, Dr. Bob Nash,
George Sweet, Matt Smith,
Marie Wears, Gordon Tebut,

 Lead sponsor of this publication: Shortland Horne Residential Ltd

A special thank you to my eldest daughter, Samantha, as Assistant Editor of this book, for the many hours she has spent proofing the content. To all the above individuals, family, friends, contributors and organisations – a simple, but heartfelt thank you and an apology to any individual or organisation I have missed.

John Edward Clarke OBE

Introduction

As I write this Introduction to the first complete history of Caludon Castle and its Manor, I reflect with some emotion and a little pride on my forty-five year journey since first putting pen to paper to create this book whilst a teenage pupil at the school that still proudly bears the castle name.

I am often asked the question – why has it taken you such a long time to publish it?

My reply usually turns this question on its head by responding with another question: 'More importantly, why has it taken so long for Caludon's history, over eight centuries and more, to be chronicled in any detail?'

The obvious answer to the latter question is simply that nobody has ever bothered to undertake a comprehensive history of Caludon. Sadly centuries of legend, conjecture and speculation have been further exacerbated by the advent of the internet, which has further clouded the historic record.

Indeed we have to go back over 400 years to the words of the loyal Berkeley steward John Smyth for the last historical account of Caludon and this was only for a relatively short period. *The Lives of the Berkeleys* by Smyth is undoubtedly a priceless detailed account of the life and times at Caludon Castle in the late sixteenth and early seventeenth centuries. It provides an amazing insight into the social history of the Berkeleys at Caludon when the castle and its park had reached its zenith.

A major reason that the words for this Introduction were the last penned for this 75,000 word tome is fundamentally because the path of discovery about Caludon and its owners is never ending. Even in the latter stages of completing the book, we uncovered new facts, new twists and turns, which had to be incorporated into the chapters of Caludon's colourful tapestry of history.

As an example, (call it fate, or even coincidence) I recently visited the historic village of Chacombe, in Northamptonshire for the wake of a dear departed friend, only to be reminded that John de Segrave, Lord of the Manor of Caludon, until his death in 1325 and the 'architect' of the first castle constructed at Caludon, had been buried at Chacombe Priory. Sadly the priory was dissolved by Henry VIII, converted into a private house, and his final resting place undoubtedly disturbed.

I also realised, just before writing this Introduction, that the 400th anniversary of the death of probably Caludon's most charismatic and colourful Lord of the Manor, Lord Henry Berkeley, was only a matter of months away. Lord Henry, godson of King Henry VIII, died at Caludon Castle aged 80 on November 26 1613, literally four centuries before the publication of this book. Fate or simply a remarkable coincidence?

Fig 1 *The castle ruin from the east; in the foreground the land is rising from the filled in moat to the platform on which the remainder of the castle buildings stood.*

Why is the story of Caludon personally so important to me?

For the first thirty two years of my life my family home was almost in the shadow of the castle ruin and no more than 200 yards from the gates to Caludon Park. So from the cradle to maturity the castle has always been a part of my life.

My passion for history was encouraged from an early age by my parents, but the big influence fuelling my interest in the castle was my discovery of the powerful status of the Lords of Caludon, who owned the castle through many centuries. They first came to my attention as an eleven-year-old at Caludon Castle School. Large wooden boards listing the names of the Lords of Caludon Castle dominated the upper walls of the school hall. I soon wanted to learn more.

My inquisitive mind (which led to a career in journalism) was soon evident and led to one of the school's senior teachers, Ernest Simpson, showing me an early account of the history of Caludon Castle, written in a thin green school exercise book, confirming the old adage – you can't tell a book by its cover.

I was hooked! I had discovered that the castle ruin and thirteenth-century park that had been my childhood playground and fields of dreams had been the former home for centuries of some of the most important aristocratic families in England.

Little did I realise that the handwritten family trees in that little green exercise book (which I still have in my possession) was to be the catalyst for a forty-five year personal mission to publish the first ever detailed history of Caludon Castle and its Manor.

My early attempts at researching and writing (pre-internet of course) the history of the castle involved regular visits to the local library and many hours researching old newspaper cuttings.

Research that opened the doors to titled families of a bygone age included the Mowbrays, Dukes of Norfolk; the Segraves, High Sheriffs of England; the Berkeleys of Berkeley Castle and more recently the Cliffords. I discovered that they were important families, amongst England's major established landowners, with pedigrees of service and loyal connections to the Crown. In addition to helping to write the pages of the military history of Britain, the families all shared one common link – as past Lords of Caludon and owners of its fortified manor house and park.

My research progressively revealed links with the Mowbrays and Shakespeare in Richard II and the famous aborted tournament on Gosford Green. An exciting discovery revealed strong evidence of a connection between Caludon and Shakespeare's 'A Midsummer Night's Dream'. Amongst other explanations, leading Shakespearean scholars suggest that this play was written and first performed by Shakespeare at the society wedding in London of the then Lord of Caludon (Lord Henry Berkeley's) son Thomas Berkeley to Elizabeth Carey.

The Caludon story would not be complete of course if it did not include the fictitious four-hundred year old legend that England's patron saint, St. George, was born at Caludon and was buried beneath its ruins. This new twist on an old myth was probably created at a performance at Caludon Castle for Lord Henry and his family in the late 1590s. The appendix containing the article by George Demidowicz separates romantic folklore from fact.

Confirmed links with other famous names in history include Thomas Malory, author of *Le Morte D'Arthur*, and William Wallace of Scotland, hung drawn and quartered by the powerful John de Segrave, Lord of Caludon and the King's Lieutenant in Scotland.

Another historic event was the visit of the celebrated sixteenth-century lutenist, John Dowland to entertain the Berkeleys and their guests when Caludon was renowned for its lavish hospitality.

The early pace of my research, and indeed desire to complete the book in those formative teenage years, was interrupted by taking the first steps on the career ladder into the world of journalism followed by over a quarter of a century running a public relations business. However, it was always at the back of my mind at all times that I had to complete the unfinished business of my book on the history of Caludon.

Looking back, my schooldays at Caludon Castle School were happy sunshine years both academically, particularly in the sixth form, and on the sporting field where I was school soccer captain. Indeed the original school developed a strong reputation for sporting success over its 50 year life, producing a pipeline of England Rugby Internationals at both full and schoolboy international level as well as some England schoolboy soccer internationals.

Its most famous sporting success was achieved by former pupil Marlon Devonish, who was the first Caludon schoolboy to win an Olympic medal - a Gold Medal in the 4 x 100m relay in the 2004 Olympics in Athens.

In recent years I have been privileged to forge close links with the newly-built school as an Associate Governor and have been delighted with the interest shown by senior staff and pupils in the book, as well as their continued support for the Friends of Caludon Park committee.

Caludon Castle School has now indeed built a deservedly high reputation for its educational standards and results and bears the modern Caludon Castle brand proudly as an Academy.

The Friends of Caludon Park committee has been a tremendous influence and an example of how a committed group of local residents can work hand in hand with their local authority, schools and local and national agencies such as English Heritage as well as the police. A park has been created that is a first class social amenity whilst at the same time its status as a historic site has been protected.

The progress of the book after 2006 took giant steps forward with the involvement of two professional writers, initially Stephen Johnson, an experienced historian on manorial matters, who diligently undertook the first stage research of the book. More recently the baton was passed to George Demidowicz, a well-known local building and landscape historian and an author of several books and academic papers. Now an Honorary Research Fellow at Birmingham University, George was for twenty-one years Coventry City Council's building conservation officer. He has found much new information for the book, working closely with me in a real team effort.

So after forty-five years some might think my Caludon project, a labour of love which has been entirely self-funded, is concluded. After all we now have, at long last, an authoritative, professionally researched and written historical record of Caludon Castle and its Manor.

On the contrary, although the first chapter in my lifelong dream to celebrate Caludon's history is now a reality, there are still more pages to write and more work to be done.

Plans are in the pipeline to write a book dedicated to the life of Lord Henry Berkeley, which will analyse all the detailed Berkeley financial accounts at Caludon during his long tenure as Lord of the Manor.

The Caludon Society will soon be launched to promote the history of Caludon Castle and the manor and to support the continuing good work of the Friends of Caludon Park committee. Our friend and loyal supporter, Lord Clifford of Chudleigh, has kindly agreed to be our Patron, maintaining the long association of the Clifford family with Caludon when they were Lords of the Manor from the late seventeenth to the early nineteenth centuries.

Suffice to say, my personal mission to promote the Lordship of the Manor of Caludon and its history continues, with the objective of introducing more people of all ages to the wonderful story that is symbolised by the present romantic ruin, all that is left of its great chamber block. This once overlooked the Caludon pool, long ago drained, that was probably styled on the much larger mere of nearby Kenilworth Castle.

The book may now be finished, but its legacy will hopefully encourage increased interest in the history of the castle and its owners and even greater awareness of the unique attractions of its historic park and its place in local and English history.

Suffice to say, Caludon has indeed been an inspiration in my life and as a consequence my coat of arms (Frontispiece) proudly bears the motto:

***Caludon Meus Instinctus* ~ Caludon My Inspiration**

I sincerely hope that the inspiration I have experienced and enjoyed through my lifelong involvement with Caludon will be shared through this book for many years to come, from the children who excitedly play in its park in the shadow of the castle ruin, to readers eager for information about the castle's past and its place in English history.

John Edward Clarke OBE
Caludon House
Autumn 2013

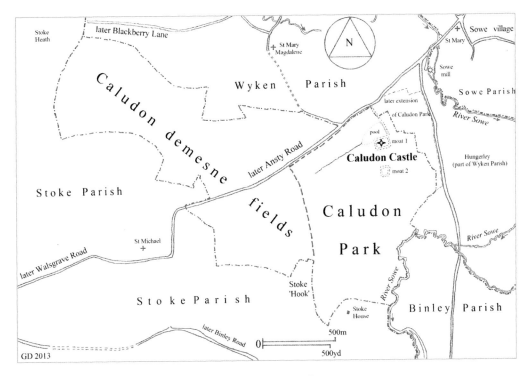

Fig 2 *Plan of Caludon manor with neighbouring ancient parishes*

A Note on Caludon Manor and Estate.

The term Caludon manor has two meanings: firstly the manor as a jurisdiction with rights to hold a manorial court, to impose fines, to collect rents and to extract minerals from below the ground. Secondly the manor was a physical entity or landed estate. In Caludon's case, this consisted of two parts: a large relatively compact area lying within the ancient parish of St Michael's containing the castle, the park and its demesne, the latter divided by the present Ansty Road. There were other much smaller and isolated areas of the estate mostly in the parishes of (Walsgrave-on-) Sowe, Wyken, Foleshill and Exhall.

This book concentrates on the largest single unit, the core of the estate, which was surrounded in a clockwise direction by the parishes of Wyken, Sowe, Binley and Stoke (Fig 2).

Caludon Castle

A romantic sandstone ruin...
rising sentinel against the winter sky,
Whilst bright sun casts down golden rays
across once magnificent moat.
Mirroring eight hundred years of history
Unveiled before you ... Caludon Castle.
Legendary birthplace of St George of England,
Now ruin standing proud whose ancient walls
bear witness to a noble past from a bygone age,
Deafening silence, though history calls.
Where was once, upon a time
A Great Hall, filled with laughter, merriment
Of titled Lords and Ladies therein
Feasting in sumptuous style
From long tables laid before them
A banquet of venison and game, fruits of the land
The spoils of hunting in the Park
At early dawn
And from a corner the gentle lilt of music lifts the air
The celebrated Lutenist Dowland playing from the stair
Before the Lord and Lady of the Manor, family and guests
Nobly served by seventy servants, all loyal to the test.
Ghosts of distinguished names past
Echoes of Segrave, Mowbray and Berkeley
Powerful families of the land.
Mowbray, Duke of Norfolk and Bolingbroke,
Whose battle at Gosford Green was ended by the King,
And celebrated in Shakespeare's own hand.
Such richness of nobility,

Chapters of a story from a colourful historical tapestry
Woven through the centuries at Caludon
A rich inheritance, indeed
From a time gone by, but sadly
No longer witness
To the eye.
And today, children play, in the Park
Tiny silhouettes dwarfed by the long shadows
of the sunkissed castle ruin
Gazing in wonderment
at a monument of days long past,
Dreams of a romantic age,
One can only imagine
But in time, childhood memories
That will surely last...
Lordship of the Manor of Caludon,
Seat of titled families
who made their mark
on centuries of British history.
Proud heritage impossible to sever,
Lords and Ladies of Caludon
Thy name will live on
Forever....

John Edward Clarke OBE
2009

Fig 3 *Pen and ink and watercolour of the castle ruin by Robert Overy 1982*

CHAPTER I

The Origins of Caludon Castle and Manor of Caludon
~ The Earls of Chester and the Segraves c.1200-1359

One of the abiding features of English social history is the tendency of a man who has made good in the town to celebrate his good fortune through the purchase of a country estate. Many of the great stately homes and handsome houses perched on hillsides and surrounded by parkland can be attributed to this tendency and although it reached its peak in the eighteenth and nineteenth centuries, the practice of moving to the country actually began in the medieval period.

After the Norman invasion of 1066, the new regime found that in order to subdue a restless population they needed a network of castles and fortifications to let the locals know that within these rising stone walls were the new rulers of the land. Castles were an all too visible manifestation of the feudal system, which had developed in the Anglo-Saxon period and been consolidated by the Normans, with the baron in his castle collecting dues from the local population and smaller landholders. At first the castle was used primarily in a military capacity but, after a fairly short period, its form changed to incorporate new functions. The sturdy walls which had once threatened the population became a place of safety in time of war where the townsfolk and others from the surrounding area could protect themselves and their livestock.

Within a hundred years of the Norman invasion there are examples of castles already falling into decay as the original reason for their existence disappeared. In Coventry for example, the eleventh-century castle, probably of the classic motte and bailey form, experienced a great deal of warfare in the early Norman period, but by the end of the twelfth century it had been reduced to ruins and was not reconstructed. The town was growing quickly and the land was redeveloped along a new street appropriately called Bayley Lane. Another major Norman fortification in the area, at Brinklow, east of Coventry, was thought to have been abandoned a hundred years later. Its well-preserved motte and bailey provides a good local example of the probable appearance of the lost Coventry castle.

Defensive fortifications using massive stone walls were developed to a high level of sophistication during the reign of Edward I. Massive and complex military edifices such as Conway and Caernarfon in North Wales were constructed as a vital part of a campaign of conquest by the English king. In England castles remained largely in the hands of local barons, but, in the long stretches of relative peace during the fourteenth century, domestic comfort became as important as solid defences. Here lie the origins of the 'Great House' and in the absence of an existing blueprint for a noble family house, the castle continued to be occupied, but with more convenient domestic facilities. Defensive features, although no longer as necessary, became a status symbol to be imitated by the lower ranks of the nobility. New homes needed to look like castles and a large number of houses and unfortified structures were crenellated. This did not necessarily mean the addition of curtain walls, towers and battlements; a few crenellated parapets, a gatehouse and moat may have sufficed. The house at Caludon was reconstructed as a fortified manor house, a consequence of the need of its owners to consolidate their social position in early fourteenth-century medieval England.

Today Caludon lies within the boundaries of suburban Coventry (Fig 4), but when the Normans arrived, soon after their defeat of Harold at Hastings, the greater Caludon area consisted of a considerable amount of woodland and waste with a few scattered farmsteads. It is not known for certain what sort of settlement Coventry was, since only an extensive rural component was assessed in the Domesday Book, William the Conqueror's great compendium of English estates drawn up by his commissioners in 1086. It is possible that the relatively new town was omitted from the survey. Caludon was not included in the Domesday Book and it probably formed part of the Earl of Chester's manor of Coventry (later Cheylesmore). Historically Caludon formed a detached parcel of the Coventry parish of St Michael (coinciding with the Earl of Chester's local domain) and was only incorporated into the parish of Wyken in 1884. The clear and separate descent of the manors of Caludon and Wyken indicate that, if they had previously been one unit, the separation occurred well before the end of the twelfth century. Furthermore Wyken is not mentioned in the Domesday Book and was first recorded in the early 1100s as the site of a chapel on the estates of the Earl of Chester.

The feudal system was characterised by layers of administration and service. When Caludon emerged as a separate manor some time around the turn of the thirteenth century, it was subject to the manorial court of Cheylesmore, although to what extent this was binding over the lords of Caludon is open to debate. By the end of the fourteenth century it seems to have become a largely symbolic relationship, as the Caludon territory had evolved its own manorial administration. As late as the sixteenth century, however, an annual rent of 12d was still being paid by the lords of Caludon to Cheylesmore.[1]

Prior to the Norman invasion the land which would later encompass Caludon was possessed by a figure synonymous with Coventry, Lady Godiva. Godiva (or *Godgifu*, as she is less glamorously but more correctly known) was the wife of Leofric, Earl of Mercia. She is famed, of course, for riding through the streets of Coventry naked, an act she performed in order to free the town's inhabitants from paying a toll to her husband. The story was first told by thirteenth-century monks and became popular in the area in the seventeenth century. Godiva was a devout Anglo-Saxon woman of high birth, however, and the story is best considered to be a legend.[2] What is certain is that the original land which later formed the manor of Caludon was part of her extensive estates. According to Richard Goddard, Godiva's lands included the 'parishes of St Michael's, Ansty, Binley, Exhall, Foleshill, Shilton, Stivichall, Stoke and Wyken.'[3] It was these settlements, or 'vills' which made up the jurisdiction of the lordship of Cheylesmore. Godiva died in about 1067, but

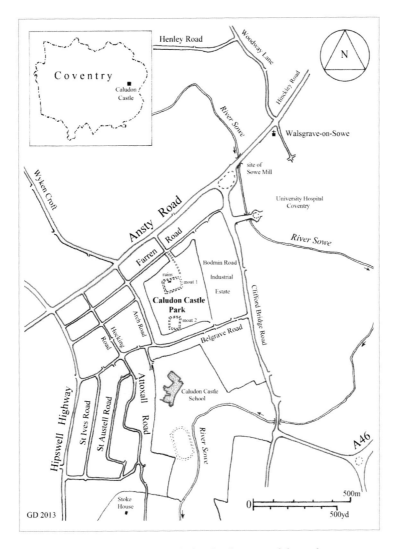

Fig 4 *Location plan of present Caludon Castle ruin and the park*

once William had subdued Warwickshire, he seized much of her land for his own to be distributed amongst his followers. The manors around Coventry may well have remained in the hands of the crown until the reign of William Rufus, which commenced in 1087. During his reign the manor of Coventry was granted to Hugh d'Avranches, the first Earl of Chester, a powerful magnate whose estates were accumulated over two decades and included land liberally distributed across the midland and the northern counties. He granted many of his manors out for the use of his followers and in this way he was able to build up a loyal retinue. He retained some of his estates for his own use as 'demesne' land (demesne – land directly managed by the lord and not tenanted) and these included the Coventry manors. With the accession of William Rufus, Hugh's political stock rose

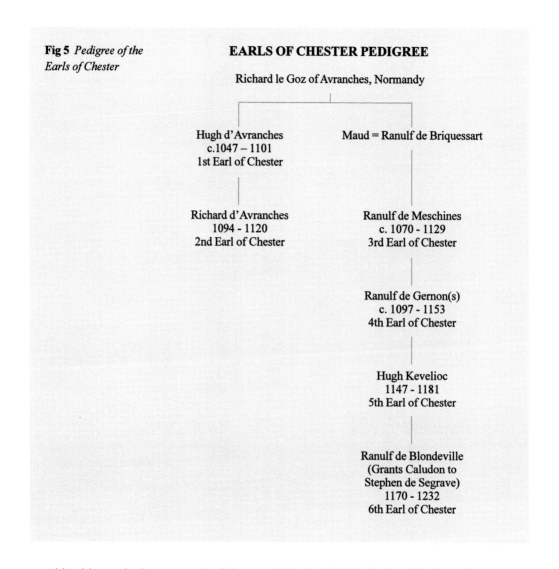

Fig 5 *Pedigree of the Earls of Chester*

EARLS OF CHESTER PEDIGREE

Richard le Goz of Avranches, Normandy

Hugh d'Avranches
c.1047 – 1101
1st Earl of Chester

Maud = Ranulf de Briquessart

Richard d'Avranches
1094 - 1120
2nd Earl of Chester

Ranulf de Meschines
c. 1070 - 1129
3rd Earl of Chester

Ranulf de Gernon(s)
c. 1097 - 1153
4th Earl of Chester

Hugh Kevelioc
1147 - 1181
5th Earl of Chester

Ranulf de Blondeville
(Grants Caludon to
Stephen de Segrave)
1170 - 1232
6th Earl of Chester

considerably, no doubt as a result of him remaining 'unblinkingly loyal in the major baronial rebellions of 1088 and 1095.'[4] At his death in 1101, the Coventry estates descended to his son, Richard, who died in the wreck of the White Ship in 1120, a tragedy which saw the death of the cream of young Norman aristocracy, including the heir to the throne, William the Atheling. After Richard's death the land which was to become Caludon passed to his cousin, Ranulf de Meschines, but his lordship was short, a mere nine years, before his death in 1129 (Fig 5). His successor, Ranulf de Gernon, had a troubled relationship with King Stephen and fought him in 1141. This was a period of civil violence and the Earl publicly favoured the party of the Empress Maud, daughter of Henry I. Ranulf was, however, a pragmatic man, his support going only as far as he could secure his valuable lands. For instance, he fought a battle against Stephen's son Eustace, at, or near to Coventry in 1147, presumably in defence of his many manors here and at his other important market town

Fig 6 *Contour map of Caludon Castle area with modern day street plan overlaid; Belgrave Road runs along the flat-topped summit of the low hill, once bare, that is the origin of the name, Caludon*

estate at Lincoln two years later. He did not appear to defend the lands of other nobles. After Ranulf's death in 1153, his son and heir, Hugh Kevelioc, proved more careless with his inheritance and, after joining a rebellion against Henry II in 1173, his estates were confiscated. Such was the Earl's power that they were soon restored after Hugh was readmitted to royal favour, but he died soon afterwards in 1181.

Hugh was succeeded by his eldest son, Ranulf de Blondeville, who consolidated the family's position as one of the greatest landowners in England. His status and power naturally gave him a position at the very the highest levels of state politics after attaining his earldom. Sensibly, he proved to be a loyal servant of Richard I and after the King's death in 1189, backed Prince John to succeed to the throne.

The earliest known mention of Caludon is difficult to date, but has been placed between 1190 and 1200 and may be as late as 1209. Listed among the charters of the Earls of Chester is a short request of notification to 'his constables, castellans and bailiffs of Coventry of his grant to William Marshall of land formerly held by a certain 'Liegrus' and a meadow below Caludon.'[5] William

Marshall was the Earl's steward who is known to have died before the autumn of 1209.[6] What this document does tell us is that 'Caludon', as a geographical entity, existed before 1200, in the hands of 'Liegrus' whose identity is unknown. The description of the meadow being *'below Caludon'* suggests that the land lay lower than the place, Caludon. The name means 'bare hill' in Old English (*calu-dun*) and as such must have been a distinct topographical feature. [7] A 'dun' hill is flat-topped and would describe the summit of the land that rises gradually to the south in the present day park to a summit in the vicinity of Belgrave Road (Fig 6).[8] To the south a shallow dip in the topography is followed by another broader flat-topped hill in the area at the south end of Attoxhall Road, near the junction with Harry Rose Road. To the

Fig 7 *Segrave coat of arms*

north the land slopes gently down to the present castle site, situated on a minor stream course, and to the south and east the land descends to the River Sowe. Either this stream, which we shall call the 'Caludon brook' for convenience, or the Sowe could have been the location of the meadow 'below Caludon'.[9] In the meantime, however, Caludon, whatever the place name signified at the time, remained in the possession of the Earl of Chester.

Although Ranulf's relationship with King John was soured by huge losses of land in Normandy when the English were evicted in 1204, the King rewarded his Earl's loyalty with a swathe of estates in 1205. Over the next ten years Ranulf became an unstinting supporter of the King. A young lawyer and bureaucrat, named Sir Stephen de Segrave, was working within the Earl's circle at this time (Fig 7). Segrave's father had held land directly from Ranulf at their family home at Seagrave in Leicestershire and Stephen was reported to have been a 'close familiar of the earl.'[10] The young man's rise was rapid and by 1217 (a year after the accession of the boy king Henry III) he had become a prominent justice. He sat in judgement at Westminster and undertook the new King's business in Norham castle, Northumberland, and Sauvey castle in Leicestershire, among other places. In 1218 Stephen was given custody of half the honour of Leicester whilst the Earl of Chester was away on crusade. The Earl had backed John through the civil war of 1215 and had fully supported Henry III's accession and so found himself in a position of considerable power in England in the early 1220s. Segrave will have risen to further prominence as a result and benefited from his master by way of land grants (Fig 8).

According to the Victoria County History for Warwickshire, Caludon was granted to Segrave 'at the end of the twelfth century', a dating derived from Dugdale's *Antiquities of Warwickshire*.[11] Dugdale describes Segrave as holding Caludon by the service of providing one sparrowhawk per year. Peter Coss's scholarly analysis of the origins of Caludon manor provides a most useful starting point.[12] He argues convincingly that Segrave's interest in the Caludon estate did not begin until the period after 1217 when most, if not all, of Stephen's gifts from the Earl of Chester belong. In 1218 he received custody of half of the honour of Leicester, while Ranulf de Blondeville was away fighting in the crusades and was eventually appointed as one of the Earl's executors. Ranulf returned from the Crusade in August 1220 and the grant to Stephen de Segrave may have been made quite early after this date.[13]

Fig 8 *Pedigree of the Segraves*

SEGRAVE PEDIGREE

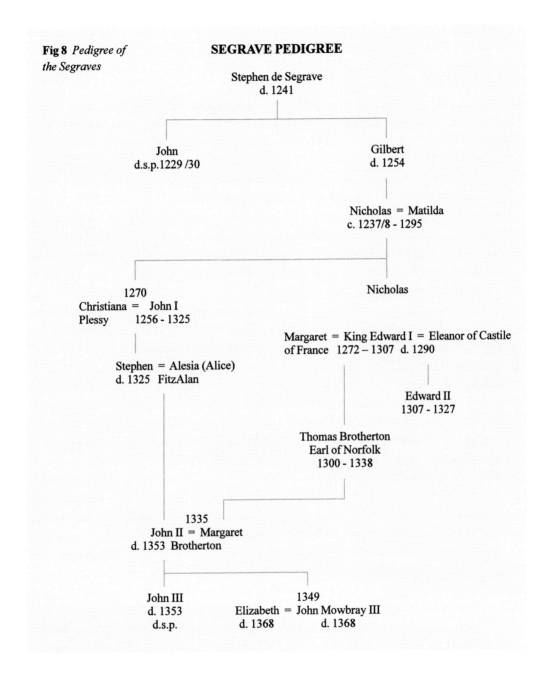

Stephen de Segrave
d. 1241

John
d.s.p. 1229 /30

Gilbert
d. 1254

Nicholas = Matilda
c. 1237/8 - 1295

1270
Christiana = John I
Plessy   1256 - 1325

Nicholas

Margaret = King Edward I = Eleanor of Castile
of France   1272 – 1307 d. 1290

Stephen = Alesia (Alice)
d. 1325 FitzAlan

Edward II
1307 - 1327

Thomas Brotherton
Earl of Norfolk
1300 - 1338

1335
John II = Margaret
d. 1353 Brotherton

John III
d. 1353
d.s.p.

1349
Elizabeth = John Mowbray III
d. 1368   d. 1368

Ranulf may have been rewarding services rendered whilst he had been away, but we shall never know the actual circumstances of the grant of land in Caludon to Segrave. In exchange Stephen was required to provide a sparrowhawk annually, reflecting Ranulf's passion for hunting.[14] Until recently this grant has been known only in a much abbreviated form, but another more detailed sixteenth-century copy has been found.[15] The grant was of 140 acres of land, but excluding 14 acres and one rood (a quarter of an acre) of land, which the Earl wished to retain (Fig 9). The use of the acre measure usually denotes arable land and was not normally applied to woodland or waste. The grant, therefore, could not have applied to the land that was eventually to become Caludon Park, but to an area of land already cultivated, perhaps not long cleared or 'assarted' from the waste. Coss considered that the land was a wilderness, in effect a licence to clear for cultivation, but this view is no longer tenable in view of the details of the grant.[16] No longer can the park be seen as the first development in the grant area followed by the creation of demesne (the lord's directly managed arable fields). The demesne, which from later sources is known to have been located on either side of the road from Coventry to (Walsgrave-on-) Sowe, was probably already in existence and Stephen de Segrave quickly set about creating a park on its south-east side.

Some of this area was certainly more akin to the wilderness that Coss described and was probably used as common pasture by the local tenants, particularly from Wyken. Other parts of the area were arable or meadow and already granted by the Earl of Chester to his retainers and administrators. The 14 acres and 1 rood of land retained by the Earl can be accurately located by description of its boundaries. It lay 'between Walter of Coventry's meadow (to the north) and Stoke field opposite Binley' (to the south) (Fig 9). The present Stoke House lies in the former Stoke field, which formed the southern boundary of Caludon. This boundary today can be seen as the tree line between the Stoke House complex and Richard Lee Primary School. Binley village, now absorbed into Coventry, stands directly to the east of the former Stoke field beyond the River Sowe.

In this period Stephen de Segrave was intent on creating a park, primarily for hunting rather than any aesthetic reasons. He probably began near the present site of the castle (not in existence at this time) and the hill that rises to the south, an area of waste adjacent to his demesne and nominally part of the territory of Wyken. He subsequently needed to acquire land from his neighbours farther to the south, which had already benefited from grants provided by the Earl of Chester.

Fortunately a number of these are known, as they were copied into a fifteenth-century schedule of deeds and charters, known as the Segrave Cartulary, which has survived. These can be used to reconstruct in part the development of Caludon Park in the thirteenth century (Fig 9).[17] Most of the deeds of this time are undated, but a rough date range can be assigned using the known dates of the grantor or grantee appearing in the charter. By great fortune two of the original charters that were summarised in the cartulary have survived and were recently found in the Clifford estate archive in Devon. These are an important discovery, as the extra information that they contain, including the names of witnesses, can help date the documents more precisely.[18] The deeds, now known to be the earliest extant for Caludon (1220s-early 1230s), reveal the efforts that Stephen de Segrave was making from the earliest time to extend his park.[19] Both relate to land that was taken in from his neighbours.

The first is an agreement between Stephen de Segrave and Walter of Coventry, the same Walter that was mentioned in the original grant from the Earl of Chester (see above). Walter owned a meadow between the River Sowe and *Caludon wood*, which Stephen wished to take into his park at 'Kalwedon' and to enclose it with a hedge to help preserve the wild animals for hunting.[20] Walter of Coventry had succeeded William the Marshall as the Earl of Chester's bailiff and died at the latest

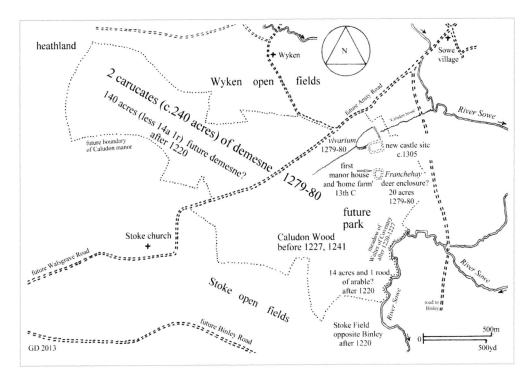

Fig 9 *Plan of the early medieval landscape of Caludon, c.1200-1300*

in 1227.[21] The agreement allowed Walter to enter his former land in the park and mow and carry away herbage and hay between March and June each year. He was also allowed to enter the park via a gate constructed conveniently opposite Stoke field, for he held land in Stoke at this time.[22] Walter's meadow could only have been located at the south end of Caludon, bordering on Stoke field and the Sowe, and may have been the same meadow that bounded with the 14 ¼ acres that the Earl of Chester had retained earlier (Fig 9). With the River Sowe to the east, *Caludon wood* must have lain to the west and perhaps the north.

The second charter records an exchange of land between Richard Hall (de Aula) and Stephen de Segrave. The latter was to receive a meadow 'below the park of Calwdon' for all his land in Spanne (Spon End). The location of Richard de Aula's meadow is, however, uncertain. In an earlier deed, dated to the late 1220s-early 1230s, Stephen de Segrave had obtained land in the 'vill' of Spon which must have been used in this transaction. The Segrave-Hall exchange may, therefore, have taken place only a few years later, perhaps in the early 1230s.[23] Two important witnesses appear on all three of these charters.[24]

The two original charters are the earliest record of the existence of Caludon Park, dating back nearly 800 years. There are several others only known in summary form and not so easily dated, the latest possible year being 1241, the year of Stephen de Segrave's death. The land in question consisted of woodland, meadow or arable confirming that the southern part of Caludon was a

Fig 10 *The original southern upper moat at Caludon, now overgrown with trees. The very gentle slope upwards from right to left rises to the summit of Caludon hill at Belgrave Road*

landscape both of clearances and woodland. Walter fitz Richard granted to Stephen all his part of *Caludon wood*, Philip fitz Miles his meadow below *Caludon wood* and Ranulf of Stivichall granted three furlongs (*culturi*) of arable land and a meadow that bordered on Stephen's own *Caludon wood*.[25]

Segrave was not, however, incorporating all his land in the area into the park. Coss drew attention to a grant of five acres and three roods of land made by Segrave to Saer de Stoke, dateable to the 1220s.[26] The land lay between *Caludon wood* belonging to Walter of Coventry and land that Stephen had granted to Robert of Stoke, also in Caludon. Interestingly it is revealed that Stephen had obtained the assart (recently cleared land) and an adjacent meadow from the Earl of Chester and in view of its location it could have formed part of the Earl's 14 ¼ acres retained by him in the original grant to Segrave (see above).

The agreement with Walter de Coventry strongly indicates that the park was being extended at its southern end, the only part of Caludon territory where the Sowe river and Stoke field form a boundary. Locating the other charters is more difficult, as meadow could lie both on the Sowe and on the 'Caludon brook'. *Caludon wood* appears to occupy a substantial part of the west side of the future park.

There is a geographical logic in suggesting that the earliest part of the park was created at the north end in the vicinity of the castle ruins. The other moat to the south, which has also survived in the present park, needs now to be considered, a site almost entirely neglected in previous writing on the subject (Figs 10 and 11). It lies upslope and uncomfortably close to the castle site. It is unlikely, therefore, to post-date the castle, but this proximity may be explained if the reverse were true: that this was the original site of the Segrave house in Caludon, perhaps established more for the purposes of a hunting lodge than a manorial seat. It was later abandoned for the present castle site owing to its small size and poor water supply.

Even if the demesne was created before the park and the area was not the wilderness that Coss envisaged, his main conclusions still stand and are worth quoting in full (author's brackets). [27]

> ...Caludon was a newly created estate of the early thirteenth century, consisting essentially of parkland and demesne. It was carved out of uncultivated land in and near the territory of Wyken. There was no village, however, and there were virtually no tenants. The Segrave demesnes of Caludon and Wyken were cultivated... by famuli (full-time estate workers).

The demesne lay on either side of the Walsgrave Road, about two and a half miles from Coventry, walkable within an hour from Cheylesmore manor when it belonged to the Earl of Chester. Once in Segrave's hands, it appears that the decision was made to build a local base, which initially acted as a hunting lodge, but developed quickly into a manor farm. There was room on the half-acre moated platform for all the necessary buildings. The Segrave estates were already extensive at this time and other manors provided the main residence such as at Seagrave in Leicestershire, the family's original home. It appears that within twenty years they began to favour Caludon and saw

Fig 11 *View from the south end of the park over the upper and lower (now castle) moats*

it as a place to live rather than just to visit for hunting trips. The estate had expanded by further purchases requiring administration, which was best delivered 'on the spot'.

In 1239 Stephen de Segrave received a papal confirmation of a gift of tithes made by the rector of the church at Coventry (St Michael's) to his free chapel built at Caludon manor.[28] The tithes were payable from Segrave's entire 'demesne… in Caludon'. A much later Coventry priory cartulary (c.1410-11) actually names the tithable fields and these lay in the area already described as lying on either side of the road from Coventry to Sowe (Walsgrave Road).[29]

There is no reason to believe that Segrave's chapel could not have been built on the higher moat site. There is more than enough room here for a house, chapel and other ancillary buildings. It measures 70m east to west and 77m north to south.[30]

Further details from Stephen de Segrave's illustrious biography provide the background, if not the motivation, to his creation of a hunting park, the recognised status symbol of a man enjoying a meteoric rise to considerable power and wealth from relatively modest knightly origins.[31] This was achieved essentially as a lawyer and a bureaucrat. Once Henry III had ascended to the throne in 1216 Segrave's importance and offices rapidly grew, a reflection of his 'competence to discharge legal and judicial functions.'[32] Caludon was granted around this time and developed as his wealth and influence increased. In these circumstances many would be willing to part with land in order to gain favour with a man obviously so well-connected. Stephen was granted the custody of Sauvey castle in Leicestershire in 1220 and the Sheriffdom of both Essex and Hertfordshire from 1220 to 1224. During this period he was also Sheriff of Lincolnshire and from 1228 Buckinghamshire, Bedfordshire and Northamptonshire. From 1228 to 1234 he once more served as Sheriff of Warwickshire and Leicestershire. This intensive period of administrative duties must have made many great demands on Segrave, but it also gave him the opportunity to amass land and estates. Following his Warwickshire Sheriffdom, his presence in the area continued to be felt since he was responsible for the repair of the nearby Kenilworth Castle. In 1233 he received custody of this important stronghold for life, after the fall of its previous custodian, Hubert de Burgh.

In 1230 Henry III left England for Brittany and Segrave was appointed as one of several regents, a position of great power for someone who was only a knight. In addition to this role he had been showered with custodies of castles: Dover, Rochester, Canterbury, Windsor, Odiham, Hertford and Colchester, many of which included lucrative incomes. In around 1232 he was elevated to the position of Chief Justiciar and became heavily involved in the factional politics which had begun to split the royal administration. Segrave allied himself with Peter des Roches, a royal favourite, against a party centred around the 3rd Earl of Pembroke, Richard Marshal. This was a dangerous political game and Segrave quickly became associated with a faction accused by the opposition as being 'evil'. Although he counselled the King against Marshal and his noble friends, the Earl was far too powerful a magnate to be side-lined and Segrave himself commanded little in the way of personal support, nor could he afford to provide for it. After a brief struggle Henry and Marshal were reconciled and Segrave was dismissed from his royal offices at the Earl's insistence.

Sir Stephen was stripped of five of his manors, but Caludon was not included in this list. It may be that he was spared from losing it, but his home manor at Seagrave was razed to the ground. In

June 1236, however, Segrave returned to royal favour, which was no doubt hastened by a payment to the King the year before of £1,000. Given the destruction of his family home, it is possible that Segrave withdrew to his other manors, including Caludon, during his period of political exile. His close connection to the area is reflected in his patronage, in the form of grants made to the nearby abbeys of Stoneleigh and Combe.

Sir Stephen's return to royal circles was as sudden as his departure. According to the chronicler Matthew Paris, he became a dominant if rather mediocre figure in the regime and he remained so until his death in 1241.[33] Paris describes Segrave as a rather selfish individual who was interested in furthering his own career over consideration for others. He was apparently easily led, an unfortunate trait in an age of factionalism, but he was generally respected as a lawyer. He was succeeded in his estate by his second son Gilbert, who had followed his father into royal service and took part in Henry III's campaign in Brittany in the early years of the 1230s (Fig 8).

Although his father was a rich man, Gilbert earned his own fortune through his service and he was rewarded in 1232 with custody of the castle and Manor of Newcastle-under-Lyme in Staffordshire and a few months later Burton, in the same county. He was severely affected by his father's temporary fall from grace and was only reinstated to favour after Stephen's death. Like his father he served on the King's Bench and in the legal service of the crown, accompanying the King to Gascony in this capacity in 1253. Ironically Gilbert's death in 1254 was the most notable event in his life. Whilst on a diplomatic mission for the King, he was travelling with a number of nobles, including the Earl of Warwick, when the band was attacked by the inhabitants of the town of Pons in Poitou. Although the Englishmen assured the locals that they had safe passage from the French King, Louis IX, they were seized and taken to the town. Their captivity does not seem to have been comfortable since Gilbert de Segrave rapidly grew ill and died within a couple of weeks.

Whilst he lived Gilbert had continued his father's acquisition of land to expand the park at Caludon. Around 1250 Walter de Coventry, probably grandson of his namesake mentioned above, granted to Gilbert de Segrave a meadow called *la lake* below or within (*infra*) the park.[34] This meadow can be identified with the field, *Lake Meadow*, recorded in the several later surveys and in the 1815 sale particulars (see later chapters).[35] Today this meadow is occupied by the lower part of Caludon Castle School and its playing fields.

At the time of his death Gilbert's son and heir, Nicholas, was a minor (aged 16 or 17) and so was made a royal ward. The medieval institution of wardship was a lucrative money spinner for both the King and his nobles. Wealthy minors were placed in the hands of those who were usually willing to pay a high price to the crown and in return the holder of wardship would be entitled to the income of the lands of their wards. Although the system was often open to great abuse, it was secure enough to enable most estates to remain in the hands of the rightful owners and so give lasting stability to noble landownership. Caludon, along with the rest of the Segrave estates, was placed in the temporary possession of Prince Edward and it is from this period that there is an excellent record of the accounts of the manor at Caludon, which were lodged with the Prince's exchequer at Bristol.[36]

The account, dated from September 29 (Michaelmas) 1257 to 22 April 1258, reveals that Caludon had developed in the space of about fifty years into an estate containing both the original arable demesne and a new park administered from a manorial centre. Caludon lacked the classic third element of the medieval manor, however, tenants living in a nucleated village or other rural settlements who farmed their own holdings. In the economic period before the Black Death (1349-50) known as 'High Farming', the tenants on many manors were servile, owing labour service on the demesne and a host of other dues and obligations to the lord of the manor.

As well as the manor house, there would have been a 'home farm' with barns and granaries needed to store and distribute the produce from the fields, some consumed by the manorial household, the remainder sold for cash revenue. At Caludon, as mentioned above, *famuli*, or full-time workers cultivated the land rather than tenants who owed labour service. They would also have needed accommodation, although some may have lived in the surrounding settlements such as Wyken and (Walsgrave-on-) Sowe.

The accounts were prepared by Luke of Caludon, an employee of the Segrave family, who also collected information on the family's other local estates at Thurlaston and Brinklow. He records gathering £4 10s 7d in assize rent, but since the period of the accounts is only seven months we would need to more or less double this to get a real value of the yearly collection. Only a fraction of these came from Caludon although rents from the whole estate were paid centrally at Caludon. Other sources of income included 3 shillings for pleas and perquisites (payments made at the manorial court) and 24 shillings from the rent of Wyken Mill. Even very small payments are recorded, such as 6d for six hens that had been paid in kind for rent in Coventry. The account also includes the prices fetched for the sale of the estate produce: 41s 3d for wheat, £8 10s for rye, and £7 11s 10d for oats. This reflects high prices in a year of poor harvests and it was found that almost as much had been spent on buying wheat seed as had been made in selling its own wheat. In fact extra rye, wheat chaff and barley had to be bought to feed the estate workers. Even the land of wealthy men barely scraped by above subsistence level in many years and, although Coss is correct in his assertion that it is very difficult to assess the profitability of the Caludon estate from such a short period, Luke's records do reflect the general failure of the English crop during the summer of 1257.

Other details of the account show that running a thirteenth-century estate required attention to detail and close regard to maintenance. Worn equipment, such as harnesses was sold off and even animals no longer at the peak of health were discarded. Payments were made for horseshoes, for mending a wheel and ploughs as well as for the forging of new ones. Craftsmen such as blacksmiths and ploughmen were paid for their work and wages appear in the Caludon accounts for hired labour to undertake threshing and winnowing. Luke, the bailiff, paid himself 41s 8d in expenses, a considerable amount of money in this period.

The well-organised manorial accounts at Caludon imply the existence of a home farm and the upper moated platform was certainly large enough to accommodate house and farm plus a small chapel. Without archaeological evidence we cannot know when the upper site was abandoned, but there is compelling evidence that we look to a later event, a half century later, to explain the 'big move' downslope.

By 1262 Nicholas had reached adulthood (aged c. 24-25) and he entered into agreement with the neighbouring Lords of Wyken, the Langleys. The latter were to renounce all their rights to common pasture which they claimed in Segrave's Caludon lands and 'in the park there enclosed by hedges and ditches.' In exchange Nicholas would relinquish his right to pasture in *La Wyke* (Wyken) and in two furlongs there.[37] The importance of this concord lies in the fact that over a considerable area of waste in Wyken and Caludon rights of common pasture had evolved. As the land was cleared for agriculture and the park developed by the Lords Langley and Segrave respectively, these intercommoning rights had become a hindrance to their use and for mutual benefit they were extinguished. Caludon Park, as surmised above, had at least in some part been carved out of an area of common pasture.

The details of Nicholas de Segrave's life are better known than his father, Gilbert. In March 1257 the young Nicholas de Segrave, Lord of the Manor of Caludon, was reported as being ill at Windsor castle whilst being in service to the King. He is described as being a King's squire and details of the royal accounts show that within the household he received an allowance of three horses, three boys and meat, fish, wine and candles.[38] On 18 April 1258 Nicholas paid a fine of 300 marks (around £200) to obtain his father's lands and perform homage to them. In return he was given permission to take formal 'livery' or possession of his estates, including Caludon.

In the early part of the 1260s national tensions arose between the barons and the King. The former party was led by Simon de Montfort, the Earl of Leicester. Segrave was a neighbour of the Earl and was evidently sympathetic to his cause since he soon joined his party. The roots of the conflict can be found in the mismanagement and incompetence of Henry III's reign during the 1240s and 1250s. The baronial party grew tired of his grandiose plans, usually ending in failure and sought a reversion to the rule of the Great Council, which had governed England during Henry's minority in the 1220s and 1230s. In 1258 the King entertained the idea of making his second son, Edmund, King of Sicily and agreed to pay Pope Alexander IV 135,000 marks for the privilege. Sicily was already ruled by a King and in reality the payment was made merely to earn the right to send an army to oust him. For many of the barons this was a plan too far and when the King tried to raise money for the quest from his barons he was met with refusal and instead presented with a series of reforming demands, known as the Provisions of Oxford. These curtailed Henry's personal power and increased the influence of the barons. In the ensuing political and ultimately military struggle, Segrave firmly allied himself with de Montfort. When peace between the Earl and King was made in December 1261, Segrave was counted among those who were required to put his seal to the agreement. According to the chronicler, Thomas Wykes, despite Nicholas de Segrave's continuing support in public for de Montfort, in May 1263 he was knighted by the King at Worcester and accompanied him on a military expedition to Wales. In 1264 simmering discontent between Henry and his barons boiled up into war when the arbitration of the French King, Louis IX, on the original dispute resulted in a verdict in favour of the English King. The civil war ended in the Battle of Lewes on 14 May 1264. Segrave is recorded as fighting for the barons on that day but no details have survived of his endeavours. The battle ended in a resounding victory for de Montfort and it placed the governance of England in his hands. As a prominent supporter, Segrave was rewarded with the custody of Rockingham Castle and the forests between Oxford and Stamford Bridge in Lincolnshire. De Montfort's administration barely lasted a year. Henry quickly regained his military strength and Segrave found himself on the losing side at the Battle of Evesham on 4 August 1265. After the battle he was captured and taken before the King.

Nicholas de Segrave had much displeased his monarch, who accused him of being 'the King's enemy' and stripped him of his lands, including Caludon. These he then placed in the hands of his son, Prince Edward. Nicholas was incarcerated, but in 1266 he appears to have escaped and was part of a rebellious force which, for a time, held out on the Isle of Ely in Cambridgeshire. After winning a conclusive victory over his baronial opponents in July 1267, the King was all but penniless and urgently required money from the very men he had recently been fighting. Segrave was therefore given the chance to buy back his property at a charge of five times its annual value. Having effectively re-purchased royal favour, Nicholas de Segrave wisely remained in the background before leaving England altogether in 1270 for a crusade to the Holy Land. Sadly his exploits in the Middle East are lost and he was back in England in 1277. The new King Edward I recognised his foreign experience and utilised him for a number of military missions during the remainder of that decade and the 1280s.

The first known survey of Caludon manor is the entry in the Warwickshire Hundred Roll (1279-80) in the time of Nicholas de Segrave.[39] It consisted of two carucates of land (approximately 240 acres) and one park with a *vivarium* (fish pond) called *Franchehay* (Fig 9).[40] The carucates are usually interpreted as the demesne, which has been identified as lying to the west and north-west of the park. It appears that since about 1220 the area had expanded from 140 acres to about 240 acres, reflecting an energetic policy of demesne expansion. A total of 240 acres would cover a large portion of the remainder of Caludon outside the confines of the park, the total being nearly 300 acres in the nineteenth century.

The park according to the survey measured 20 acres and its small size is puzzling in view of all the effort that had been made in previous years to extend an existing park. *Franchehay* was in fact a deer 'hay', a hedged or fenced enclosure constructed to breed and confine deer. A sizeable area of former waste - woodland, scrub and common pasture - could have formed the more extensive and informal park. The Hundred Rolls essentially recorded land holdings that owed service and rent and this kind of land was not generally included in a survey.

The *vivarium*, a pond for breeding fish, could be identified with the pool that used to lie on the north side of Caludon Castle and linked with the moat. It was drained away long ago, but the dam still exists and the driveway leading to the castle passes along it. The fish pond was constructed to the north of the upper moat, exploiting the small tributary stream flowing eastwards into the River Sowe (the Caludon brook).

There were only two tenants at Caludon in 1278-9, John de la Haye who held a freehold plot of three acres and Robert de Stoke holding 'certain land' for a yearly sum of 7s. It is not known where their holdings were situated, but an earlier Robert Stoke had his land near *Caludon wood* (Fig 9). The productive land remained largely as meadow and arable though Segrave's income was supplemented by the ownership of two mills nearby, at Henley and Sowe.

Throughout this period Nicholas de Segrave was involved in a number of military campaigns, no doubt in a bid to retain the favour of the new King, Edward I. He was called to serve in a number of English expeditions in Wales in 1277, 1282 and again in 1294 and travelled to Gascony in 1295, although, once more, there are no specific details of his actions during these campaigns. He appeared at a number of Edward's parliaments, but has often been confused with his second son Nicholas, who was also growing in importance. The younger Nicholas seems to have been involved in Edward's northern campaigns against the Scots and was given custody of both Dumbarton and Ayr Castles in 1291. In 1295 he was summoned to Parliament as Nicholas de Segrave junior.

Both men seem to have been used in both military and bureaucratic capacities which took them away from their lands and estates for long periods of time. They would have had to rely on their local bailiff for the efficient and good running of Caludon and it is unlikely that any major rebuilding took place at this time. Nicholas junior received a wide variety of commissions from military duty in Scotland to diplomatic missions to the court of the Archbishop of Cologne.[41] He undertook an investigation into the administration of the Isle of Man and also headed an inquiry into the state of weirs on the River Trent. In spite of these distractions, the Segraves continued to tend to their own estates and develop them economically. In July 1292 Nicholas, the elder, received an extensive grant of rights for many of his manors.[42] For Caludon he received the right of free warren, which Barsby describes as '...a right to keep beasts and fowl of warren on land.'[43] This was an economic asset since it gave the lord of the manor exclusive right both to hunt and kill the animal but also to protect the animal from being killed. Animals covered by free warren rights included hare, rabbits, and roe deer. A variety of birds were also allowed: quails, partridges, ducks, herons and woodcocks amongst them and given that Caludon was possessed of a pool it is likely that the Segraves would have sought to keep water birds on it. Rabbit warrens became very popular, but they had to be kept away from arable. There may still have been plenty of space towards the south end of the estate, but even in such areas they were often fenced in to prevent the rabbits nibbling away precious woodland saplings. The scope of the grant provides a good indication of the geographic spread of Segrave lands throughout the eastern Midlands. Other Segrave manors granted the same right were Bretby, Rosliston and Cotes-in-the-Elms in Derbyshire, Staunton in Huntingdonshire, Cold Overton, Seagrave, Sileby and Diseworth in Leicestershire and Chacombe in Northamptonshire, all counties where the Segraves had held political positions. Nicholas de Segrave died at Canterbury in 1295 but was buried at Chacombe Priory, Edward I giving two cloths of gold to lie over the body.[44]

The documents on Caludon unfortunately do not tell us how often the Segraves stayed at Caludon and whether it was a favoured house in their extensive, but scattered estates. In 1288 Nicholas's wife, Matilda, was recorded as being in Warwickshire and may well have spent some time at Caludon. On this occasion at least, her visit was not a pleasant one. In August of that year a special investigative court, known as Oyer and Terminer, was appointed to hear a complaint from Sir Nicholas that his wife had been attacked and thrown from her carriage at Exhall, a few miles north of Caludon. According to Segrave a group of around forty men and women had seized his wife and tossed her onto the roadside. They had then taken away a long cart on which were laden food and other goods. The sheer number of assailants seems to rule out a simple highway robbery and raises the possibility that the Segraves were unpopular in Warwickshire, or certainly in this area of the county. Perhaps they made for tyrannical landlords, or it was Matilda herself who had provoked the violence through some unknown act.

After the death of Nicholas the elder in 1295 Caludon passed to his eldest son John (Fig 12). Born in 1256, the first official record of him occurs in 1270 when at the age of 14 he married Christiana the daughter of Hugh de Plessy, whose grandfather, John Plessy, Earl of Warwick, had been a prominent supporter of de Montfort. The marriage seems to signal that old loyalties remained important and intact after Simon's defeat. John de Segrave was keen to placate the new regime of Edward I and like his father, was employed in military campaigns in Wales, Ireland and Scotland. He spent most of his time from 1297 in fighting and subduing the Scots and

JOHN DE SEGRAVE.

Fig 12 *Seal of John de Segrave 1300-1301*

entered into the close service of Hugh Bigod, Earl of Norfolk. In 1302 his good work in Scotland led to his appointment as constable of the strategically vital castle at Berwick. Later that year he was made the king's lieutenant in Scotland at a time when a truce between the two nations was about to be broken. In the following September John was ordered to march an English force to Stirling castle and in 1304 he increased pressure on the Scots by organising a series of raids throughout the kingdom, launching them from his base on the border. At one point during this activity he was captured by the Scots but was rescued soon afterwards. He found himself hunting William Wallace, known to the modern world through the Oscar winning Mel Gibson film 'Braveheart'. John was among the 'dastardly' Englishmen that captured Wallace in the spring of 1305, although it is sometimes forgotten that he was aided in his capture by that other great Scottish hero, Robert Bruce. Segrave himself led the transportation of Wallace to London that summer and he appeared as one of the justices at his trial. Wallace's fate was not an enviable one. He was hung, drawn and quartered, the constitutional death assigned to traitors. The four parts of his dead body were sent to Newcastle, Berwick, Stirling and Perth. Segrave was handed the grisly task of transporting the remains, a commission for which he was paid 15 shillings. After dealing with his executed foe, Segrave relinquished his lieutenancy of Scotland and returned to England. There followed a rash of charters in his name and grants for his land so it appears that he required this time away from duty to put his estates in order.

Among his grants was a charter from Edward I to fortify, or crenellate, his manor house at Caludon. We can only guess how the original house might have looked. Manor houses of the thirteenth century were of varying types: aisled, or without an aisle with their hall on the first or ground floor. At Caludon it may have been constructed of the local sandstone or alternatively of cheaper timber-frame. Given the fact that the Segraves had greater and more extensive estates in other counties, and that their principal estate was in Leicestershire, it seems doubtful whether any of the heads of family had lived here for any significant time until this point. The manor house may have been a residence of a minor or younger member of the family and housed the head of the family only when he was on a procession from estate to estate. For most of the time perhaps it functioned as the headquarters of the Caludon bailiff.

Segrave's copy of the original licence to crenellate, dated 2 February 1305, has recently been found in the Clifford estate archive at Ugbrooke in Devon (Figs 13 and 14).[45] King Edward I granted to John de Segrave senior licence to ditch and build an encircling wall of stone and lime around his manor house and to crenellate the walls. He had already obtained a similar licence in 1301 for his manor house at Bretby.[46] Licences to crenellate are now understood to have been granted more as a status symbol, 'a mainly symbolic representation of lordly status' than an expression of control over the fortifications of barons and nobles.[47] The royal seal conferred an extra cachet, which was eagerly sought and appreciated.

Fig 14 *The endorsement on the original licence to crenellate Caludon Castle with the seal of Edward I 1305*

The great castles of England, except the royal strongholds, were owned by the most powerful lay magnates and therefore fortifications, battlements and towers came to have a social

Fig 13 *The original licence to crenellate Caludon Castle granted John de Segrave in 1305*

meaning as well as the obvious defensive function. Castellation had become an architectural expression of noble rank. Regardless of symbolic and social value, there is good reason to believe that the licence was implemented in a most radical way, by the digging of a new moat and construction of entirely new buildings, with the architectural pretension of a fortified manor house. Work at Caludon might have started before the licence was issued. The site chosen, about 200 metres downslope of the original moat, was assured of a better water supply, as the fish pond had already proved, and the water of this pool was cleverly incorporated so that it was level with the water of the new moat. The new moated area (1 acre) was twice the size of the upper moat, which might have become cramped over time. Grander buildings would certainly have needed more space.

The castle moated platform in fact appears to take a bite out of the south side of a once bigger pool. It is interesting to speculate that the new Caludon was inspired by Kenilworth castle, situated only a few miles away, where on a much bigger scale a large body of water, the Mere, wrapped round the south and west side of the defences and integrated with the massive outer moat. At Kenilworth the castle is approached from the south across the Mere dam, at Caludon from the north along the much smaller dam, but both no longer hold back water. In recent years, however, flooding due to heavy rainfall temporarily recreates the appearance of the former Caludon 'mere' (Fig 15).

After 1308 John de Segrave took up official responsibilities within reach of his Midland estate. He appears to have been disenchanted with life in the North and likewise, evidently, his wife, for he did not return there until the 1320s. Remarkably, she received a special payment from the crown for the trials she had suffered in accompanying her husband in Scotland. In January 1308 Segrave attended the coronation of Edward II and three months later was given custody of Nottingham Castle and the responsibility as Justice for the forests of north England. His authority was then extended to Scotland and Cumberland. Glimpses of Segrave come from official documents, which tell of his deeds and responsibilities, but little of the man. He was a man holding great power under the new King, who was capricious in his choices of counsel and caused great disaffection among the established nobility. For the time being Segrave remained loyal, however, but there is evidence that the King's unpopularity was affecting his subjects. In 1315 Segrave made a complaint to Edward II that both he and his garrison of men at Nottingham had been forced to seek refuge at their own castle by the townsfolk. This was no spontaneous uprising since to signal it the town bell had been rung. The gates of the castle were torn down and Segrave and his men assaulted. They secured themselves against their attackers, but were then besieged for eight days. Segrave's bitterest complaint was that he had not been allowed access to provisions. The citizens of Nottingham had reacted to some provocation, perhaps caused by Segrave himself or by an official decree he had been obliged to enact.

Despite mounting opposition to Edward, for the period from 1318 to his death in 1325, Segrave remained a loyal servant of the King. Edward's rule had been largely incapacitated by his poor judgement of character. Early in his reign he had promoted his favourite, Piers Gaveston, to power in the face of the incredulity of the barons and he repeated the blunder a few years later when he promoted the cause of the Despencer family. This provoked the enmity of the most powerful noble, Thomas of Lancaster, and Segrave was drawn towards supporting him. He was warned by the King not to join what had quickly turned into an armed rebellion and in 1322 was commanded to raise

Fig 15 *View in 2007 from the former dam, now the park entrance driveway, over the site of the former Caludon pool or mere; this returns to its historical appearance in times of flooding.*

troops for the King in Warwickshire. It is unclear if Segrave took part in any action against Lancaster and he may have decided to keep a tactful distance from the hostilities. After Lancaster's defeat, Segrave remained on military duty, primarily in Scotland, until his death in 1325.

There are a few contemporary documents which link John de Segrave directly to Caludon. Four charters are known to have been signed at Caludon in his name, signifying that at least part, if not a substantial amount of new construction, such as the great hall, had been completed to enable the business of estate administration to be regularly conducted.[48] Even if the new Caludon moat and building had been constructed before 1325, the year of his death, we have no way of knowing how involved John was in their planning and implementation. John had many brothers (five) and sisters (six) with whom he might have had to share the various family residences of the Segrave estate. This may be the reason that Caludon rose in prominence at this time. It is possible that John selected Caludon for particular attention, transforming and embellishing it on a new site. There is also a hint that his son, Stephen, was allowed a role as there is an intriguing, but undated, deed in which two local men grant to Stephen, heir of John de Segrave, two blocks of selions (open field strips) in Wyken, one of which stretched between the Wyken demesne as far as Caludon Park.[49] This transaction was perhaps designed to obtain a setting for the new moated site by expanding northwards into Wyken territory. Stephen, however, was only to outlive his father by two months.

The inquisition after John de Segrave's death confirms that Caludon was one of his properties, and the house was described as a fortalice (*forcelletum*) surrounded by water.[50] The use of this word suggests a small or minor fortress, more akin to a fortified manor house, especially if compared with the great strongholds of Kenilworth and Warwick nearby. Nevertheless, the licence appears to have been implemented.

In 1325 Caludon descended unexpectedly from John to his grandson John, owing to the death of Stephen. John the younger was only a minor (aged 14) when he inherited and John de Bolingbroke, the escheator of Warwickshire, was commanded to place Caludon in the hands of John's mother, Alesia.[51] An escheator was a royal official responsible for confiscations of landed estates without heirs on behalf of the King. Caludon manor was valued at £19 19s 11d. In return for possession of the estate and its income, Alesia was required to pay the exchequer 24s 9d, the excess value of her dowry. The inquisition into the manor repeated the extent (survey) of a few months earlier in describing Caludon Castle again as a *fortalice* surrounded by a moat.

This being the high watermark of the feudal system, a number of records from the fourteenth century highlight that the Lords of the Manor and Castle of Caludon themselves were still required to make homage to their 'overlord.' As has already been noted, Caludon had been carved out of land which had belonged to Ranulf Blondeville, the Earl of Chester and he remained as the 'overlord' of the Caludon manor, the higher rung on the feudal ladder. After the death of the last Earl of Chester, his remaining Coventry properties were divided between four surviving nieces. One of these, Cecily, was married to Roger Montalt, who became the overlord of Caludon even though his social status, as the Earl's steward, was not equal to that of the Caludon lords. The Segraves were required to make yearly payments to Montalt. This is confirmed by the inquisition of 1325 which shows that John de Segrave held Caludon manor for a 1/4 of a knights fee and 12d from 'Robert de Monte Alto'.[53] Although the sum was small, petty even, it was an important symbol of feudal order and fealty, the acknowledgement of the authority of a superior lord. This tie to the Montalts lasted until at least 1348, but by the death of the last Segrave in 1353 the overlordship had passed to Queen Isabella, wife of Edward II.[54]

The last Segrave, John, had a short but eventful life. We know little of his early years save that on the death of his father at the age of ten he was left in the care of his mother, Alesia (Alice). In 1335 he made an advantageous match with Lady Margaret Brotherton, the sole heir of Thomas Brotherton, Earl of Norfolk, who had administered his estates as ward. Thomas was the second son of the late Edward I (d.1307) by his second marriage. This brought him not only a huge swathe of land, consolidating his territorial position, but he was also to enjoy familial ties to the royal house. In the context of the 14th century, this gave Margaret an uncommonly powerful position within her union and she appears to have actively used this power to obtain a jointure of her husband's estates after his death. Whatever had been built on the new moated site in the years after its construction, we might look to the period when John de Segrave junior owned Caludon (c.1335-1353) for the construction of the impressive two-storey great chamber range of which only one small section of wall survives. It appears to be modelled on the Great Hall at Kenilworth, the magnificent royal castle with which John's wife, Margaret, granddaughter of Edward I, had close dynastic connections. Segrave property transactions continued to be signed at Caludon, this time in the name of John junior (1334, 1336, 1338, 1343), one of which included John's widowed mother, Alice.[55] We also know that the manorial court was being held there in 1328.[56]

Although Caludon was a home it does not appear to have been an especially happy one. In 1350 Margaret travelled to Rome to ask the Pope in person for a divorce from John. We can only guess at the source of the marital strife since the union itself was one for normal familial convenience and the production of heirs. Margaret was arrested for her troubles, having travelled abroad without obtaining a licence, and reached Rome in the company of Sir Walter Mauney, who was almost certainly her lover. On her return she was summoned, together with John de Segrave, to the King's presence to explain her behaviour. This must have been an embarrassing encounter for all concerned, but particularly for Segrave. Even if he had been acquainted with the details, it must have caused him much discomfort for the affair to be so publicly aired. The King had Margaret 'honourably' imprisoned in Somerset and confiscated her personal property. Within months, however, she was freed from house arrest and in 1353 divorced from Segrave, who died in the same year aged just 38. Within a year she had married Mauney.

Segrave's sole heir from his union with Margaret was to be his daughter, Elizabeth, for his son, John III, also died in 1353. She had married John, Lord Mowbray, in 1349 and it was to the Mowbray family that Caludon subsequently descended.

Chapter 1 – NOTES

1 Coventry Archives (subsequently CA) BA/A/1/7 f. 185v

2 *Victoria County History of Warwick*, Vol 8, (1969) 242-3, (subsequently VCH Warwick, Vol 8)

3 Richard Goddard, *Lordship and Medieval Urbanisation: Coventry 1043-1355*, (2004) 25

4 C. P. Lewis 'Hugh d' Avranches' article in the Dictionary of National Biography

5 Geoffrey Barraclough (ed.) *Charters of the Anglo Norman Earls of Chester, c.1071-1237, The Record Society of Lancashire and Cheshire, Vol 126* (1988), no 252; Peter Coss, *Lordship, knighthood and locality, A study in English society C.1180-C.1280*, (1991) 96

6 op. cit., Coss, (1991) 34

7 J E B Gover, A Mawer (eds.), *The Place-Names of Warwickshire*, (1936) 192

8 Margaret Gelling, *Place-Names in the Landscape*, (1984) 140-158

9 The Caludon Brook was later dammed to make a fish pond followed by the Caludon Castle moat alongside with which it formed one body of water.

10 Nicholas Vincent, *Peter des Roches: An Alien in English Politics, 1205-1236*, (1996) 315

11 op. cit. VCH Warwick Vol 8, 242; William Dugdale, *The Antiquities of Warwickshire*, (1730) 128 (subsequently Dugdale 1730)

12 op. cit., Coss, (1991) 93-102

13 Iain Soden, *Ranulf Blondeville, The First English Hero*, (2009) 93-95

14 ibid., 97

15 op. cit., Barraclough,, nos 366, 366a, Stratford Birthplace Trust Record Office, (subsequently SBTRO) DR10.1409, ff 351; the 16 th-century copy, made by Arthur Gregory of Stivichall, appears to be very close to the original and combines 366 and 366a in the Segrave cartulary listed by Geoffrey Barraclough.The grant also included the right for the men of Caludon to pasture in the earl's wood, for which a charge of 12d per year was levied.

16 op. cit., Coss, (1991) 97

17 British Library (subsequently BL) Harl MS 4748; an analysis of the Segrave cartulary reorganised by location was completed by Dr Samantha Letters in the second volume of her PhD, see Samantha Letters, A history of the Seagrave family c.1160-1295, with an edition of the calendar of the Seagrave Cartulary (1997) PhD, University of London

18 Another of Peter Coss's substantial Coventry studies has proved invaluable here: Peter Coss, *The Early Records of Medieval Coventry*, (1986)

19 Clifford Archive, Ugbrooke, Devon (subsequently Clifford), W(E) 1/20

20 Clifford, W(E) 1/9

21 op. cit., Coss, (1991) 37

22 ibid, 66-68; Clifford W (E) 1/3

23 op. cit., Coss, (1986) no 407

24 William de Sancto Edmund and John de Riparariis (Riparus) were closely associated with Stephen at the time, William being under-sheriff of Warwickshire for him in 1229, succeeded by John in 1232, op. cit., Coss, (1989) note on p. 205,

25 op. cit., Samantha Letters PhD; BL Harleian MS 4784, nos 287, 269 (confirmed in 1295 no 324) 314

26 op. cit., Coss, 96-7

27 op. cit., Coss, (1991) 102

28 *Calendar of Papal Registers relating to Great Britain and Ireland*, Vol 1: 1198-1304, (1893) 184; op. cit., Samantha Letters PhD, no 517; a much fuller 16th-century version can be found at SBTRO DR10 1409, f 351

29 The National Archives (subsequently TNA), E164.21 ff.59v; Coss, (1991) 97; the three fields were *Michilfild, Littulfeld and Asshmore, which can be identified as the later Ashmoore, Litle Field and Stubble Field* (1668)

30 Ian Fisher, 'Archaeological geophysical survey at Caludon Castle, Coventry, West Midlands,' Northamptonshire Archaeology (June 2008), 2

31 Most of the biographical details on the Segrave family have come from three extremely useful sources: a), op. cit. Samantha Letters, vol, 1 b) David Smith's notes on the Segrave family accompanying A2A entry for Berkeley Castle Muniments, c) Robert Hill, Seagrave history 1086 to 1760, (2008) Seagrave history website: Leicester villages .com

32 op. cit., Vincent, 315

33 William Hunt, 'Sir Stephen Segrave' in *The Dictionary of National Biography*.

34 op. cit., Samantha Letters, PhD, no281; BL Harl MS 4748; SBTRO DR10/1409 f 351v

35 Clifford, W(L) 1/7, 1815 Sale particulars of Caludon estate

36 TNA SC1094/11/ m20; op. cit., Coss, (1991) 100-102

37 op. cit., op. cit., Samantha Letters, PhD, no 290; BL Harl MS 4748; SBTRO DR10/1334; Nicholas still retained rights of common pasture in *La Wyke* and the two furlongs after harvest and in every third fallow year. The Langleys were obliged to maintain a hedged route through to this area for Segrave's cattle.

Chapter 1 – NOTES

38 Helen M Jewel, 'Nicholas of Segrave - first Lord Segrave' in *The Dictionary of National Biography*

39 Trevor John (ed.), *The Warwickshire Hundred Rolls of 12879-80, Stoneleigh and Kineton Hundreds*, (1992) 144-5

40 Christopher Curie, 'Fishponds as Garden Features, c 1550-1750,' *Garden History, Vol 18, No. 1,* (spring 1990) 22

41 J S Hamilton, '*Nicholas Segrave' in The Dictionary of National Biography*

42 *Calendar of Patent Rolls, Edward I, 1281-1292,* 1893), July 14 1292

43 A W & C Barsby, *Manorial Law,* (1996) 116

44 op. cit., Robert Hill, Seagrave history, see n. 29

45 Clifford , W (E) 1/3; another copy was enrolled in the Patent Rolls and published in, *Calendar of Patent Rolls, Edward I, 1301-1307,* (1898) 314. There is no evidence that the licence was renewed in 1354, as claimed in a newspaper article, c.1882 (Coventry Archives, Lowe's Newspaper Cuttings, Vol 3) and repeated in VCH, Warwick Vol 8, 121

46 op. cit., Seagrave history.

47 Charles Coulson, 'Hierarchism in Conventual Crenellation,' *Medieval Archaeology, Vol 16,* (1982) 72

48 SBTRO DR10/637 (1317); Berkeley Castle Archive (subsequently Berkeley) BCM/D/5/74/19 (1317); BCM/D/5/79/5 (1318); BCM/D/5/87/2 (1323)

49 Clifford, W (E) 1/9

50 *Calendar of Inquisitions post Mortem, Edw II*, Vol VI, (1910) no 699, 429

51 *Calendar of Close Rolls, Edward II 1323-1327*, Vol 4 (1898) 454

52 *Calendar of Inquisitions post Mortem, Edw II ,* Vol VI, (1910) no 700, 433

53 op. cit., Barraclough, no 366a; this annual charge derived from a grant of right of pasture to Caludon men in the earl's wood at Coventry

54 *Calendar of Charter Rolls* ,1341-1417, Vol 5 (1916) 105

55 Berkeley, BCM/D/5/69/5 BCM/D/5/37/3; BCM/5/78/2; BCM/D/5/1/15

56 SBTRO DR10/649

CHAPTER 2

Caludon and the Mowbrays
1359-c.1494

Fig 16
Mowbray coat of arms

On February 4 1359 Sir John de Mowbray (III) was called upon by Edward, the Black Prince, to do 'fealty for the Manor of Caluedon and other lands in the county of Warrewyk, the Manor being held of the prince as of the Manor of Cheilesmore.'[1] Fealty was a pledge of allegiance from an inferior, Sir John, to his superior, the Prince and formed the cornerstone of the feudal system. It provided a 'contract' between the two parties at their different levels in the hierarchy. The record makes plain that, although the lordship and castle of Caludon descended to Elizabeth, the heir of the Segraves, the law had dictated that it was to be her husband, Sir John, who would be recognised as the Lord of the Manor of Caludon.

We are fortunate in knowing in some detail the make-up of the manor over which Sir John exercised his new lordship. At the behest of the state, after the death of John de Segrave III in 1353, an inquisition was carried out to establish the nature and extent of his estates, which due to his premature death passed to his brother-in-law, John Mowbray III (Fig 17).[2] The manor of Caludon is described in terms of its productive demesne land, land which is farmed directly for the benefit of the lord (Fig 18). There was no mention of the castle nor was the park surveyed, but some of the field names can be reconciled with earlier and later surveys. Mowbray's demesne was divided into three divisions. The first consisted of three parts. A field of 27 acres was situated 'in the land of the park', in other words in the park itself, and *Parvus campus* (identifiable as the later *Little Field*) containing 36.75 acres lay near the park. *Middelfeld* (possibly a small part of the later *Michel Field*) together with the other two, measured just over 101 acres (Fig 19). Most of these fields appear to have been located on the north side of the Ansty Road. The second part of the demesne was more or less the same size (100 acres), divided between a large field of 65 acres and a second of 34 acres named as *le Moneriddingge*, and must have been situated to the west of the first group, again on the north side of Ansty Road. Lastly there was another large field called *Assemor*, measuring just over 104 acres, whose position is fortunately without doubt, as the later *Ashmoore* lay to the west of the park and the south of Ansty Road. It was associated with some 'ploughland to the mill', (6 acres). In 1668 there was a field called *Millers Ashmoore*, which strongly suggests that there was a mill in the vicinity.[3] A small

Fig 17
*Pedigree of
the Mowbrays*

MOWBRAY PEDIGREE

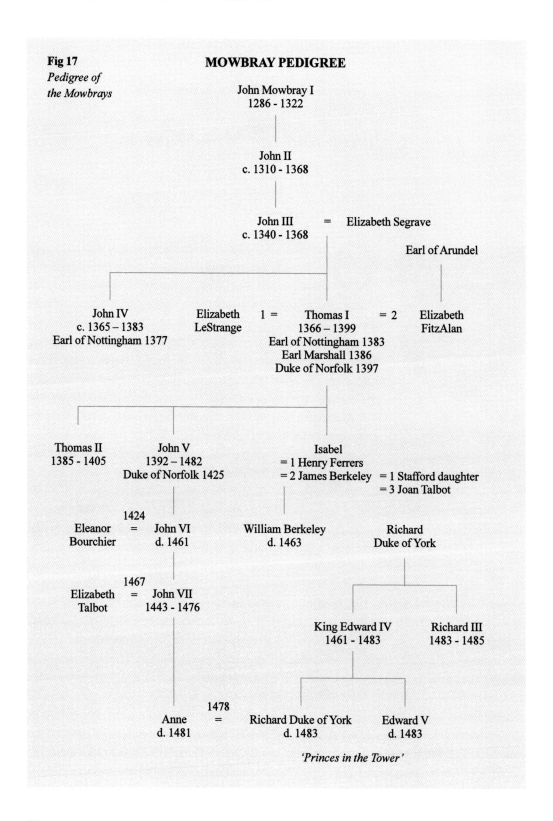

John Mowbray I
1286 - 1322

John II
c. 1310 - 1368

John III   =   Elizabeth Segrave
c. 1340 - 1368

Earl of Arundel

John IV   Elizabeth   1 =   Thomas I   = 2   Elizabeth
c. 1365 – 1383   LeStrange   1366 – 1399   FitzAlan
Earl of Nottingham 1377   Earl of Nottingham 1383
          Earl Marshal 1386
          Duke of Norfolk 1397

Thomas II   John V   Isabel
1385 - 1405   1392 – 1482   = 1 Henry Ferrers
          Duke of Norfolk 1425   = 2 James Berkeley   = 1 Stafford daughter
          = 3 Joan Talbot

          1424
Eleanor   =   John VI   William Berkeley   Richard
Bourchier   d. 1461   d. 1463   Duke of York

          1467
Elizabeth   =   John VII
Talbot   1443 - 1476

          King Edward IV   Richard III
          1461 - 1483   1483 - 1485

          1478
Anne   =   Richard Duke of York   Edward V
d. 1481   d. 1483   d. 1483

'Princes in the Tower'

stream used to flow along the east boundary of *Ashmoore* into Stoke parish. With no evidence of a mill in this part of Caludon, it is likely that it was situated just across the boundary in Stoke. The combined total of the demesne was about 311 acres, a figure that compares closely with a total of 297 acres measured using the late nineteenth-century edition of the large scale (1:2500) OS map of the area.

Demesne meadow was also identified, but was scattered about the manor; the '25 acres below the park' was probably *Lake Meadow* on the River Sowe, now part of the playing fields of Caludon Castle School. The other meadows were at *platbrigge*, in *Mildnis*, and near Sowe bridge.

Given their size it is likely that these large demesne fields were 'open'; ploughed in strips for practical purposes (drainage), but unlike the open fields of tenant land, not subject to a highly divided tenurial division. As single blocks of cultivated land, they may have been enclosed by ditches and hedges. The meadow would have provided excellent feed and watering for livestock, being fed by the Sowe river.

The summary statement referred to rents, adding up to £18 per year, of properties constituting the 'sum of the total rents of Caloudon to them of his members'. From later surveys we know these rents came in the main from properties in the neighbouring manors of Wyken, Sowe, Binley and Foleshill, although many were to be found in Coventry. These rentals include a 'messuage in Earle Street' rented to Peter de Egiffeeld (Edgefield) for 2s 6d and a room and a storeroom held for half a mark (6s 4d). Peter Baron held part of a shop on Broadgate and Gregor Sutor had a complete shop on the same street. There were a number of other shops also owing rent in Broadgate as well as in Spon Street and Dog Lane. A crossbowman, Philip Balistarius, tenanted a shop in Cheylesmore, on the edge of the city near the manor house (now the Coventry Registry Office).

In many cases manors were not compact land units, but included outlying lands and rents which contributed to their incomes, and Caludon was a prime example. The other scattered fragments, the 'members' of the Caludon manor had been acquired over time by purchase, exchange and inheritance. There was however a contiguous core consisting of the park and its demesne.

Sir John Mowbray (III) was descended from a family which could trace its ancestry back to the 7th century in the person of a Swede, Olaf Ingjaldsson. His descendants eventually helped to invade and settle the area in northern France, which became known as Normandy. Roger d'Aubigny came to England in 1066 and his descendants in turn became one of the great medieval English families. They anglicised their name to Mowbray in the twelfth century and in 1295 Roger de Mowbray was ennobled to become a baron. His son John (I), born in 1286, had suffered during the reign of Edward II (1307-1327) for opposing the rise of the Despencers, the immensely powerful Earls of Winchester. He forfeited much of his land to Edward and eventually his life. After supporting the rebellion of the Earl of Lancaster in 1322 he was captured at the Battle of Boroughbridge and drawn and hanged as a traitor at York on March 23 of that year. His son John (II), a twelve year old, was imprisoned for his father's rebellion. After his eventual release he wisely served Edward III loyally and successfully until his death from the plague in 1361.

John's son was also named John, the third in this Mowbray succession and the first to have a connection with Caludon (Fig 17). He was born at the family estate at Epworth in 1340 and first enters the state record at the time of his knighthood by the King and the Duke of Lancaster in July 1355. This

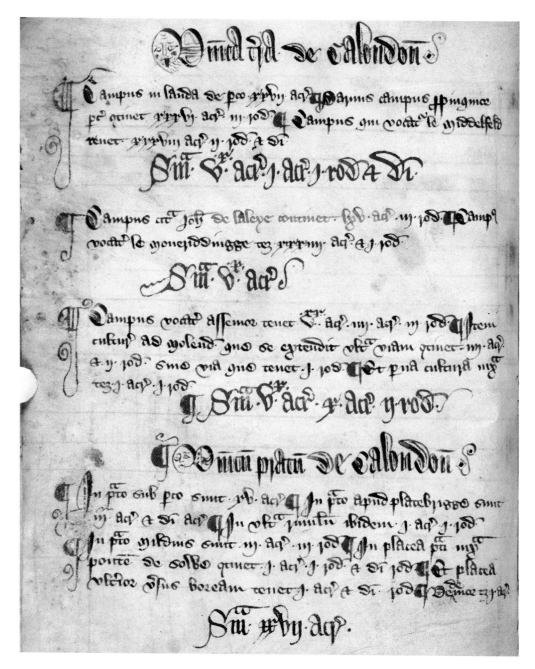

Fig 18 *Extract from the Caludon feodary or survey 1353*

was on the occasion of the King's trip to France to meet with Charles of Navarre. When he was just three years old a marriage was proposed by his family between John and Audrey Montague, one of the numerous descendants of Edward I. This was to be a double wedding, with John's sister Blanche marrying Audrey's brother, Edward. The plan failed to come to fruition and so instead, in 1349, John married Elizabeth Segrave. There appears to have been some friction between the Segraves and Mowbrays. John's uncle, the earl of Lancaster, was required to seek dispensations from Pope Clement VI to allow the marriage to take place. Given the litigious nature of the era, there may well have been a dispute between the two families involving their estates. A marriage between the families was sometimes used as a way of settling differences.

Very little is recorded of John III's life. He was not greatly involved in politics or public life, although he was summoned to parliament as a baron between 1362 and 1366 and in 1367 he received a licence to nominate attorneys to look after his estates and affairs when he left for Europe on Crusade. Soon after crossing Europe in 1368, he was captured and killed by Turks somewhere near to Constantinople. Almost twenty-eight years after his death, in 1396, his son Thomas was able to take possession of his father's remains and arranged for them to be them transported back to England for burial.

The inquisition that followed John's death on Crusade was made in December 1369 and it was found that he had held the Lordship of the manor of Caludon 'by the courtesy of England and the inheritance of Elizabeth his wife and daughter and heir of John Segrave Knight.'[4] According to the record, the manor included 'a several (enclosed) fishery and a park' and was held of Prince Edward by a knight's fee and 'service of a sparrowhawk or 12d'. The sparrowhawk or 12d charge can be traced back to the original charter of c.1220 from Ranulf de Blondeville to Stephen de Segrave (see Chapter 1).[5] By this time such a service was very often rendered in name only, sometimes converted to cash payments, a process known as scutage. A payment of 6s was also made to the prior of Coventry, patrons of St Michael's church in Coventry; this charge had been agreed in 1239 to enable tithes to be collected locally to support the chapel at Caludon.

The inquisition gives a passing insight into the state of the manor at this time and prominent in the description is the existence of both a park and a fishery, most likely the fish pond on the north side of the castle. The park was a visible symbol of a medieval landowner's success and aspirations. It distinguished his estate from many others principally farmed by his tenants.

Parks were by no means an usual feature of the medieval landscape. It is estimated that there were over 3,000 parks in England in 1300, but they were reserved only for the wealthy.[6] The park at Caludon is known to have contained an enclosure for deer, the deer hay or enclosure mentioned in 1279-1280 (see Chapter 1). Fallow deer were the most popular and convenient deer to keep and the mixture of grassland and trees was designed to foster their upkeep and care. Keeping and hunting deer and consuming venison at the table were symbols of success and status and this living resource was needed to be jealously guarded. Caludon would have required park keepers or parkers to protect the stock, particularly from poachers.

Fish was an important part of a nobleman's diet and it is likely that the catch from Caludon pond would have found its way into the dishes served at the castle. It was highly valued as a gift if given to neighbouring landowners. The main fish pond lay on the north side of the castle integrated with the moat. Even today after heavy rain water gathers in this hollow between the castle ruin and the gardens of Farren Road to form a small mere (Fig 15).

After the death of John de Mowbray (III) in 1369 Caludon passed to his four-year-old son, also called John (IV). Both John, and his younger brother, Thomas (born in 1366) were minors and therefore valuable wards at the time of their father's death. The young Mowbrays were given over to the care of their great-aunt, Blanche Wake. She became the de facto Lady of the manor of Caludon until such time as her eldest ward came into his majority at the age of twenty-one or was given a special dispensation by the King. Blanche was well connected, being both a cousin to the King and the daughter of Henry of Lancaster and as an historical figure she is best remembered for her role in a dispute with Thomas Lisle, the Bishop of Ely, which broke out during the 1350s. A running argument over boundaries in their neighbouring Huntingdonshire estates erupted into an ugly skirmish fought between retainers on both sides. Blanche complained to the King, and a commission to investigate the trespass by Lisle's men onto Lady Wake's Manor of Colne, which had originally sparked the fight, was granted. At the resulting proceedings the Bishop was found guilty and fined £900. Lisle evidently did not take the matter lightly and was later indicted for inciting the murder of one of Blanche's retainers. Not surprisingly Lisle fled to France before he could be prosecuted but not before he was stripped of his estates and possessions by the King.

At the coronation of Richard II in 1377, the young John Mowbray, Lord of Caludon, was elevated to the Earldom of Nottingham. A special clause was inserted into the charter of creation which specified that ... 'all his lands and tenements whereof he was then possessed should be held sub *honore comitali*, and as a parcel of this earldom.'[7] Sadly, John's youth and his early death in 1383 at the age of about eighteen meant that he made little impact as a nobleman. The celebrity of the Mowbray name came instead to be embodied in his younger brother, Thomas, who was just a year younger than John and was made second Earl of Nottingham on February 12, 1383. Through his mother, Thomas was related to Richard II and having spent a great deal of time with the young King the two youths became close personal friends. Their great mutual pleasure was hunting and a year before his brother's death, Richard granted Thomas the valuable right to hunt in the royal forests. The King's personal intervention was instrumental in securing a good marriage for Thomas and a bride was chosen; Elizabeth, the daughter of John, Lord le Strange of Blakemere. A further gift conferred on Thomas by King Richard was membership of the Order of the Garter, granted once his friend had succeeded to his earldom. As a second son, Thomas Mowbray could not have expected to have received this honour and so, mindful of this he staged a procession in London to mark his brother's memory a year after his death. The ornate throng snaked its way through the busy streets of the capital, making its way to John's final resting place at Whitefriars in Fleet Street.

Thomas was still a minor (c.17 years of age) and therefore in no position to take control of his inheritance. There is no doubt also that he reserved the majority of his time for service at court and attendance on the King. Richard even allowed Mowbray to keep his own apartments at both Eltham and Kings Langley Palaces so that he could remain in close contact with the King. The management of his estates fell to others with drastic consequences, particularly on Caludon.

In the early and mid 1380s Caludon suffered major damage by the hand of William Bagot of nearby Baginton. He had been awarded with John of Gaunt, amongst others, the wardship of certain of the estates of the young John Mowbray, and when he died, the wardship of his brother, Thomas. William, an extremely ambitious local landowner, and later to be known as one of the three infamous 'evil consellors' of Richard II, enjoyed the patronage of the Earl of Warwick and many other baronial families. In 1385, however, he was called to account for the damage he had caused at Caludon. The document is the first to describe some of the buildings at the castle.[9]

> ... in the time of John de Moubray ... William Bagot did waste the Manor of Calughdon... He pulled down and carried away a tiled building of four bays inside the bridge, which cannot be rebuilt for £10. He carried away a bell worth 20s, hanging in the chapel of the manor. He pulled down and carried away a tiled building of seven bays outside the bridge, which cannot be built for £12, and a barn of five bays roofed with straw which cannot be rebuilt for 100s.

As well as this wholesale demolition of property at the castle Bagot then proceeded to remove a huge amount of timber:

> ... He felled and sold a wood called 'Newhewen', worth £40; and for lack of fencing the buds (tendrones) and shoots are wasted by beasts to the damage of 100s. In the wood of the manor called 'Dedemoor' he wasted ash trees worth 100 s and felled and wasted 100 oaks worth 40s. He felled and wasted 60 oaks worth 40s in the park of the manor. All this 'waste, sale and destruction' was said to have been carried out during the lifetime of John de Mowbray except for the felling of the oaks which was done 'in the time of the present King and the said Thomas.

This is not an unusual story of a guardian taking advantage of his ward's relatively powerless position and exploiting the estates temporarily under his control. John Mowbray had in fact shortly before his death in 1383 granted William Bagot the manor of Crick in Northamptonshire, but any gratitude for this was not demonstrated - quite the reverse.[10] William might have seized his chance to asset strip Caludon in order to improve his own castle at Baginton. More strange was the fact that William Bagot's relationship with Thomas was not impaired, and he was to retain Thomas's confidence for the rest of his life.[11]

In any event the record itself reveals interesting details of the manor which would not be found elsewhere. It shows there to have been present buildings both within and without the moat crossed by a bridge. It can be assumed that the more important buildings were located on the moated platform, the obvious hall and apartments not being mentioned, and that the more utilitarian structures such as the 'home farm' complex, e.g., the barn, were arranged in a courtyard on the outer side of the moat (east).

The felling of the considerable number of trees would have produced a large amount of timber for new buildings which could have been erected at Baginton or on his other local estates (Wolston and Draycote). The wood, Newhewen, can be identified as it was later a field at the western extremity of the Caludon demesne, situated on the east side of Stoke Heath and (part later called Barras Heath) (Fig 19). *Deedmore* is better known from the modern road name, but its actual location was in Caludon near Henley mill (Sullivan Road).

Moving to the wider political world, Thomas Mowbray was immersed in intrigue at this time. He was a confidant and advisor to the King and Richard, like his predecessor, Edward II, was capricious and open to influence. He gathered around himself a coterie of young nobles and favourites. This caused consternation among the older lords, who considered themselves the wisest and most appropriate counsel. The Duke of Lancaster was concerned enough openly to accuse Richard's youthful advisors of having too much of a 'malign' influence over the King.[12] He had good reason for his suspicions since he had good intelligence that a number of them, including Mowbray, had plotted to kill the Duke in early 1385.

Lancaster's accusations did nothing to halt Mowbray's advance: Richard simply ignored them and in January 1386 he granted the title and position of Marshal of England to Mowbray. The title of Marshal, or Earl Marshal, as it later became, was one of the high offices of medieval government, connected most closely with the King's military organisation and his horses and stables. Today the title resides with the Dukes of Norfolk and is concerned chiefly with genealogical matters as head of the College of Arms. In the thirteenth century it had been held by the Earls of Pembroke and subsequently vested in Mowbray's great grandfather, Thomas Brotherton. When granted to Mowbray, however, the office became inheritable.[13] As was often the case, no sooner had the Marshal reached a career pinnacle at court, than he began to lose the affection of the King. Richard was a deeply suspicious and jealous man. He came to distrust Mowbray soon after his marriage to Elizabeth FitzAlan, the daughter of the Earl of Arundel. His first wife, Elizabeth le Strange, had died only a few months after their marriage and this second match did not please the King. Firstly, Arundel did not approve of the King's choice of counsellors and made his distaste for them public. Richard was fearful of Arundel's ultimate intentions. Secondly, Thomas had not sought a licence from the King in order to marry, a requirement for all nobles. In a fit of petulance, the King ordered Mowbray's lands to be distrained (confiscated) until the Marshal had agreed to seek and pay for a marriage licence.

Unsurprisingly, Mowbray quickly became disillusioned with the King, not merely for temporarily dispossessing him of his lands, but also because Richard had turned his attention to new favourites, such as Robert de Vere, the Earl of Oxford. He naturally felt side-lined at court and increasingly sought the company of his father in law whereby they could hatch schemes to secure their own promotion. In March 1387 he accompanied Arundel on one of the most celebrated acts of piracy in English history. The two Earls commanded a sea borne attack on a Franco-Flemish wine fleet off the coast of Margate. They easily overcame the merchants and made away with 8,000 tuns (casks) of wine. After shipping their booty home they sold the wine off at 4d a gallon to register a handsome profit. Their actions aroused both outrage and jealousy amongst their peers as well as causing a major diplomatic incident. When the pair next attended court, instead of the rapturous reception they had expected, Richard proved reserved and cold, whilst others at court simply turned their backs on the two 'pirates'.

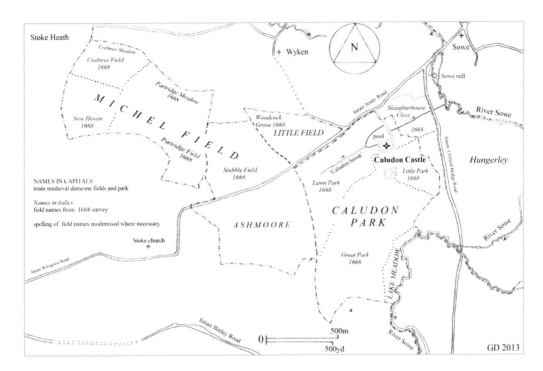

Fig 19 *Map of the ancient Caludon Park and demense identifying field names*

It was fortuitous that the disgruntled Mowbray had been pushed aside at court, since late in 1387 a powerful array of nobles, including the Earls of Gloucester, Warwick and Arundel combined to declare that five of the King's confidants, including de Vere, were guilty of treason. At Hornsey, north of London, they drew up their forces in a show of strength against the King with Mowbray eventually choosing to join them. In panic De Vere was sent by the King to raise his men in Cheshire, but his army was defeated at Radcot Bridge on December 20 by the 'Lords Appellant', as the rebels became known. Mowbray had hastened to the fight with his own men, but arrived on the field too late to take part in the battle. In victory the Appellants returned to London, seized the court and established the 'Merciless Parliament' to deal with the King's 'evil counsellors'.

Mowbray's reticence and underwhelming support for the rebels continued and he remained suitably appropriately unenthusiastic in public. Consequently when divisions emerged within the Appellant faction, ultimately causing its collapse, he managed to escape the fallout. The King acted swiftly to retake full control in 1389 and, needing all the support he could muster, Mowbray was forgiven and received favourite status once more.

Relying on his renewed influence, Mowbray became one of most powerful men in England and added considerably to his own fortune. In addition to his existing estates, including Caludon, he was granted a number of lucrative, manors, sinecures and offices. He was appointed Captain of Calais and Chief Justice of Chester, Flint and North Wales. In Ireland, during a campaign with Richard II during the year 1395, he was granted the wealthy Lordship of Carlow. During this period the receipts from his many properties were estimated to be worth around £14,000 per annum. The core of his estate lay in East Anglia, but he had manors in Warwickshire as well as a group of estates centred on Melton Mowbray in Leicestershire. There was also a host of manors in Lincolnshire and Yorkshire, as well as the huge manor of Chepstow in south Wales. Mowbray was a rich man and an impressive figure. In an age before media celebrities, men like Mowbray provided power, glamour and fame. He was especially renowned for his brilliance at tournaments. In the spring of 1390 he won the honours at a major tournament staged at Smithfield in London after jousting with the Earl of Moray. The sport took him across Europe and his movement between countries was cleverly utilised by Richard who engaged Mowbray in secret diplomatic missions. The most notable of these involved Mowbray contacting the imperial diet at Frankfurt to discuss Richard's ambitious plan to have himself crowned Emperor of the Holy Roman Empire. For a time it appeared that Mowbray would become the most powerful man in England save the monarch, but his sudden downfall was as swift and spectacular as his sudden revival.

In 1397, after circling his enemies for months, the King finally swooped on them and arrested the Earls of Gloucester, Warwick and Arundel. A month later the three were brought before eight of the King's prominent supporters, including Mowbray, for formal charges of treason to be presented. It is difficult to know how Mowbray felt about his father-in-law's predicament, but any lingering affection seems to have evaporated in the cause of expediency. On 21 September Arundel was tried, convicted and executed.

Mowbray was viewed by the remnants of the Appellant faction as a traitor for his part in Arundel's death, but even before the execution he had implicated himself in an even more serious act. During the period leading up to Arundel's trial Mowbray had been holding Thomas, Earl of Gloucester captive at his castle in Calais. When he was ordered to bring Gloucester to Parliament, he sheepishly went before his peers to announce that he had indeed held Gloucester 'in my custody' but that, unfortunately 'in that same prison, he died.'[14] Mowbray then read aloud a rather convenient sounding confession that Gloucester had supposedly provided, admitting to the truth of all Richard's claims against him. In fact the matter was rather more unpleasant than a simple death in custody; which, after all, was a common occurrence in fourteenth-century prisons. It soon became apparent that Gloucester had, in fact, been murdered by Mowbray's valet, John Hall, on his master's orders. Indeed, Mowbray is said to have forced Hall to carry out the deed on pain of his life. Furthermore, it then became clear that Mowbray himself had been acting on orders from the King and had feared for his own life, a defence he would later use to mitigate his part in the crime.

The affair, understandably, caused a sensation in England. Opinion of Mowbray plunged even lower just days after his announcement to Parliament: using this occasion Richard, with no thought to subtlety, raised Mowbray to the Dukedom of Norfolk. The King was clearly relishing his victory and, in an even more unseemly gesture, handed Mowbray huge swathes of Arundel's estates, most notably the Honour of Lewes in Sussex.

Mowbray was no fool. He knew that his power and wealth were held at the whim of a monarch of both dubious morality and capricious loyalty. Although Richard had accepted Mowbray back to court in 1389, it is likely that the King had never truly forgiven him or placed in him his full trust.

By December 1397 Mowbray had realised that the King was about to turn his wrath upon him and was in fear for his life. Intrigue and rumour of his impeding downfall were rife and it was almost perverse of him to have chosen this moment to make a serious error in judgement. One morning, on meeting Henry Bolingbroke, the son of his enemy, John of Gaunt, Duke of Lancaster, on the road from London to Brentford, he spilled out his concerns that he was marked man and feared that he was about to pay for his disloyalty at Radcot Bridge. Bolingbroke naturally reported the details of the conversation to his father, who in turn recounted them to the King. Mowbray soon discovered Bolingbroke's betrayal and lost his nerve completely. He tried and utterly failed to have Gaunt assassinated and vowed revenge on Bolingbroke for breaking his confidence. For his part, the King promptly stripped him of the marshalcy and ordered his officials to seize Mowbray's estates. By the end of February 1398 he had been incarcerated in Windsor Castle.

On 16 September 1398 a writ was issued to Guy Spyne, the escheator of the counties of Warwickshire and Leicestershire, for an inquisition to be held into the composition of lands held by Thomas Mowbray, Duke of Norfolk. The escheator's function was to assess the value of property that automatically passed to the King during a minority of an heir (wardship) or for the crime of treason. This property was 'escheated' or returned to the King's possession, a process which dated back to the Norman Conquest of 1066. Under feudal law the King was the ultimate holder of all land in his realm (the tenant-in-chief) and any estate was held by his nobles and landowners in return for military and other services. Accusations of betrayal often led to the confiscation of estates by the Crown, a most useful source of income and means of reward for others in favour by their redistribution. The escheator Spyne's return made in 1398, provides another useful survey of Caludon manor. It was described as:

> a fortress (*fortelettum*) of no net yearly value, divers closes of pasture formerly arable namely 'Henleye', 'Michelfield', 'Stubyfeld', 'Littelfeld', and 'Asshemour' containing 3 carucates of land worth £13 6s. 8d. yearly.[15]

These fields were 'let at farm', in other words rented out, and the names are familiar from the earlier surveys of the demesne lands (see above and Chapter 1) (Fig 19). The significance here is that the fields were rented and not directly cultivated from the 'home farm' at Caludon Castle. This change reflects the wider economic disruption that had taken place after the Black Death (1349-50) and possibly the wastage caused by William Bagot. Generally demesne cultivation collapsed owing to the lack of labour, both servile and paid, and the outbreak of this disease caused the loosening of the bonds of serfdom, a process that accelerated during the fifteenth century. At Caludon it had become easier to lease the demesne in parcels to local tenants, whether of the manor itself or of other neighbouring estates.

The survey of the meadow closely follows the detail of the 1353 Feodary (see above). The meadow, *Lakemede* (on the River Sowe) is mentioned again, confirming that it was managed as a separate entity within the park for its valuable hay crop (Fig 19). There was another meadow in nearby 'Bynley' on the opposite side of the Sowe and a meadow in Wyken. Three other meadows

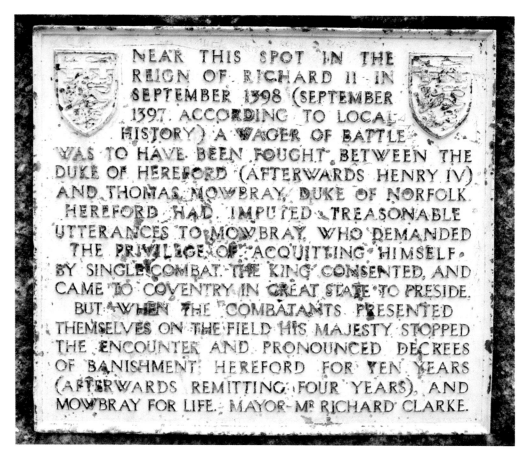

Fig 20 *The Mowbray – Bolingbroke tournament plaque at Gosford Green, Coventry.*

are recognisable from the earlier Feodary: at *Sowebrigge*, *Platebrigge* and *Midelmede*, only the first recognisable as being near the bridge over the Sowe on the road to the village of the same name (now Walsgrave on Sowe). The park attached to the castle may also have suffered depredation since, it was claimed, it had no value above the keep of the game. Of even more interest is the fact that the whole manor of Caludon was let to Sir William Bagot for £26 pounds per annum who had devastated Caludon in the early 1380s. It is not certain when this lease was made by Thomas Mowbray himself or swiftly after the Crown had seized the Mowbray estates.

The date of the inquisition is significant since this was the same day (16 September 1398) on which Mowbray and Bolingbroke were due to fight a trial by combat at Coventry precipitated by mutual insult and accusations. Mowbray had given himself up to the King in February 1398 in order to explain himself fully and plead his case in person. At the same time he was imprisoned in some style at Windsor Castle. Later he was transferred to the great wardrobe by St Paul's Cathedral (rooms where royal clothes and jewels stored). Despite his confinement, Mowbray whipped up a storm of invective against Bolingbroke, who had remained a free man. The dispute caused great problems for King Richard, who tried in vain to have the two reconcile their differences. He urged them to meet in April 1398, but when Bolingbroke confronted Mowbray at Windsor he produced even more charges against the Duke; these included accusations that he had stolen money given to him by the King for governing Calais and, more seriously, the oft repeated charge that Gloucester had been murdered on his order. The meeting is famously recreated in the first scene of Shakespeare's Richard II, when Bolingbroke accuses Mowbray of having received:[16]

> …eight thousand nobles
> In name of lendings for your highnesses soldiers,
> The which he hath detained for lewd employments'
> Like a false traitor and, injurious villain.

Mowbray is enraged by Bolingbroke's 'false passage of thy throat' and though he admits to neglecting Gloucester's welfare, he denies killing him. The King eventually tires of the bickering and orders that their personal conflict be resolved by combat, armed with lances and on horseback. He then commands that the two men should:

> Be ready, as your lives shall answer it,
> At Coventry, upon St Lambert's day.
> There shall your swords and lances arbitrate
> The swelling difference of your settled hate.

The realistic but deadly joust was fixed for 16 September, 1398, the same day as the escheator's inquisition. What this says of Richard's thoughts on the outcome of the trial by combat is open to interpretation.

Mowbray came to Coventry with his retinue and lodged at Caludon Castle before the trial by combat. It was but a short distance from Gosford Green, where the combat had been arranged (Fig 20). On the morning of 16th he rode forth from Caludon on his warhorse which was clad in 'crimson velvet embroydered with Lions of silver and mulberie-trees' and made his way towards the Green for what promised to be one of the most splendid events at the culmination of the fourteenth century.[17] A spectacle of this magnitude was rare even for an important city such as Coventry. For the occasion both Mowbray and Bolingbroke had ordered bespoke armour from the finest manufacturers in Europe. The former's attire originated in Milan, whilst the latter's was shipped from Germany. Both men took the field in their magnificent array before an expectant crowd, including the King and his nobles as well as a host of onlookers (Fig 21). Whether Richard had planned his next move is difficult to determine. In Shakespeare's version, the King appears to have baulked at the prospect of either man being killed, '…for our eyes do hate the dire aspect of civil wounds plough'd up with neighbour's swords.'

As the two Lords readied themselves for the fight, Richard caused an audible gasp by suddenly announcing that there would be no battle. In what appears to be either an almighty compromise or a carefully calculated punishment, he called both men before him. Richard announced that as King, he alone was able to judge a man accused of treason. Since he did not really wish to harm either man he hesitated at capital punishment and instead banished Mowbray from England for the rest of his life whilst Bolingbroke was exiled for ten years, a mistake he would ultimately rue. He ordered that Mowbray's land be forfeited and the order was issued on that same day for the seizure of Caludon. Both men were given until 20 October to remove themselves from the country. Given the speed in which the orders were received, it is likely that the King had prepared the whole charade beforehand and primed his officials to take swift action to secure the estates.

Mowbray, Lord of Caludon, left on October 19 and within a year (22 Sept 1399) he had died of the plague in Venice. After his departure disturbances

Fig 21 *An imaginary reconstruction of the Mowbray – Bolingbroke tournament at Gosford Green, Coventry, where the duel was aborted by Richard II.*

had broken out at Caludon Castle. A few days after the Duke's death an order was sent out to the Mayor of Coventry, Geoffrey Hampton, to enquire 'about certain wastes and other damage committed in the Manor of Caloudon.'[18] It is a possibility that Mowbray's remaining retinue had ransacked the manor in order to prevent it passing in whole to the King or the tenant, William Bagot, judging by his past record. Furthermore the tenants and labourers themselves had taken the opportunity to make mischief following the disgrace of the castle's owner. The record is frustratingly silent on details of the events or the results of any investigations that Hampton was able to carry out.[19]

A month after the order to Hampton, the King finally had his men in place in Warwickshire; Thomas Rempston, John Leek and William Jorse. They were all from Nottinghamshire and were ordered to keep the Mowbray estates, including Caludon, in the King's name until Thomas's heir, Thomas II, came of age.[20] At the same time it was confirmed that the grant by Thomas Mowbray to William Marshall (Marchall or Mareschal) for life of the 'keeping of his park of Calowden would stand.'[21] Marshall was one of Mowbray's yeomen of the chamber and had also been earlier Keeper of the Mowbray park at Haweness in Bedfordshire. However, the custody of the park was claimed a few days later by William Riffane, by the force of a later grant than William Marshall's, dated 17

March 1398, which also appointed him Lieutenant of the Manor and Castle, the custody of which had already been granted to John Kingsley (Kingeley) for life. The grant, confirmed by letters patent, reveals two principal offices at Caludon, one running the park (the park keeper), the other the manor demesne and the other tenanted land comprising the estate (effectively the bailiff).[22] The immediate outcome of these conflicting claims both supported by later letters patent is not known, but it appears that John Kingsley was ultimately to survive in office (see below).

On 18 November 1399, the manor was again surveyed, this time as part of the official inquisition following Thomas Mowbray's death. It was found to still be held of the King 'as of the Manor of Cheylesmore, by the service of a pair of guilt spurs or 12d yearly', the 12d having been paid from c.1220 for the right to pasture in the earl's wood, whatever was left of it at this time.[23] The old payment in kind of a sparrowhawk appears to have been converted to a pair of spurs, although in reality the money equivalent was probably only actually being paid. The inquisition also mentions that in 1389 a grant of £20 per year had been made from the manor to Thomas de Clynton, confirmed by letters patent in 1399.[24] Clynton was one of Mowbray's knights and his £20 per annum from Caludon was confirmed which also paid for 'two yeoman in his household with a bouche a court.'[25] Meaning literally, 'to have a mouth at court', the privilege of *bouche a court* was an ancient tradition that allowed Clynton and his two yeoman to eat at Caludon should they be passing and require hospitality. The official nature of the grant may have been a way of allowing Clynton to check up on what was happening at the Castle in the absence of its young master, Thomas.

Thomas Mowbray (II) never got to enjoy the spoils of his rightful inheritance. Born in 1385, he was raised in the royal household of King Richard. Merely eight months after his exile, Henry Bolingbroke returned to England as the Duke of Lancaster, in June 1399. Richard was chased from London, support draining away from him as he went. Eventually he surrendered to Bolingbroke at Conway Castle and was deposed in October 1399. The new King sought to overturn many of Richard's later actions, amongst them the young Thomas Mowbray's elevation to the Dukedom of Norfolk, which was annulled. The much coveted post of Marshal of England was handed over to the Earl of Westmorland. Mowbray estates were dismembered and given over to supporters of the new Lancastrian King. Although he was allowed the title of Earl Marshal as a courtesy, Thomas was never permitted to be styled 'Duke' like his father and his income was vastly reduced. Henry did not, however, revoke the seizures made by Richard of the Mowbray estates. Whilst the manor at Caludon had been put in the care of William Riffane and others, other estates were retained to provide for Margaret Brotherton, the elder Thomas Mowbray's grandmother, who had been created Duchess of Norfolk in 1397. Evidence suggests that the Duchess herself retained as much as a third of the manor of Caludon, though grants up until 1405 seem to show this share was held on behalf of Thomas the younger.[26] Crucially, unlike other Mowbray properties, Caludon was not removed from the family's ownership but instead continued in an administrative limbo between the King and the Mowbrays.

Thomas II was allowed to enjoy the title of Earl of Nottingham and expected to 'keep his head down'. He deeply resented the treatment he and his family had received, however, and this led him to join an anti-Lancastrian rebellion led by two northern factions, the Percy family (led by the Earl

Fig 22 *Portrait of John Mowbray, Lord of Caludon, 2nd Duke of Norfolk (1392-1432); based on an engraving by Wenceslaus Holler of a full length portrait in painted glass in St Mary's Hall, Coventry, now lost*

of Westmorland) and a grouping around the Archbishop of York, Richard Scrope. The rising was a miserable failure, the King having been fully aware of it from his network of spies. Thomas was easy prey for Henry, who lured the hapless Earl to a supposed meeting with Westmorland and arrested. He was hanged as a traitor at York on June 8 1405 before reaching full age.

Caludon was again officially forfeited to the King, but it is unlikely, in reality, to have passed out of the control of his officials. Despite their official grip on the property, the King's men had difficulty in persuading inhabitants of the manor to make certain payments. Four months after Mowbray's death, the King issued an order to the 'farmers, receivers or other the occupiers of the Manor of Caloughdoun' to pay what they owed to John Kingsley, the custodian of the castle.[27] It was claimed that Thomas Mowbray had granted 20 marks per annum to his squire, John Kingsley, for life out of the income of Caludon, confirmed by the King by letters patent on 9 June 1405. They had not paid Kingsley since 9 June, the day after Mowbray's execution. It is not known how long this resistance to paying this charge continued. The King's stewards may have struggled for some time to keep their tenants in order and extract an income in order to satisfy the King and pay what was owed to Margaret Brotherton. Although in the hands of the King's officials, the estate was potentially the inheritance of the new Earl of Nottingham, John (V), the second son of the exiled Duke, who had been born in Calais in 1392 (Fig 22). As a minor he received a limited allowance from the King. In January 1412 he married Katherine, daughter of Ralph Neville, Duke of Northumberland and in the following year he was allowed full livery of his estates. This was a massive landholding including the Mowbray patrimony. Even after this time it seems that the Crown retained an interest in Caludon perhaps as a means of guaranteeing Mowbray's loyalty .

Unlike his troublesome father and brother, John Mowbray was publicly loyal to the House of Lancaster and busied himself with fighting in France for Henry IV and Henry V. He took part in the major campaigns of the period and was present at the sieges of Caen, Louviers and Rouen between 1417 and 1419. He only returned to England in August 1422 after the death of Henry V and from this point became increasingly involved in securing full possession of his lands. The accession of the infant king, Henry VI, would only have made his task easier.

There is little information on Caludon during this period and it is not known whether Mowbray spent much time there. For many decades, with absent or exiled owners, replaced by royal officials or their henchmen, it is difficult to imagine the castle undergoing any major improvement or expansion. In fact the reverse was more likely - neglect and over-exploitation. The return of the Mowbray estates from the Crown in 1413 may have finally brought a halt to the many years of decline.

John Mowbray (V) had few political commitments, even after managing to regain the Dukedom of Norfolk in 1425. In the same year he came to live at Framlington Castle in Suffolk and lived in relative obscurity until 1432. This may have been the price he paid for the return of his titular dignity.

The Crown's remaining interest in Caludon is likely to have been a third of the manor as recorded in a writ of 1425.[28] A year after the Duke's death an order went out to the escheator of Warwickshire to remove 'the King's hand ... from the Manor of Caloughdoun, which is held of others than the King.'[29]

The new Mowbray heir at Caludon, John (VI), was a minor at the time of his father's death (1432) and control of his lands was given over to his warder, Humphrey, Duke of Gloucester. By 1438-9 John (VI), Duke of Norfolk, was considered lord of the manor as he headed the Caludon court records in these years.[30] In July 1444 John granted Caludon to feoffees (trustees) these being John Stafford, Archbishop of Canterbury, Eleanor, his wife, Duchess of Norfolk, and Humphrey, Earl of Stafford, created Duke of Buckingham on 14 September 1444.[31] They were all inter-related, Buckingham being Eleanor's maternal half-brother and John Stafford a kinsman, the illegitimate son of another Humphrey Stafford (of Southwick, Hants). The motive for transferring the estate to feoffees is not certain, but it explains why John and Humphrey Stafford appear at the head of Caludon manor court proceedings in the years 1445-1447.[32] It has been suggested that the grant was a jointure settlement for Eleanor Bourchier, whom he had married over twenty years earlier in 1424.[33] The Duke of Buckingham was soon to figure prominently in an infamous and well-documented incident which propelled Caludon to the forefront of local and national politics and ultimately into the history of English literature.

The young John Mowbray (VI) had been a 'troublesome young man... leading a disorderly life with a retinue of equally disorderly followers.'[34] Eventually his outlandish and unruly behaviour was apparently brought under control in 1436 by being sent abroad on 'national service'.[35] He travelled with Gloucester to take part in the relief of Calais, which had come under siege by the Duke of Burgundy. Following this he was sent on a number of high profile political missions in Europe. At home he found his political position in East Anglia eclipsed by William de la Pole, who was created Duke of Suffolk in 1448. Mowbray concentrated a great deal of his domestic energies in countering Suffolk's threat to his position within East Anglian society and this led him to neglect traditional family estates in the Midlands and the North.

There is certainly little to suggest that he spent much time at Caludon Castle. 'The essential character of the family estate was that it was dispersed, with nearly 150 properties in 25 counties, Wales, Ireland and Calais.'[36] When in England he in fact preferred to reside in Lincolnshire. In the preceding decades, as suggested above, the confusing intermix of distant royal overseers and absent landowners was not conducive to the improvement and development of the Caludon estate. The consequences of these years on the estate are difficult to judge, however, and we have no information on the state of the castle buildings. On the other hand, the administration of Caludon shortly after the three feoffees were appointed does appear to have been well organised, as the court records will testify (see below).

Caludon is pulled from relative obscurity by a most unexpected figure: Thomas Malory, before he wrote *Mort D'Arthur*, a major work in early English literature, was a felon and poacher who caused much damage in Caludon Park.

Despite the fact that there has been much scholarly debate on the identity of Malory, modern opinion seems to have reached a consensus.[37] The author of Mort D'Arthur, the great medieval romance from which we have absorbed the majority of the legend of King Arthur, was the same

Thomas Malory who personally led an attack on Caludon manor in the summer of 1451. Thomas Malory held the manor of Newbold Revel in Monks Kirby, Warwickshire, but also owned land in Northamptonshire and Leicestershire.[38]

The evidence to support the claims that this Thomas Malory was the celebrated author rests on his repeated reference to the consequences of imprisonment in his work. The Malory of Caludon fame was no stranger to the gaoler and first came to the attention of the authorities in 1443, when he was charged with assault and theft by Thomas Sprotton of Northamptonshire.[39] In the 1440s Malory was the subject of a complaint made by Katherine, the Lady Peyto. She claimed in Chancery proceedings that Malory and a number of other armed assailants had entered her manor of Sybertoft in Northamptonshire and driven away four cattle to his own house in Warwickshire. E. K. Chambers argued that in the legal chaos of the 1450s this may have been Malory's way of reclaiming a debt, but the matter is more complicated than this, wrapped up in the vacillating allegiances and rivalries of Warwickshire and the national political scene. Malory sought the protection of the most powerful local magnates, but this was not constant and he moved from the affinity of one to another as different opportunities arose.

The political background on the national scale was the conflict between the houses of Lancaster and York. In 1451 a warrant for Malory's arrest was issued by the Lancastrian, Humphrey Stafford, Duke of Buckingham and feoffee of Caludon. Malory was arrested for theft in July of that year and committed to the Sheriff of Warwickshire at his house in Coleshill. Within two days of his incarceration, and probably with the aid of at least one of his captors, Malory was able to escape and swim the moat that surrounded the house. Two days later the fugitive entered nearby Combe Abbey, insulted the abbot and his monks, and carried off large sums of money, together with jewels and valuables.[40]

This was one of a number of attacks that Malory and his confederates had made over the previous months in the area around Coventry. In the previous years he had broken into the house of Hugh Monks and raped his wife, Joan. At Combe he had secreted himself with twenty-five men in the woods surrounding the abbey. This action has been interpreted as a failed plot to assassinate the Duke of Buckingham. Malory was wrongly convinced that Buckingham was staying at the abbey at the time. Five days before his arrest Malory broke his way into Caludon Park, and caused havoc. He was accused of stealing six does and causing £500 pounds of unspecified damage. The accusations against Malory were presented in the form of a plea and delivered by attorneys on behalf of the Duke and Duchess of Norfolk (John and Eleanor), the Archbishop of Canterbury and the powerful figure of Humphrey, Duke of Buckingham.[41] The latter had gathered sixty mounted yeomen at Atherstone and he himself rode out to arrest the wanted men.[42]

Independent corroboration of Malory's attack on Caludon Park has recently been found and is a hitherto unknown source. Very fortunately a number of court rolls for the manor of Caludon for this period has survived in the Clifford estate office at Ugbrooke, Devon. A court held at the beginning of November 1451 describes the event, but differs from the petition account. There are two different versions of the court record, although Thomas Malory is clearly described in both as 'of Newbold in the parish of Monks Kirby.'[43] Both also state that the incursion took place on St

Anne's day, 26 July, the same date as given in the petition, the latter using the alternative saint's day of St Margaret the Virgin. It was said that Malory broke into the park and with many armed men killed two deer and removed their carcasses (6 deer were killed according to the petition). Although most of them were unknown, two accomplices were identified by surname, Podmore and Gryffyn, both yeomen of Warwickshire.

The second account leaves out the names of the yeomen and writes up the account in a more formal way declaring the action as disturbing the king's peace. It repeats the figure of two slaughtered deer and adds that enormous damage had been caused. This was in fact not the first time that Malory had attacked the park. In 1446 it was reported that Malory had killed a buck on 8 September, but the actual year was not given.

Interestingly, in 1451 mortality of deer had risen dramatically for reasons other than Malory's incursion; it was reported that twenty bucks and does in the park had died of 'murrain' and that the king had killed another fourteen deer.

Malory's action could be interpreted as an attack on the interests of Buckingham, who he held to be his chief local enemy. Christine Carpenter argues instead that a dispute between Malory and the Mowbrays led to the Caludon attack rather than a grudge against Buckingham.[44] She claims that at the heart of the struggle was a property dispute with Combe Abbey, whose land bordered the estates of Malory; the dispute spread to include Norfolk, another neighbouring owner and Buckingham felt obliged to intervene to demonstrate that he still carried authority in eastern Warwickshire, going as far as to ride out to apprehend Malory. The attack on both Combe Abbey, which came under the protection of the Mowbrays, who held the advowson (right to present the rector or vicar), and Caludon itself suggests that Carpenter may well be correct and that Mowbray, not Buckingham was the target of Malory's wrath.

Ultimately the prosecution of Malory for his activities at Caludon was never carried through, although he was incarcerated for most of the next eight years in various prisons, including Newgate, Marshalsea and the Tower of London. By this time instability in political life had brought about a malaise in the legal system, as the conflict between the houses of Lancaster and York began to intensify. Finally, in November 1455 Malory received a pardon for his offences from the Duke of York, who was acting as Protector whilst Henry VI was incapacitated by illness. Given Buckingham's allegiance to the Lancastrian cause, Malory may have passed himself off as a Yorkist to save himself. Subsequently his case falls into further obscurity and he leaves our story. Mowbray did not recoup his losses.

The court rolls that recorded Malory's raid on Caludon Park cover a decade before the notorious deed.[45] They reveal what appears to have been a relatively efficiently run estate with courts being held at regular intervals. In the majority the Lord of Caludon was acknowledged within the main body of the text as John, Duke of Norfolk, but in one, dated 1445, the feoffees John Stafford, Archbishop of Canterbury and Humphrey Stafford, Duke of Buckingham, were identified at the head of the court record. The principal business of the court concerned the transfer of tenancies and the running of the park and the name of Caludon's main official appears in all the rolls . In 1440 John Savey junior was described as the custodian of the manor and park, but by 1449 he is described as 'farmer of the manor', implying that he had leased the whole of the estate from John Mowbray VI. John Hochens was mentioned as a previous custodian. Mowbray's chief steward was John Broughton, who issued many instructions to John Savey during this decade, particularly in relation to the park. Broughton was one of the parties in the grant of Caludon to the feoffees in 1444.[46]

The park at Caludon figured prominently in the records, particularly as a source of raw materials. Whole trees were cut down and loppings removed to repair tenants' houses on the estate in Stoke (1440, 1444), Styvechale (1444, 1447) and Henley mill itself (1440). A barn, farther afield in Thurlaston, now near Draycote Water in Warwickshire, was supplied with twelve oaks (1445). John Savey was also required to make repairs at Caludon itself, using two oak trees from the park to make palings for the fence enclosing the park (1445), the first confirmation of the existence of the park pale or fence. In the year before he mended the dam (or head) of the pool on the north side of the castle, then called *Calowdon pole heed*.

The greatest danger the deer faced was disease, the all-encompassing 'murrain', which caused their death in great numbers (18, 1444), (22, 1445) as well as the twenty that died in the year of Malory's attack (1451).

The courts typically recorded changes of tenancies, an opportunity for the lord of the manor to earn income from entry fines. The information is given in some detail, providing the names of the outgoing and incoming tenants, often relations, and also describing the tenants' landholding. In January 1448 Robert Nevell and his wife, Jolina, passed their holding onto their daughter, Agnes. It consisted of three fields called Littelstobyfelde, (Little Stubbyfield) 'lying next to the lane that led from Coventry to Sowe (Ansty Road)'; another of their fields lay below Newhaven. Both these fields have already been identified from earlier surveys and we know that they were situated on the north side of Ansty Road then interestingly called a lane, rather than a highway(Fig 19). At this time the lane was not the major route to Leicester as it was later to become.

In 1445 John Savey, 'the parker of Calowdon' took on a holding consisting of various blocks of open field strips (selions) in *le Cowelesewe*, (Cowleasow), *Oxonfeld*, three selions and a butt (irregular shaped block of arable strips) in the same field called *persones londe*, and eight selions and seven butts in *Hungerlowe*. This entry is illuminating as it clearly describes the scatter of open field or common field strips that characterised medieval arable cultivation. In this area of Warwickshire the open fields were to be gradually enclosed, creating a landscape of hedged fields, a process that was piecemeal, but mostly complete by the time Parliamentary enclosure swept through south Warwickshire in the late eighteenth and early nineteenth centuries. The selions of *Hungerelowe* provide the earliest known reference to an area of land to the east of Caludon, later Hungerley Farm, now encircled by Dorchester Way (Fig 19). We now know that it originated as an arable open field of Wyken. The reference to *persones londe* (parson's land?) in *Oxonfeld* is interesting, as a later survey of Caludon in 1595 states that *Oxe Close* or *Personne Lande* had by this time been enclosed into the park.[47]

The mid fifteenth century was a period of intense civil strife in England, now referred to as the Wars of the Roses. The Lancastrian King Henry VI fought the rebellious house of Edward, Duke of York. Mowbray had supported Henry throughout the early 1450s, but his support was always tacit and his watchword was caution. In 1454, after the outbreak of warfare, he was asked to counsel the King but declined claiming ill-health. Nevertheless he remained a nominal supporter of the King. At the Battle of St Albans, in May 1455, he brought his forces up short of the action and entered the town only after the fighting had all but ended. This enabled him to come to early terms with the Duke of York who had won the battle. For the next few years he withdrew to self-imposed provincial obscurity and travelled abroad on several pilgrimages to Europe and the Holy Land.

His main rival in East Anglia, the Duke of Suffolk, had been executed in 1450 and Mowbray now sought once more to dominate the political life of Norfolk and Suffolk. But in such a rich and prosperous area of England he was often thwarted by other rich nobles and his lack of influence at national level and his repeated absences abroad reduced his powers of patronage. Colin Richmond considered that Mowbray was idle and failed to wield his influence with authority: 'he contributed nothing after 1439 towards preventing the loss of either Normandy or Gascony.'[48] As the English possessions in France were thrown back towards the Channel they slid into civil war and political chaos. Mowbray sought to protect his estates and fortune by remaining uncommitted. He did not even put an army in the field when warfare broke out in 1459 and was only roused to change sides and to support the Yorkists after their victory at the Battle of Northampton on 10 July 1460. He had seen his friends captured or killed and realised on which side of the Pennines the future lay. On 3 March 1461 he duly took his place alongside a select group of nobles who approved the ascent of Edward, Duke of York to the throne and acted as Earl Marshal at his Coronation. It was the deepest of ironies that having finally committed to one side, he died on 6 November 1461 before he could fully share in the spoils.

The fourth Duke of Norfolk, John Mowbray (VII) was seventeen when his father died and was viewed by his contemporaries as something of a prodigy. Unlike his father, who had been able to steer a relatively neutral course through the previous decades of strife, this Duke stood firmly in the Yorkist camp. Their victory, which had secured its possession of the throne, was achieved at the bloodiest battle ever seen in England, at Towton on 29 March 1461. Although Mowbray was not personally involved in the battle, he and his men were used in the mopping up operation, which continued for several years afterwards. His fortunes then ebbed and flowed with the course of the civil war. When the Lancastrians forced Edward to flee England in 1470, Mowbray was arrested and expelled from office as Henry VI was restored to the throne. On Edward's successful return in the spring of 1471, Mowbray fought with him at the Battle of Tewkesbury (4 May) and rode with him when he re-entered the capital in triumph. Despite his bravery and loyalty on the field of battle, Edward kept the young Duke at arm's length from the politics of the court.

Mowbray was suspected of having poor judgement and generally supposed to be weak-willed. He was also hamstrung financially by his long lived grandmother and mother, in whom much of the family estate was vested, severely restricting his income. In the 1470s he sold off numerous far-flung estates, but even with this injection of funds his yearly income was far less than his peers, smaller even than his own mother. It is no wonder then that in this period his interest in Caludon waned and it became a backwater, no longer receiving financial or administrative investment and geographically set apart from the Duke's more important estates in the East of England.

After John's (VII) death in 1476, Caludon and the rest of the Mowbray lands were entrusted to Mowbray's wife, Elizabeth Talbot, daughter of Sir Gilbert Talbot, the first Earl of Shrewsbury. Elizabeth had originally been granted these lands in 1467 as part of her jointure.[49] The manor and castle of Caludon was leased by Elizabeth to a kinsman, Sir Humphrey Talbot, and for a while the Talbot family became the *de facto* 'Lords of Caludon'. The heir to the estate was the couple's three year old daughter Anne, whose potential wealth raised immediate interest in noble circles. The King, now Edward IV having returned to the throne, saw great opportunities in marrying Anne to his son, Richard, Duke of York, and an arrangement was reached after Elizabeth was greeted with favour at court. Elizabeth, however, negotiated with some skill with the King. She craved a suitable dower for herself and expected the King to disinherit William, Lord Berkeley. The latter was a natural heir to Anne, through the marriage of John Mowbray's (V) sister, Isabel, to James Berkeley, William's father. The Berkeley family had been involved in an interminable land dispute with the Mowbrays for a generation. With his eyes on the Mowbray inheritance, Edward readily agreed and Anne Mowbray (aged five) and Prince Richard (aged four) were married at Westminster Abbey in January 1478 in perhaps one of the most melancholy and tragic ceremonies in English history. The tiny bride lived for just four more years and Richard for only five. In 1483 he was famously murdered as one of the two princes in the Tower of London, almost certainly on the orders of Richard III, his uncle and brother of Edward IV.

With the death of the child heiress, Anne, the Mowbray family passed into extinction and their estates were left to be divided. Caludon then passed to the family in whose possession it would witness its greatest days - the Berkeleys.

Chapter 2 – NOTES

1   *The Register of Edward the Black Prince, England* 1351-1365, Vol 4 (1933) f 158d, 259

2   'Feodary of the Manors and lands of John de Segrave, Baron Segrave (d. 1353), in cos. Leicester, Warwick, Derby, Huntingdon.' British Library Add. MS 37671. A feodary was a survey of landed estates and its income.

3   Warwick Record Office (subsequently Warwick RO) CR1097/87

4   *Calendar of Inquisitions post Mortem*, 39-43 Edward III, Vol XII, (1938) no 397, 381

5   See note 13, chapter 1

6   Oliver Rackham, *The History of the Countryside*, (2000), 123

7   John Burke, *A genealogical and heraldic history of the extinct and dormant baronetcies of England, Ireland and Scotland*, (1841) 387

8   Sir William Bagot, (bef. 1354-1407), of Baginton, Warw, historyofparliamentonline web site; Linda Clark, 'Sir William Bagot,' Dictionary of National Biography.

9   *Calendar of Inquisitions Miscellaneous*, 1377-1388, Vol IV, (1957) no 299, 169

10 See note 8

11 ibid.

12 C Given-Wilson 'Thomas Mowbray - first duke of Norfolk', Dictionary of National Biography

13 The office is still held by Mowbray's descendant, the present Duke of Norfolk.

14 op. cit., Given-Wilson, Dictionary of National Biography

15 *Calendar of Inquisitions Miscellaneous, 1392-1399*, Vol VI (1963) no 388, 233-4

16 From 'Richard II' in *The Illustrated Stratford Shakespeare*, Chancellor Press, (1982). 364

17 op. cit, Dugdale, 128

18 *Calendar of Patent Rolls* Henry IV AD 1399-1401, Vol I, (1903) 44

19 In 1401 Geoffrey Hampton denied that he had received the commission, *Calendar of Close Rolls Henry IV*, 1399-1401, Vol I (1927) 386

20 *Calendar of Fine Rolls, Henry IV* 1399-1405, Vol XII (1931) 10 Nov 1399

21 op. cit., *Calendar of Patent Rolls*, 1399-1401, 90; William Marshall's original grant from Thomas Mowbray was dated 11 June 1396

22 op. cit., *Calendar of Patent Rolls*, 1399-1401, 102

23 *Calendar of Inquisitions post Mortem*, Henry IV, 1399-1405, Vol XVIII, (1987) no 269, 78-9

24 ibid.

25 op. cit., *Calendar of Patent Rolls* 1399-1401, 28

26 *Calendar of Close Rolls, Henry IV*, 1402-1405, Vol II, (1929) 210

27 *Calendar of Close Rolls Henry IV*, 1405-1409, Vol III (1931) 26; see also *Calendar of Patent Rolls Henry IV* AD 1405-1408, Vol III, (1907) 46

28 *Calendar of Close Rolls Henry VI*, 1422-1429, Vol I, (1933) 215

29 *Calendar of Close Rolls Henry VI*, 1429-1435, Vol II, (1933) 198

30 SBTRO, DR10/2444

31 Berkeley DCM/D/5/78/3; Carole Rawcliffe, 'Humphrey Stafford, first duke of Buckingham (1402-1460),' Dictionary of National Biography

32 SBTRO, DR10/2322

33 Notes on Mowbray Estate accompanying Berkeley Castle Muniments listing, BCM/D, on A2A (Access to Archives)

34 Colin Richmond, 'John Mowbray (VI) third duke of Norfolk (1415-1461),' Dictionary of National Biography

35 ibid.

36 ibid.

37 The literature on Malory and his rampages around Warwickshire and elsewhere is extensive, with Caludon featuring prominently: P J C Field, *The Life and Times of Sir Thomas Malory*, (1993);Elizabeth Archibald and A S G Edwards (eds.), *A Companion to Malory* (1996); Felicity Riddy, *Sir Thomas Malory*, (1987) 1-6; Christine Carpenter, 'Sir Thomas Malory and Fifteenth Century Local Politics,' *Bulletin of Institute of Historical Research*, 53 (1980) 31-43; A C Baugh, 'Documenting Sir Thomas Malory,' *Speculum*, Vol 8 (1933) 3-29; one dissenting voice from the Warwickshire identification of Malory is Gweneth Whitteridge, 'The identity of Sir Thomas Malory, Knight Prisoner,' *Review of English Studies*, Vol 24, 95 (1973) 257-265

38 P J C Field, 'Sir Thomas Malory (1415x18-1471)' Dictionary of National Biography

39 E K Chambers, *English Literature at the Close of the Middle Ages*, (1945) 200

40 op. cit., Chambers 201

41 op. cit., Baugh, 20-21

42 op. cit., Field, Dictionary of National Biography

43 Clifford 3, Manorial 10/4, court rolls 1439-1451

44 Christine Carpenter, *Locality and Polity: A Study of Warwickshire Landed Society 1401-1449*, (1992)

45 op. cit., Clifford 3, Manorial 10/4

46 op. cit., Berkeley, BCM/D/5/78/4

47 Clifford W(E) 1/30

48 op. cit., Richmond, Dictionary of National Biography

49 Berkeley, BCM/D/1/1/20

CHAPTER 3

The Berkeleys at Caludon
c.1494-1631

Fig 23
Berkeley coat of arms

Following the death of the last Mowbray heir, the lordship and castle of Caludon came to the family which would elevate the estate to its zenith of wealth and importance - the Berkeleys. Before tackling the complicated story of this transfer of ownership, it is worth providing some historical background on the Berkeleys, one of the most powerful aristocratic families in medieval England. It is fortunate that their castle at Berkeley is today the repository for an enormous family and estate archive, which has greatly aided the research on the history of Caludon.[1]

The Berkeleys enjoyed an ancient lineage and by the end of the fifteenth century were one of the few noble families which had survived from before the Norman invasion through their earlier kinship with the FitzHardings. Maurice de Berkeley was granted Berkeley Castle in 1189 and descendants remained as its lords, gradually enlarging both the castle and the estates. Although wealthy, the family were relatively marginal participants in national politics. They, nevertheless, took part in the wars, rebellions and rivalries of the thirteenth and fourteenth centuries. Thomas de Berkeley was captured by the Scots at Bannockburn in 1314 and in 1321 his son Maurice joined the fight against Edward II and the Despencers. His successor, Thomas, was noted for his extraordinary wealth. He was involved in the most infamous event in the family's history, when in September 1327 the deposed King Edward II was imprisoned at Berkeley Castle and was murdered there. Legend has it that in punishment for his supposed sexuality a red hot iron poker was run into the King's rectum. Although tried for his part in the murder, Thomas de Berkeley was acquitted by Edward's son, Edward III. Thomas's son, Maurice was a chivalrous and valiant warrior for Edward III, but died in 1361 of wounds he had received at the Battle of Poitiers in 1356.

Through Thomas, Maurice's son and heir, the family reached the peak of their influence and power. He held numerous important positions under Richard II and Henry IV, including acting as one of the Regents of England in 1416 when the King was fighting in France. On his death in 1417, however, the Berkeley patrimony broke apart, the Lordship of Berkeley going to his nephew James, son of his younger brother, James, who had died in 1405 fighting under Owen Glendower. After a

Fig 24 *Pedigree of the Berkeleys*

BERKELEY PEDIGREE

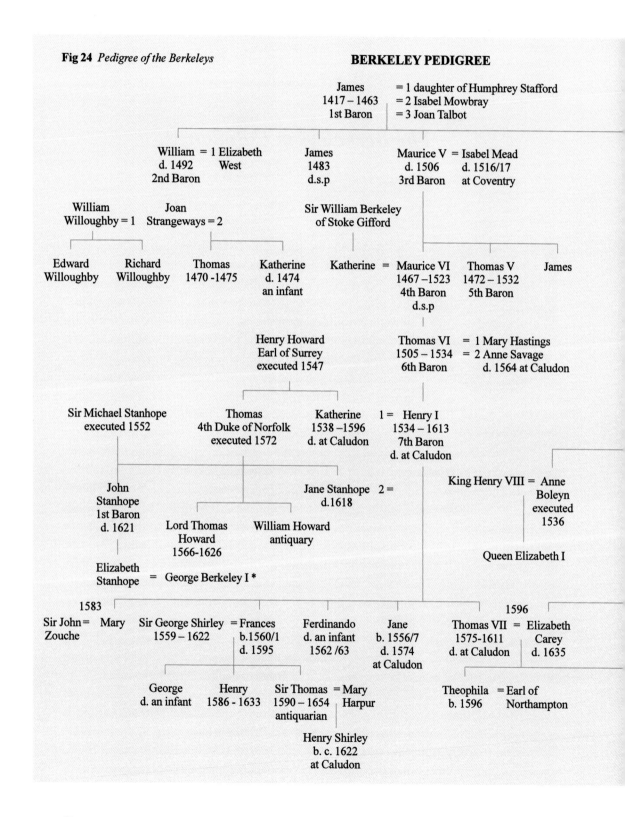

James
1417 – 1463
1st Baron
= 1 daughter of Humphrey Stafford
= 2 Isabel Mowbray
= 3 Joan Talbot

William = 1 Elizabeth
d. 1492   West
2nd Baron

James
1483
d.s.p

Maurice V = Isabel Mead
d. 1506   d. 1516/17
3rd Baron   at Coventry

William
Willoughby = 1

Joan
Strangeways = 2

Sir William Berkeley
of Stoke Gifford

Edward
Willoughby

Richard
Willoughby

Thomas
1470 -1475

Katherine
d. 1474
an infant

Katherine =
Maurice VI
1467 –1523
4th Baron
d.s.p

Thomas V
1472 – 1532
5th Baron

James

Henry Howard
Earl of Surrey
executed 1547

Thomas VI = 1 Mary Hastings
1505 – 1534 = 2 Anne Savage
6th Baron   d. 1564 at Caludon

Sir Michael Stanhope
executed 1552

Thomas
4th Duke of Norfolk
executed 1572

Katherine
1538 –1596
d. at Caludon

1 = Henry I
1534 – 1613
7th Baron
d. at Caludon

John
Stanhope
1st Baron
d. 1621

Jane Stanhope 2 =
d.1618

King Henry VIII = Anne
Boleyn
executed
1536

Lord Thomas
Howard
1566-1626

William Howard
antiquary

Queen Elizabeth I

Elizabeth
Stanhope = George Berkeley I *

1583

1596

Sir John = Mary
Zouche

Sir George Shirley = Frances
1559 – 1622   b.1560/1
                d. 1595

Ferdinando
d. an infant
1562 /63

Jane
b. 1556/7
d. 1574
at Caludon

Thomas VII = Elizabeth
1575-1611   Carey
d. at Caludon   d. 1635

George
d. an infant

Henry
1586 - 1633

Sir Thomas = Mary
1590 – 1654 Harpur
antiquarian

Theophila = Earl of
b. 1596   Northampton

Henry Shirley
b. c. 1622
at Caludon

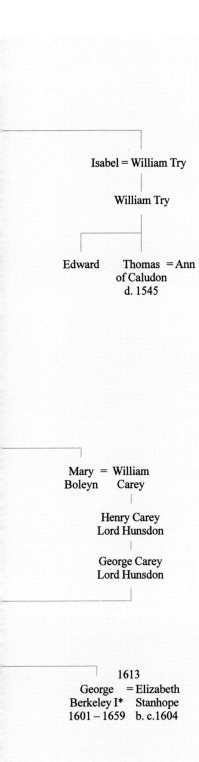

Isabel = William Try

William Try

Edward   Thomas = Ann
           of Caludon
           d. 1545

Mary = William
Boleyn   Carey

Henry Carey
Lord Hunsdon

George Carey
Lord Hunsdon

          1613
George   = Elizabeth
Berkeley I*   Stanhope
1601 – 1659 b. c.1604

short-lived marriage and childless marriage to Humphrey Stafford's daughter, he married Isabel Mowbray, sister of John Mowbray V in 1423-4. This union instigated the eventual Berkeley claim on the Mowbray estates, as a consequence of which their eldest son, William, took centre stage (Fig 24).

William's personal life was as chaotic as the age in which he lived. Unusually, he left it late to marry and was forty-one when matched in 1466 with his first wife, Elizabeth, the daughter of Reginald West, Lord de la Warr. The marriage floundered almost immediately and Berkeley sought a divorce. The reasons for this are not entirely understood, although it has been suggested that he conveniently found the excuse that Elizabeth was his second cousin in order to hasten the proceedings against her. This was a convenient legal screen to cover the fact that his wife had not been able to provide a male heir. For her part, Elizabeth appealed in vain against the divorce to Pope Paul II and letters approving the dissolution of the marriage were granted in November 1467. A year later, Berkeley married Joan, the widow of Sir William Willoughby, and this union did produce an heir. Thomas Berkeley was born in 1470 and was prepared from an early age to take on the duties of an heir to a great noble family. In 1475, aged just five years old, he was made a Knight of the Order of Bath and soon afterwards betrothed to Mary, the daughter of William Herbert, the Earl of Pembroke. A double tragedy struck the family as Thomas died shortly afterwards, followed by his younger sister, Katherine. Joan died in 1484 and within two years Berkeley had married once more, his third wife being Anne, daughter of John Fiennes, Lord Dacre. The fact that this marriage was no more successful in producing heirs helps explain his decision to leave much of his estate to the King and give the rest away. Another factor was his indebtedness to the Talbot family, into which his father, James, had married after the death of Isabel, William's mother.

But first we must return to the Mowbrays, and in particular the last John (VII) with whom William Berkeley had in fact enjoyed good relations (Fig 17). The King of England, Edward IV, had insisted on intervening in the extraordinarily complex succession of the Mowbray estates. Edward arranged with John Mowbray VII for his inheritance to pass to the King's younger son, Richard, Duke of York, through his marriage to Anne Mowbray, the sole heir of the last John Mowbray (see Chapter 2). John's cousin, William Berkeley, as son of Isabel, John's great aunt, possessed a claim on the inheritance, but in order to be released from bonds that he owed to the Talbots, this entitlement was relinquished first in favour of Richard, Duke of York, and then to the Duke's father, Edward IV, reverting to William only if the royal line failed to produce heirs. Edward IV died in 1483, followed by the deaths in the same year of his young sons, Edward V, who reigned only for a month, and Richard, Duke of York. It is assumed that they were murdered in the Tower of London, the main suspect being Richard III, the boys' uncle. As a consequence of this notorious event, William Berkeley's claim on the Mowbray estates presumably reverted to him, but in 1485 he felt obliged to grant a reversion of his estates to Richard III, an arrangement that was annulled by the death of the King at Bosworth in August 1485.

William made an auspicious beginning in his dealings with the new regime. When Henry VII was crowned on 30 October 1485 Berkeley attended as the 'Bearer of the Third Sword' and was made Lord High Steward and Earl Marshal for the occasion. In the following year he granted out swathes of old Mowbray land in south Wales and the Marches to William Stanley, who had intervened with the King in order to secure the Marshalcy for Berkeley. In the same patent, granted in February 1486, he is described as being elevated to the Marquessate of Berkeley. In December 1487 Berkeley made provision, to settle almost his entire estate on the King and his heirs should he die childless. His dismemberment of his Mowbray inheritance earned him the nickname, William 'Waste All' from the family historian, John Smyth.[2]

In view of the fact that William was childless these arrangements were more than a simple expression of sycophancy towards the monarch. In return for the potential gift Henry ratified Berkeley's elevation to Marquis, the seventh such title created. William had by now almost entirely abandoned any interest in his estates and he made numerous other grants, parcelling out manors to retainers and royal courtiers. He spent all his time at court and lived at Westminster. Another motive underlying his vigorous attempts to alienate his Berkeley and Mowbray inheritance was his disapproval of the marriage of his brother and heir presumptive, Maurice, whom he was determined to disinherit. Smyth noted that William complained about the 'obscure parentage of Lady Isable (Isabell) which he vainly called base'.[3] (see below).

When massive feudal estates are partitioned, dissipated and alienated, it can be difficult to trace the fate of one small fragment such as Caludon. Until recently there was uncertainty about the date when the actual transfer of ownership from Mowbray to Berkeley took place, the Victoria County History proposing some time in the decade between the death of Lady Anne Mowbray in 1481 and 1491.[4] New evidence has come to light from deeds lodged in the Clifford archive in Ugbrooke House, Devon, that provide details for the first time on the process by which Caludon was transferred to the Berkeleys.

Caludon had originally been granted in 1467 to Elizabeth Talbot, wife of John Mowbray VII, Duke of Norfolk, as part of a marriage settlement for the duration of her life (see Chapter 2).[5] She apparently managed to retain Caludon, despite the efforts of King Edward IV to obtain the Mowbray lands for his younger son, Richard, Duke of York (see above). In 1486 the widow Elizabeth, Duchess of Norfolk, with many of the trustees mentioned in the earlier jointure, quitclaimed (renounced) her interest in Caludon with Kyngton (Kineton, Warks) to William Berkeley, 'Earl Marshall and Duke of Nottingham.'[6] In 1488 William granted Caludon to Edward Willoughby and Richard Willoughby, stepsons from his third marriage to Joan, nee Strangeways, and widow of Sir John Willoughby.[7] This was grant 'in reversion' in which a sequence of heirs was identified, each inheriting for life following the death of the previously named heir. The Willoughby brothers were beneficiaries of William Berkeley's attempts to dispossess Maurice, his brother, of his inheritance. In this case, however, Humphrey Talbot was already holding Caludon for life, on a lease, according to Smyth, granted by John Mowbray (VII), Duke of Norfolk.[8] Two years later the reversions were confirmed by fines and two copies of the original fines (final concords) of 1491 have now been found. They recorded that William, Marquis of Berkeley, had granted Caludon to John Skille, probably as a feoffee (trustee) and that John in turn was to settle the estate in reversion on William Berkeley for life followed by Edward Willoughby and his brother, Richard.[10]

William Berkeley died childless in 1492 and despite all his efforts, his brother, Maurice (V) was able to recover fifty of seventy Mowbray manors, including Caludon. The survival of another final concord, dated 1494, confirms that new feoffees had granted Caludon to Maurice and Isabel, his wife, for their lives and for the lives of their heirs.'[11]

There are now no grounds to believe that Caludon passed to the King in accordance with the agreement of 1487. The evidence of the deeds cited above, supported by Smyth, confirms that Maurice Berkeley was in possession of the castle and its estate by 1494.[12]

It is not known who lived at Caludon in the tumultuous years of the last quarter of the fifteenth century. Sir Humphrey Talbot, the supposed leaseholder may have been a resident, but there is no direct evidence. The administrators and bailiffs of Caludon's absentee aristocratic landlords might have made it their home, as had been the case many times previously. These men probably had local Coventry connections, but their names have not been passed down in the historical record.

According to Smyth, Maurice Berkeley did not visit Caludon until the turn of the sixteenth century (1500-1501), an event remembered by him owing to the fact that that the Abbot of Combe had ignored the arrival of the Berkeley lord locally.[13] Maurice expected to be entertained by the Abbot as a descendant of one of the founders of the abbey in the same way that Thomas Mowbray had been honoured over a century earlier. Berkeley was so enraged that he resorted to Chancery proceedings to prove his lineage. Smyth expressed some sympathy for the Abbot in not being aware of Berkeley's 'discent' and so might the authors here many centuries later, who have struggled to explain as clearly as possible the intricate and interconnected family trees that were Maurice's 'discent'. As the arbitrators found in Maurice's favour, the Abbot, duly chastened, received him with 'due observances....procession and solemnities,' a practice that continued until the dissolution of the monastery in 1539.

It is difficult to believe that a lay lord would resort to the law in order to receive deference from the head of a monastic order, but Maurice was determined to receive the respect that he considered his right, conscious of the fact that his status had been much reduced by the actions of his brother William. Although he was styled 'Lord Maurice', he was unable to claim the Marquisate of Berkeley or the Earldom of Nottingham and these titles became extinct. His early political career had been largely played out in the shadow of his brother and little of real consequence has been recorded of Maurice's public life. He served as a knight to the body of Edward IV, but, although a prestigious title, this position seems to have been the limit of his influence at court. Given his brother's profligacy, Maurice never possessed the funds to advance socially and politically, unlike William. Even his marriage betrayed his reduced status. Isabel was the daughter of Philip Mead, an alderman of Bristol, who had served as Lord Mayor of that city on three occasions, but could claim no great noble lineage. Isabel was by no means poor as she brought property to the marriage, which she had inherited from her brother Thomas - lands such as Thornbury in Gloucestershire and Wraxall, Ashton, Bedminster and Tickenham in Somerset. As mentioned above, his brother, William, could not forgive him for his lowly marriage.

Smyth provides considerable genealogical information on Maurice and Isabel, but direct information on Caludon is sparse and can only be surmised.[14] They had three sons, Maurice (VI), Thomas (V) and James and one daughter, Anne. Thomas was eventually to inherit the estates re-assembled by his father, as the oldest brother, Maurice, died without issue. Maurice (V) died in September 1506, aged 70 and Isabel in 1516-7 (8 Henry VII), also aged 70.[15] Both were buried at the church of the St Augustine Friars in London and an extensive account of Isabel's funeral was left by Thomas Try and recounted by Smyth.[16] Try was a distant cousin of Maurice and a trusted administrator (Fig 24); Isabel had appointed him as her receiver general (chief estate accountant) after her husband's death.[17] Shortly before her death, Isabel and her son, Maurice (VI), granted Caludon to Thomas Try for the term of his life. We will return to Try's tenancy of the lordship and manor, as it marked an important stage in its development.[18]

Isabel Berkeley died in Coventry in 1516-17, but Smyth does not explain why she happened to be there. She may have taken ill and collapsed on her way to or from Caludon, although it had already been leased to Thomas Try a few years before. Her funeral, most likely organised by Try, illustrates the lavish ministrations and obsequies accorded to deceased noblewomen at this time. On the Wednesday of her death until the following Monday one company of priests succeeding another in attending her body continuously chanting prayers and singing dirges (funeral songs). Meanwhile the bells of all of Coventry's churches, St Michael's, Holy Trinity, St John's and the cathedral priory of St Mary's were rung, costing a shilling a peal. Most of the peals were rung at Bablake, because this building was the nearest to where she lay. The exact place of her death is, unfortunately, not known. On Sunday, her 'horse-litter' was prepared and her coffin was conveyed to the largest church in Coventry, the cathedral priory of Coventry. Thomas Try had needed four days to organise the magnificent funeral cortege. At the head there were thirty women wearing her livery and black gowns with kerchiefs upon their heads, one ell each in length (c.45 inches) having raw edges to show they were cut out of new cloth, every woman bearing a wax taper of one pound in weight. They were followed by thirty-three 'crafts', presumably members of the craft guilds, carrying two hundred torches. Next came the friars, white and grey, with their crosses and after them the lights of the 'crafts'. Priests, numbering one hundred, likewise carrying crosses, preceded the hearse. Thirty of her own servants in black gowns, carrying waxen torches, were arranged about her 'horse litter' and behind it walked 'five gentlewomen mourners.'

This impressive procession was followed in its wake by a host of city officials; the Recorder, the Mayor of Coventry and the Aldermen; the Sheriffs, and the Wardens and Chamberlains. It made its doleful passage to St Mary's (soon to be destroyed by Henry VIII), where Isabel was placed before the high altar to the sound of a solemn dirge. The party then moved on to St Mary's Hall where a lavish feast of 'cakys, comffets and ale,' followed by a second course of 'marmelet, Snoket (both sweets), redd wynne and claret' and a third course of 'wafers and Blanch powder with Romney and muskadele.'[19] The next morning the whole procession set off once more in the same order for the final destination of St Augustines in London, but via the road to Caludon, where presumably many local dignitaries paid their last respects and departed home. This time the noblemen and women were mounted on horses draped in black cloth. When they reached Binley Bridge, near to Caludon, they were met by the Abbot of Combe with his mitre, censing the hearse, and by a great crowd, allegedly numbering five or six thousand. Although these numbers may well be exaggerated, the funeral procession must have been an astonishing spectacle for the local population, who would not have seen an event like it in their lifetimes. Religious processions and celebrations punctuated the whole year, but this was organised on a greater scale than any saint's feast day or parade. The cost was undoubtedly enormous and the splendour and drama of the procession illustrates the vast chasm in wealth which existed between the Lords of Caludon and the ordinary folk who lined the city streets and the country lanes towards Caludon.

Maurice (VI) succeeded to the Lordship of Caludon after his mother, Isabel, but he would have to wait until the expiration of the Try leases (see below). Smyth gave Maurice the title, 'the Courtier', an apt description of a man who spent almost all of his working life either abroad or at court in the service of the Crown. He was born in 1467 and therefore was well advanced into middle age when he inherited his estates. He spent his childhood at Thornbury in Gloucestershire and was raised by his father. Little is known of his early life save for his marriage to Katherine, the daughter of a kinsman, Sir William Berkeley of Stoke Gifford in 1485. Maurice was not satisfied with his marriage, which failed to produce any children, nor with his domestic life at Thornbury. Within a few years the unsettled Maurice decided to seek a career as a soldier and courtier. His appearance at court coincides with the accession of Henry VIII in 1509, although he had received his first commission, as Keeper of the Kingswood Forest in south Gloucestershire, a few years before. He is recorded as being present at Henry's coronation and was made a Knight of Bath on the eve of this occasion. Shortly afterwards he was appointed as Sheriff of his home county, a position he would hold several times.[20]

In 1512 Henry VIII entered into a war with France as part of an alliance led by Pope Julius II.[21] Berkeley was appointed to serve under the Marquis of Dorset as knight of the body to the King and was one of the leading commanders of the English force which landed in France. Berkeley transported an army of 411 of his own trained men, which he gathered, trained and equipped in Gloucestershire. Many of the men were his own tenants and workers. Despite both his eagerness and efforts, Maurice did not see any action and the campaign proved largely fruitless. The English felt they had been let down after receiving only tepid support from their allies in Spain. A year later the King travelled in person with his army to France and again Berkeley and his Gloucestershire men formed part of the invading force. Maurice was once more appointed as a leading captain but on this occasion Henry utilised his commander by seeking Berkeley's advice on organising the army and Maurice obliged by providing him with a detailed paper on the subject ('Orders to be observed by the Army'). He recommended dividing the English force into three sections giving precise instructions on the breakdown of command for each third. He was evidently a man to whom even the smallest detail was important, with the Orders even covering subjects such as the administration of the military encampment, for instance, suggesting that each morning 'the trumpets shall give warning, every man to take downe their Tents.'[22] Evidently Berkeley's paper had some positive effect for during this campaign the English army managed to capture the garrison town of Tournai. Ultimately, however, this war was as unproductive as the previous one and the actual military glory was gained by fighting the Scots instead. Henry enjoyed a crushing victory over the 'auld enemy' at the Battle of Flodden in September 1513, but Berkeley had been required to remain behind and missed the action. His loyalty and service was rewarded, however, with a special commission in 1515, once peace with France had been negotiated. Maurice Berkeley was appointed to direct a magnificent train of escort for the King's youngest sister, Mary, who was to be married to Louis XII as a consequence of the peace settlement. Considered to be one of the most beautiful women in Europe, Mary had been 'sacrificed' to facilitate the treaty between England and France. Louis was a decrepit sixty-year-old and Berkeley's expensive transfer of Mary to France proved to be a pointless extravagance. The marriage lasted only three months before a broken-down Louis died.

For Maurice (VI) this marked a high watermark in his position at court and in addition to the lieutenancy of Calais, which had been granted to him in 1514, a number of lucrative and influential posts followed. By 1520, however, he had largely given up on his military life and returned to England to concentrate on developing his estates. Although he retained much of the Berkeley inheritance, many of the family's former lands were still held by the Crown and he spent much energy in trying to prise them from Henry's grip. He was even willing to agree the holding of a number of stewardships and commissions on behalf of the King for some of the manors he was trying to recover.

The perceived indignities inflicted on his forbears seemed to weigh very heavily on Maurice. This is reflected not only in his attempts to recover land, but also in his reluctance to accept from the King the honour of a Barony and a summons to attend Parliament in this capacity. These he long resisted, considering a mere Barony beneath him, arguing that he was fully entitled instead to the ancient Berkeley Barony, which had become officially extinct. He was urged to accept the Barony by his friends Sir John Fitzjames and Sir William Denys, the former writing with others in 1523:

> ...this honor, which the king's grace by his writt hath lately called you too; Sir, wee all will
> advise you to take the honor; and howbeit that as yet yee have not the roome in the parliament
> chamber that the Lord Berkeleys have had of old time, yet wee will advise you to take this
> roome appointed to you at this time and to make noe labor of the higher roome at this time, for
> causes to longe to write:[23]

Berkeley finally acquiesced to the pressure of his friends and accepted the King's offer, but before he had a chance to travel to Parliament he died suddenly in Calais in 1523, having returned to France in 1522-3 in the service of Earl of Surrey.[24]

As mentioned above, Caludon had been leased by Maurice and his mother to the Berkeley family steward and kinsman, Thomas Try. He had travelled with his master to France and had rendered to him faithful service at the sieges of Tirwin and Tournai and at other places.[25] There is ample evidence of Try being at Berkeley's side during his various travels around England. At one point his absence was noted because he was recovering from a broken leg.

We originally learn of Try's lease from Smyth who recites Maurice's own will, which offered Try legal protection against:

> ... any person [that] should put out or molest his said Cozen Thomas
> Try out of the manor of Callowden which he hath for the Terme of his
> life by the joynt demise of him and his mother in the 5th of Henry 8th [1513-14].[26]

This clause in the will suggests that the grant of Caludon to Try might have been resented by other closer family members or heirs, whom Maurice feared would attempt to repossess the castle and its estates.

An inquisition has now come to light, dated 1528, which recites in some detail the above quoted lease to Try, giving the exact date, and revealing an important phase in the development of the Caludon Castle site.[27] It has been a considerable while since we had the name of a person known to have lived at Caludon Castle. The lease was granted on 23 March 1514 for 'true an faithfull service in tyme past done ..by our wellbilovde Cosyn Thomas Trye and also in consyderacon of the Great Charges whiche…Thomas hathe been at in byldyng and edyfying many howses upon the seyght of the said manor.' Unfortunately we do not know exactly what this 'building and edifying' work entailed, but it is likely that after many years of neglect Try made the castle habitable and more comfortable, perhaps introducing some of the new features of the early Tudor great houses such as larger windows, glazing and fireplaces. The work may also have involved renewing or rebuilding some of the service buildings. The park was specifically mentioned as part of the manor and for the fact that its hedges and palings were required to be repaired as a condition of the lease. The same inquisition goes on to recite a later lease, dated 26 January 1521, confirming Maurice Berkeley's grant of Caludon to Thomas for life, but adding another twelve years after his death, for his heirs to enjoy the property.[28] Thomas died on 10 February 1545 at Caludon, which would have taken the lease as far as 1557. The 1522 Muster Roll for Coventry (a survey of households and their wealth in case of a call to arms) confirms that 'Thomas Tre Esquire' was tenant of Caludon and that he was expected to provide horses for ten men. Assessed with him was the priest, John Wright, who was paid 'wages' besides his meat and drink but who had no goods. The names of seven servants were listed also with no goods.[29]

Try had been instrumental in retaining Caludon for the Berkeley interest. When Maurice was eventually succeeded by his brother Thomas in 1523, the new Lord Berkeley had little interest in his Warwickshire estates and seriously considered exchanging them for more land in his beloved Gloucestershire. These belonged to Richard Sacheverell, whose home base was in Warwickshire

Fig 25 *Engraving of Berkeley Castle, Gloucestershire, published by Samuel Lysons, May 1 1802*

and Leicestershire.[30] Try convinced him to retain Caludon, and the remainder of the Segrave-Mowbray inheritance in a series of letters sent from Caludon in the year 1525. Try warned Thomas that Sir Richard was not acting in good faith and that the exchange was essentially unbalanced in favour of Sacheverell and that the loss of the Segrave and Mowbray lands was a grave error. He persuaded Thomas to send officials to Caludon 'where this honest and wise gentleman soe made good his informations.'[31] Although anxious no doubt to protect both the interest and local influence of his patron, he was probably concerned about his future if he was to become a tenant of Sir Richard.

Thomas Berkeley was a very different man from his brother. Smyth names him as the 'Sheepmaster' since the nobleman spent much of his time 'living a kind of grazier's life, having flocks of sheep sommering in one place and wintering in other places as he observed the fields and pastures to bee sound and could bargaine best cheape.'[32] He was possessed of a kind of pastoral fever, developing into a keen farmer and estate manager, a world away from the military derring-do and bravado of his brother. Thomas's preference for land management and husbandry had not prevented him from fighting at Flodden in September 1513 and he had received a knighthood from the Earl of Surrey on the same day. Although by no means as politically influential as Maurice, he did hold a number of official posts, including the custody of Berkeley Castle (Fig 25), but it was the land and not the battlefield that attracted him and his official duties and service were a consequence of his rank not his personality.

Thomas's appearance in the Caludon story serves merely as background for he died in 1532 and during the whole of his Lordship of Caludon remained in the hands of Thomas Try, his lessee. He was succeeded by his son, also Thomas (VI), who had been born in 1505. Like his father and uncle he was summoned to Parliament and also retained custody of Berkeley Castle. He made a greater contribution to the history of Caludon as a result of his second marriage. His first wife, Mary, the daughter of George Hastings, Earl of Huntingdon, had died in early 1533. Within a few weeks Thomas remarried, his new wife Anne being the daughter of John Savage of Frodsham in Cheshire. It was perhaps Anne who did more than any other family member to cement the Berkeley interest at Caludon. Smyth describes her as 'a lady of masculine spirit, over-powerful with her husband, seldom at rest with herself ... Of complexion shee was of a comely brown, of middle stature'.[33] There is no doubt that Anne was a formidable personality and she came to dominate the family after her husband's untimely death, aged just 29, in 1534.

Lady Anne was determined to occupy Caludon, perhaps attracted by the improvements that Thomas Try had made. After his death in 1545 she entered into a protracted battle for the property, as it had been made part of her jointure. She refused to accept the second lease of 1521, which assigned another twelve years to Try's heirs, claiming that it was forged.[34] Thomas Horton and his mother, Ann(e), the widow and executrix of Thomas Try, would not allow Anne Berkeley to enter the premises and her response was to submit a bill to Chancery and argue the case at common law, 'calling on many witnesses. And so after two years and a half Strugling, she obtained the possession and overthrew the lease.'[35] During this period (c 1545-1548) Caludon Castle was attacked, the only recorded instance, as Anne attempted forcible entry.

> And in that space many forcible entries and riotous assaults were made, a part of the mote about the house filled with faggots, and so assaulted by the said lady, howbeit kept out both of the house and the greatest part of the Manor till tryal.[36]

Anne further strengthened her position legally as a result of an inquisition taken before the King's attorney in 1549-50, again finding in her favour, despite an appeal heard in the Star Chamber by Anne Try[e] in about 1546-7.[37] She gave evidence of another attack on her property by Lady Anne's servants. Six were named:

> who together with diverse other riotous persons to them assembled by the commandment of one Ladye Berkeley with force and armys and in manor of warre arrayed the 23th [sic] day of marche in the syxe and thryttyth yere of yor graces Raygne [36 Henry VIII, 23 March 1545/6] entered into the sayde manor of Calloughdon... and theyr not oneleye spoyled and cutte down the woddys growing...but also then wyth lyke force and armys toke 15 kye [cows] and 10 calves of the goodes and cattalles.... beying depasturing and fedyng theyre in and upon the premysses and the kye land and calves from thens dyd dryve and carye awey owte of the sayde Countye of the Cytye of Coventree into a lybertye called Chellesmore lyberyte and from theyre dyd impounde in severall poundes by force...

After more legal action Anne Try managed to recover her cattle and the matter of the validity of the original leases was then put before a jury of Coventry men. According to Anne Try, the jury found

Fig 26 *Reconstruction drawing of Caludon Castle (1550-1570) from south-east, by Pete Urmston*

in favour of Lady Berkeley owing to the pressure that she and her friends and 'allyances' brought to bear upon its members.

The dispute ensnared Gerrard Try, an illegitimate son of Thomas, who had testified in favour of Lady Anne Berkeley and as a consequence 'lost him the love of his said mother in law and of her son Mr Horton. And also kindled in them a desire to doe him any mischief.'[38] He had been left a house in Binley in his father's will and Lady Anne, 'having now possession of Callowdon she seized upon this house and lands in Binley.' Gerrard had to return from oversees to regain his inheritance, but his several petitions to Lady Anne failed, even after she encouraged him to come to Caludon after visiting her at her house in Kentish Town. Having entirely lost patience with Gerrard's pleas, she eventually threatened to 'make him burn [like] a fagott.'[39] After Lady Anne's death, Gerrard, uncowed, continued to demand the return of his Binley property from Henry Berkeley (I), Anne's son and eventually obtained possession but only by means of a lease.

Early in her widowhood Lady Anne chose to live in several places, such as Augustine Green, Bristol, Yate, Gloucestershire, and Kentish Town. She eventually settled for Caludon, spending her last few years there, dying in October 1564, aged 58.[40] Unlike a great many of her female contemporaries, she was no cosseted noblewoman and took an active and personal interest in estate management. Smyth noted that 'she would betimes in Winter and Somer mornings make her walkes to visit her stables, barnes, day houses, pultry, swinetroughs, and the like.'[41] Her baby son, Henry, born nine weeks and four days after his father's death (1534), was named after Henry VIII, who was godfather to the child. He was heir to a great fortune and she made his welfare and protection her priority. Although she was considered by some to be rather rather male in temperament, Smyth defended her, noting that she 'bee most tender hearted to her children.'[42] Anne was indulgent and did not readily let them out of her sight to the detriment of their education. She determined that her son was to be brought up at Caludon under her own guidance and throughout her life she was to remain devoted to him, the memory of her husband and her fierce Catholicism. In her public efforts to wrestle Caludon from Thomas Try's widow, Anne had needed to use her influence at court with some caution, as her son was a young child and easily removed from her as a ward of the Crown.

Although the practice of wardship was generally on the decline, it was the King's prerogative to place potentially wealthy minors in the care of the those whom he saw fit, or, as was more usual practice, with those who could offer the highest price for the control of the minors' estates until they reached their majority. According to Smyth, Henry at the age of seventeen months was already the king's ward and 'the whole of his lands under the king's rule and protection.'[43] Anne resisted all moves to make her son a ward and wrote to the King's Chancellor, Thomas Cromwell in the autumn of 1534 in order to dissuade him from this course of action, which appears to have been successful. On November 1 she wrote to him once more offering her thanks for his 'goodness'.

> Her late husband and some friends stand bound to the King for his special livery of which a great
> part is paid. As he died and took no profits of his lands, desires to have a privy seal on a bill
> exhibited to the King to discharge the rest, as Cromwell promised when she was last with him. [44]

In other words, Cromwell had promised her that the Crown would discharge any interest it had in her son or his family's estates since the Berkeleys had paid handsomely in order to take livery [possession] of them. In the following August she was forced to write once more to Cromwell politely thanking him for his 'favour', but requested again that he have her bill signed, as he had promised 'for my lord's special livery.'[45] It is significant that both the letters were written from Caludon in 1534 and 1535, Lady Anne perhaps seeking advice as 'guest' of Thomas Try, a decade before the dispute with his widow over its possession. Having managed to keep her young son, Henry, by her side, it would appear that her decision to live there towards the end of her life (late 1550s-early 1560s) meant that Henry became well acquainted with Caludon Castle as he grew into manhood.[46] Henry was aged about thirty when his mother died (1564) and these years may have created an emotional attachment to Caludon that was to last for the rest of his long life.

Anne had been a devout Catholic and the 1550s witnessed the dramatic pendulum swings between Rome and the Church of England, caused by the accession of Queen Mary (1553-1558). Ultimately the new Protestant religion triumphed with the accession of Queen Elizabeth in 1558. Like many of his noble contemporaries Henry Berkeley had been raised in the older religion and there is plenty of evidence to suggest that he made efforts to remain publicly a Catholic when it would have been more be more prudent to conceal his faith. Further evidence of his making Caludon his home lies in his renewal of the use of its chapel. In 1556 during the more congenial reign of Queen Mary this was one of his first actions on his reaching his majority. Cardinal Poole, as Legate of the Bishop of Rome, absolved him from the excommunication that had been imposed on him in his younger years during the Reformation and granted him faculty (permission):

> to use his Chapell in his Manor of Callowdon, as of ancient time before the schism his
> Ancestors had used the same: And to have a portible Altar to say masse and to receive the body
> and bloud of Christ, and to keep the same in a box covered with a faire sindon or Linen cloth,
> with a candle burning before it.[47]

In the reconstruction of the castle by Peter Urmston (Fig 26) the chapel can be seen as almost a separate building attached to the great chamber range. At the same time Henry sought permission to reclaim local tithes that had been granted by Pope Gregory so many years before in 1239 (see Chapter 1), the payment of which had lapsed after 'the late most pernicious schism.'[48] Hodges offers an interesting opinion on these actions, which she suggests were possibly for the benefit of his mother. She claims that Henry had more sympathy with the Protestant cause than he admitted.[49] This certainly rings true for having only just reached his majority, he may still have been under the influence of his strong-minded mother.

Berkeley trod a fine line between the alternating denominations of his monarchs. On the death of the Protestant Edward VI the great proportion of Berkeley lands which had been in the possession of the Crown for sixty years were finally returned on the extinguishment of the male royal line. At the coronation of the Catholic Queen Mary, Henry was made a Knight of Bath. He entered into a Catholic marital alliance in September 1554 when he married Katherine, the daughter of Henry Howard, the Earl of Surrey and heir to the Dukedom of Norfolk. This renewed the ties between the two families, but unlike many dynastic marriages there was more to this union than a political or religious advantage. His sixteen-year old bride had a strong personality in common with his mother, but they also shared and enjoyed many of the recreational pursuits of the aristocracy.

> And his wife of like honnor and youth…gave her self to like delights as the Country usually
> affordeth; wherein she often went with her husband part of those hunting Journeys, delighting
> her crossbow; kept commonly a cast or two of merlins, which sometimes she mewed in her
> own chamber; which falconry cost her husband each yeare one or two gownes and kirtles,
> spoiled by their mutings: used her longe bowe, And was in those daies amongst her servants
> soe good an Archer at butts[50]

Merlins are small falcons, trained as hunting birds and she kept a 'cast' or number of them in her room, providing nests for them in her clothes - a kirtle being a one-piece gown worn over a smock.

Although her father had been executed by Henry VIII in 1547, the Howard family had been rehabilitated during Queen Mary's reign and so Katherine proved to be an excellent match for Henry,

SEAL OF LORD HENRY BERKELEY.

Fig 27 *Seal of Lord Henry Berkeley,*
Lord of Caludon (1534-1613)

both personally and financially. Sharing their love of sports and the outdoor life, the marriage soon developed into a close and loving relationship, far removed from the calculated unions which many of his forbears had been forced to suffer.

In May 1555, although still underage, Henry was granted the Berkeley estates which had been held by the male royal line since the time of William Berkeley (Fig 27). Edward VI had died in July 1553 and Queen Mary permitted the ancient Berkeley patrimony to revert to Henry before his majority in gratitude for his support during Wyatt's rebellion in early 1554.[51] This was precipitated by the announcement of Queen Mary's marriage to Philip of Spain, to which there was considerable resistance, religious and political, Sir Thomas Wyatt of Kent, being the principal ringleader.

Hearing of the revolt, the nineteen-year old Henry Berkeley roused his tenants in Gloucestershire and formed an armed band of five hundred men with which he set off at once for the capital. By the time he was halfway there news reached him that Wyatt had been captured and the rebellion crushed.

During the reign of Queen Mary, Henry kept a household of 150 servants in livery, travelling between Yate (Gloucs), Mangotsfield, London and Caludon. It would take eight days for this train to travel from the country houses to London.[52] Within four years of their marriage the extravagant lifestyle to which they had become accustomed created an enormous strain on their finances. Henry, as Smyth so delicately phrased it, 'much over ranne his purse.'[53] Expenditure in fact exceeded income by £1500 yearly, a vast sum and Smyth explains how this profligacy was encouraged.

> by many flatterers and sicophants, as well of his own Family as out of London, Captaines, Schollers, Poettes, cast courtiers and the like….It came to pass that within two or thre years they were unknowingly cast into great debt.[54]

To clear some of his debt, Berkeley was forced to sell some of his outlying estates, although Caludon, as a favoured residence, was secure for the time being. The sales continued throughout his life, chronicled in detail by Smyth, who could clearly see how drastically the estates had been reduced by the end of Henry's life in 1613.[55]

One member of 'his own Family', who had contributed to the financial crisis, was his mother Anne. As soon as Henry took possession of his estates on his coming of age in 1556, Anne demanded a dower over and above the lands given to her in jointure by her husband, Thomas (VI). Henry, hopelessly diverted by his love of sport and other games, such as bowls, tennis, cards and dice, agreed to all his mother's demands and in lieu of dower granted her several manors in four counties and his Calais property.[56]

According to Smyth, during the first thirteen years of the reign of Elizabeth I (1558-1571) Henry and Katherine continued their peripatetic life, 'never long in one place' dividing their time between London, the Duke's houses in Norfolk and the castles at Berkeley and Caludon. It seems, however, that Caludon suddenly exerted a magnetic pull, for Smyth also states, in slight contradiction to his earlier comment, that 'the greatest part of this lord's [Henry's] abiding after his mother's death, happening in the sixth year of Queen Elizabeth [1564] was at Callowdon till his own death in the eleaventh of King James' [1613].' Caludon was already attractive to Henry as the convenient proximity of the park fed his passion for hunting:

> But his cheife delights wherin in he spent near thre parts of the yeare, were, to his great charges, in hunting the hare fox and deere, red and fallow..; And hawking both at river and land; And as his hounds were held inferior to no mans...so were his hawks of severall sorts.[57]

In July 1559 Henry journeyed with his wife from Castle Rising in Norfolk to Caludon and upon arrival he sent for his 'buckhounds' to Yate (Glos). With his pack he then set off in all directions from Caludon to parks at Berkswell and Kenilworth (Warks), Groby, Leicester Forest and Bradgate (Leics), 'And this was the course of this lord (more or less) for the thirty next somers at least [till 1589?], not omitting his own at Callowdon and in the county of Gloucester.'[58] But it was perhaps the death of his mother that caused Henry to make Caludon his home. Anne's vexatious and domineering personality by which, according to Smyth, he had a few years earlier been deceived into parting with a considerable number of estates in place of her dowry, was no longer a brooding and hostile presence at the castle. Her devotion to the old faith, six years into the reign of Elizabeth, could have caused him political difficulties and her death provided the opportunity perhaps to disperse her Catholic entourage. Financial worries may also have contributed to the decision to spend most of the year at Caludon, as progresses around the country from one house to another, accompanied by 150 servants, were extremely draining on resources.

The bailiff of Caludon at this time was one Edward Bucknam, a 'much trusted' officer, but in 1576 Henry brought an action against him for not completing the Caludon accounts for seven years after Anne Berkeley's death (c.1564-1571).[59] It was found that he had only neglected the seventh year, 'for which year hee after accompted in prison', as the record shows, seemingly a harsh punishment for the misdemeanour described. Smyth was aware of the case for it contained a 'reasonable survey of the particulars of the Manor.' This has been identified for it survives at Berkeley castle, and the date 1575 appears at its head together with Edward Bucknam's name.[60] As a rental, it unfortunately does not include any details on Caludon Castle itself, which was in the 'lord's hands.'

Knowing the religious preferences of the new Queen and the troubled history of his wife's Catholic family, Lord Henry took more care to adopt a Protestant outlook, or at least remain publicly neutral on questions of faith. It was a clearly calculated move to gift Queen Elizabeth £10 in gold every New Year throughout her life. His motivation in this direction should probably not be compared with his gifting of £5 of gold annually to his wife, also for her life.[61]

Henry's generous spirit could be judged as mere profligacy, an aspect of character that could be easily exploited by others. Robert Dudley was noted for his devious and unscrupulous acquisition of property, seeking advantage from the credulous and naïve. Henry's ancestral estate came under scrutiny from the Queen's favourite, Robert Dudley, the Earl of Leicester. He was a Warwickshire neighbour at nearby Kenilworth Castle and looked enviously upon the Berkeley estates, devising a scheme to wrest some of them from Henry's hands. His duplicity depended for a large part on Berkeley's open, friendly and trusting personality. As mentioned above, Henry had often been a hunting guest at Kenilworth and in about the year 1570, Dudley,

> With semblance of great familiarity gave him liberty without restraint over his Deere in his Parks and chace there; fairly relating unto him how it was his greatest honour.. to be discended from his ancient house [the Lisle family]; desiring that the same by some good herald might by his means be warranted unto him, with their matches, out of his evidence;[62]

Leicester was feigning an interest in their shared family history and in fact wished to examine the Berkeley muniments to establish grounds for a claim on property that had descended to Henry from the Lisle family. An unsuspecting Henry responded willingly, agreeing to let a herald inspect the relevant genealogical material at both Caludon and Berkeley. Dudley's herald, on the pretext of taking notes, took the opportunity to steal property deeds. He delivered them to Robert Dudley, who in turn presented them as evidence at court declaring that some of Berkeley's properties belonged to him through his own descent from the Lisles.

In 1572 Katherine's carefree world was shattered when her brother, Thomas the 4th Duke of Norfolk, was beheaded for treason on the orders of Elizabeth. Like his sister, Norfolk had reconciled himself to a Protestant Queen and had fought for her in the Scottish campaign of 1559-60. The seeds of his destruction lay not in religious differences, but in an almost pathological jealousy of Robert Dudley, the Earl of Leicester, upon whom the Queen had bestowed great confidence and trust. It was even rumoured that they were lovers. Howard was indignant that he had not been shown such favour and whilst serving in Scotland he devised a plan to marry Mary, Queen of Scots, a clearly provocative act, considering Mary's continuing claim to the throne of England. On hearing of his intentions, Elizabeth reacted in fury, forbidding the union and imprisoning Norfolk. Although he was subsequently released, he foolishly became embroiled in a half-hearted Spanish conspiracy to invade England and depose the Queen. The plot was, with little difficulty, discovered and Norfolk arrested, tried for treason, found guilty and subsequently beheaded. The downfall and death of her brother proved to be a bitter blow to Katherine and whilst previously she had sought many of the pleasures of life available to a noblewoman, she now went into mourning, largely withdrawing from public life.

> shee retired her self into her chamber and private walks; which each faire day in garden, parke, and other solytaries, for her sett houres, shee constantly observed: not permitting either her gentleman usher, gentlewoman, or any other of her house to come nearer to her than their appointed distance.[63]

Katherine's marriage to Henry brought little land with her as her portion and it was not until about the year 1570-1 that her jointure was settled. Through act of parliament she received a large number of manors, including Caludon.[64] At this time she had three daughters, Mary, Frances and Jane. A son, Ferdinando, had died at only two years of age.[65] Jane was to die in about 1574-5 from eating roasted apple poisoned with arsenic intended for rats. She was buried in (Walsgrave-on-) Sowe church, the cause of the accident concealed with great secrecy from her parents.

Katherine gave birth to the long awaited male heir, Thomas, on 11 July 1575 at Caludon Castle. This coincided with the illustrious visit of Queen Elizabeth to Kenilworth Castle, its owner, Robert Dudley, having created a new garden to delight and enchant the Queen. This has recently been reconstructed based upon a contemporary description.[66] Word was sent to Elizabeth, who agreed to be the child's godmother, evidence of the status enjoyed by the Lord and Lady of Caludon. Thomas spent the majority of his childhood at Caludon 'under the indulgent instruction of his mother and her waiting gentlewomen, whom in nine years they had only taught to spell and meanly read a little English.'[67] His early education had clearly been more indulgent than instructive. Edward Cowper from Trinity College then took over as schoolmaster in 1584. The event is recorded by Smyth, as he arrived a few days after Cowper on 10 November, in order to take up service in the Berkeley household, aged only seventeen. Significantly, the family was not living at Caludon, but at Whitefriars in Coventry, the former Carthusian monastery, having taken a lease of John Hales' house for three years to avoid the major building works taking place at Caludon (Fig 28).

In 1583 Thomas's older sister, Mary, married Sir John Zouche, of Codnor, Derbyshire, in this temporary accommodation. John Smyth's duties were to attend the young Sir Thomas Berkeley in his chamber, but for his first two years these were undertaken at Whitefriars. Smyth, who had been educated at the free school at Derby, was not destined to be a servant only. He may already have been recognised as a high flyer, and was probably tutored with Thomas Berkeley under the supervision of Edward Cowper. Smyth had arrived with another young recruit, William Ligon and after returning to Caludon, presumably after the building works were complete, the threesome were despatched to Magdalen College Oxford in 1589.

Fortunately Smyth made a note of the building operations at Caludon stating that they had taken place about the 22nd year of the reign of Elizabeth (c.1579-80), but it is likely they were more prolonged. As he arrived during their progress, it is likely that he was not well acquainted with buildings in their previous state.

> ...the porters lodge, the building towards the great poole on the northwest part of Callowdon house, with the brewing house, the stables and many other out houses both within and without the mot built of new; And the roofs of divers of the houses of those old castle buildings taken down and soe far altered that the whole house might bee said to have been moulded and made new;[68]

What can be surmised from this brief description? The work was certainly extensive and radical, involving many of the buildings that stood both within and without the moat. New were a porter's

Fig 28 *The surviving east range of Whitefriars monastery, Coventry; the Berkeleys resided here for three years between c.1584 and c.1586 while Caludon Castle was undergoing extensive building work.*

lodge, a building towards the great pool on the north-west part of 'Callowdon house' (location uncertain), a brewing house and stable. We do not know whether the name 'Callowdon house' was used solely for the main castle building, the hall and its chamber range. Many of the castle building roofs were renewed, perhaps having reached the end of their lives, despite the improvements carried out at the beginning of the century by Thomas Try. It appears, however, that this work was not confined to re-roofing, but also involved significant alterations and perhaps the modernisation that might have involved transforming buildings from medieval halls and chambers to a more comfortable suite of rooms. The Berkeleys, having decided that Caludon was to be their principal seat, probably felt that their house was old-fashioned and to maintain status, despite rapidly waning finances, needed to ostentatiously display the new ideas that were sweeping through the houses of the nobility as a result of the Renaissance. Without a detailed survey or building accounts it is difficult to interpret this evidence any further, but the excellent preservation of foundations discovered by a geophysical survey had permitted a speculative reconstruction of the buildings before this major work of reconstruction and modernisation began (Figs 26, 29 and 30).

A little more information is available regarding the rebuilding as the 'receipts and disbursements in the new buildings adjoining Callowdon house and of the gatehouse and of other outhouses' submitted by the overseer, John Bott, were questioned by Henry Berkeley. He was ready to dismiss

Fig 29 *Reconstruction drawing of Caludon Castle (1550-1570) from the north-west, by Pete Urmston*

him for not clearing the 'reconings', but Bott managed to avoid being discharged, since he had a hold over Katherine.[69] She had sent him to soothsayer, the 'wizard Bourne' in the forest of Arden with a letter, asking for a reply to be returned by him, but Bott had opened Lady Katherine's original letter, although forbidden to do so. He threatened to reveal the contents, if Katherine did not protect his position. The remainder of the convoluted story, given in great detail by Smyth, eventually ended with Bott's dismissal. Thomas, her son, had remained at Oxford until about 1595, during which time he contracted a fever, permanently affecting his health. He had already damaged his spine whilst playing as a boy in the Whitefriars cloisters, which caused a permanent twist to his neck.[70] After returning to Caludon he followed his father to London, where he met Elizabeth Carey, daughter of Henry, Lord Hunsdon, and married her on 19 February 1596. This was followed by a little flurry of building activity at Caludon presumably to please his new bride. Her religious devotion was satisfied by the construction between the years 1597 and 1599 of a prayer retreat somewhere in the castle grounds, 'the retired Cell of her soules Soliloqies to God her creator.'[71] For pleasures of a temporal nature she had a banqueting house constructed in the same period (1597-9) on the north side of the pool opposite the castle, presumably reached on occasions by boat.[72]

The marriage of Thomas to Elizabeth merits only one line in Smyth's history of the Berkeleys, but it has attracted considerable attention amongst Shakespearian scholars.[73] In 1895 Howard Furness proposed that *A Midsummer Night's Dream* was commissioned for and performed at an aristocratic wedding, putting forward three possibilities (Fig 31).[74] It was not until 1935, however, that the Berkeley-Carey wedding was suggested and over the years this has gained favour. By 1979 Harold Brooks felt able to state that the Berkeley-Carey wedding was the one 'which fits the largest number of facts.'[75] In 1993 an influential Shakespearian scholar, David Wiles, came out strongly for the Berkeley nuptials based on a close reading of the play's astronomical imagery,[76] but, typical of the battles that continue to rage in Shakespearian studies, the matter has not been conclusively settled, and the wedding-play theory is not accepted by all.

The most recent work on the subject by Helen Hackett best summarises the present position.[77] 'There is quite a body of circumstantial evidence, but there is no conclusive proof that *A Midsummer Night's Dream* was performed at the Carey wedding...'

The principal circumstantial evidence is as follows: Elizabeth Carey was granddaughter of Henry Lord Hunsdon, Lord Chamberlain to Queen Elizabeth and patron of the Lord Chamberlain's Men, Shakespeare's Company. 'If an entertainment were to be commissioned for the occasion then it is highly likely that he would have turned to his own players and their chief writer.' Henry died in 1595, but his son George Carey, the second Lord Hunsdon, continued as patron as and was equally likely to have commissioned the work.[78] Elizabeth Carey was also related to Queen Elizabeth as great granddaughter of Mary Boleyn, sister of Anne Boleyn, the Queen's executed

Fig 30 *Reconstruction drawing of Caludon Castle (1550-1570) from the north-east by Pete Urmston*

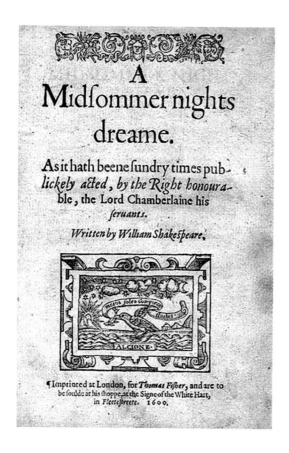

Fig 31 *Title page of A Midsummer Night's Dream' from first quarto 1600 – possibly written and first performed by Shakespeare's Company at the wedding of Lord Thomas Berkeley to Elizabeth Carey in 1596*

mother. Both Elizabeth Carey and Thomas Berkeley were godchildren to the Queen and the play contains references (much debated by Shakespearian scholars) to the reigning monarch, who may have been invited, but did not attend as surely Smyth would have noted this event. Elizabeth Carey was also known to have been interested in dreams, as demonstrated by family letters and a dedication to her in Thomas Nashe's, *The Terror of the Night*, alluded to in Shakespeare's *A Midsummer Night's Dream*.

Within two months of the marriage, now cast into the limelight by recent Shakespearian studies, Thomas's mother, Lady Katherine, was dead.[79] Two stories recounted by Smyth provide a glimpse of other aspects of her personality other than her extravagance and her love of the hunt. Whilst at Whitefriars in 1583-4 Smyth remembers as a seventeen year old crossing the gallery where she dwelt carrying a covered dish in his hands for her son's (Thomas's) breakfast.[80] He was in a hurry and attempted a courtesy at speed, which singularly failed, as Katherine called him back and demanded he practise the movement in front of her at least a hundred times. She took the matter a little further than perhaps Tudor proprieties might allow by lifting her skirts to her calves 'that he might better observe the grace of drawing back the foot and bowing of the knee.' With some irony, perhaps, Smyth remarks that this lesson sprung from her nobleness, rather than the coquettishness of a mature woman teasing a young boy 'lately come from a Country Schoole.' As a substantial part of the Whitefriars monastery in Coventry still stands today, particularly that part converted into Hales's house, it is fascinating to speculate that these events may have taken place in the long, wide room on the first floor, which had formerly been the friars' dormitory.

Three years before her death she developed what was likely to have been arthritis in one of her fingers. The Coventry surgeon suggested either lancing the bare bone or cutting off the finger at the palm, the latter requiring her strongest servants to hold her down. She declined: 'Shee held out her hand, hee did his office, shee never blenched or so much as seemed to take notice of the paine.'[81]

Katherine was eloquent in speech, a fluent letter writer, proficient in both Latin and French and played the lute 'admirably'. Towards the end of her life 'she gave herself to the study of natural philosophy and Astronomy'. Smyth acquired for her a 'globe, Blagraves mathematicall jewell, a quadrate, Compass, Rule and other instruments, wherin she much delighted herself till her death.'[82]

Her undoubted intelligence is difficult to reconcile with the poor quality of education that she provided for Thomas, her son, as already discussed earlier.

Katherine died at Caludon on 7 April 1596, aged 58 from dropsy, probably a swelling of the tissues (edema) due to congestive heart failure.[83] Her death was treated with comparable, if not significantly greater, reverence and ceremonial than that provided for Isabel, her husband's great-grandmother (see above, 1514). She was buried on Ascension Day, 20 May, in St. Michael's church, Coventry, 'with the greatest state and honor that for many years before had been seen in the Citie, or in those parts of the kingdom.'[84] Unlike Isabel's funeral over eighty years earlier, Smyth was a direct witness and contributor, writing down the funeral arrangements dictated by Lord Henry, 'mourning all the time at Callowdon in his private chamber.' Smyth was a willing participant, since Katherine had acted as his benefactress in his early years of service and education with the Berkeleys, providing him with an income of £10 per annum.

Fig 32 *Location of destroyed Berkeley tomb chests in the Drapers' Chapel of old Coventry Cathedral, 2013; Katherine and her son, Thomas, may still lie buried beneath the floor beyond the gates.*

Her body had lain from 7 April until two days before the funeral in the chamber in which she died at Caludon, whereupon her coffin was conveyed during the night to the house of Sampson Hopkin's in Earl Street, which can be identified as Great Palace Yard, destroyed in the November 1940 blitz. It stood on the south side of the street near to the present Council committee room block.

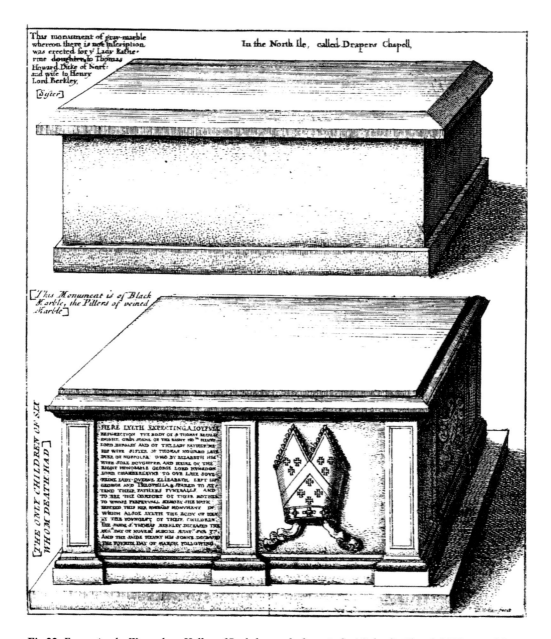

Fig 33 *Engraving by Wenceslaus Hollar of Berkeley tomb chests in St. Michael's Church 1656, now old Coventry Cathedral*

The dignitaries and mourners gathered outside the house at 10 o'clock in the morning. They were organised by heralds and moved off in procession, a quarter of a mile in length, to St Michael's Church, witnessed by massive crowds lining the streets. The grief-stricken Henry, Lord Berkeley, was not amongst them. The official mourners were so numerous that there is no room here to give details of the order in which they processed. Smyth's document provides a useful roll-call of the local aristocracy in this period, but is disappointingly brief on the officials of Coventry Corporation, its mayor and aldermen, who were placed at the rear of the cortege. The service was also described in detail, the sermon being delivered by Edward Cowper, chaplain and tutor to the Berkeley family. The procession returned to Sampson Hopkin's house in the same order that it left and thence moved on to Caludon, where, true to his generous spirit, Lord Henry Berkeley held an extraordinary wake and provided such an enormous quantity of food that 'more than one thousand poore people were plentifully fed the same afternoone' from the left-overs.[85] The scale of the wake may not simply have reflected the extravagance of the Berkeleys but the deep grief Henry felt on losing his wife. His marriage appears not to have been simply one of convenience or dynastic advantage, but fortuitously an affectionate and intimate relationship.

Katherine was buried in a vault in the north-east corner of the church in the Drapers Chapel (Fig 32). Below the Drapers Chapel there are at present two crypts, one accessible from the exterior, the other to the east completely filled with stone rubble. It is possible that she was buried in the latter. An engraving of the monument itself (by Wenceslaus Hollar), a plain grey and uninscribed marble tomb chest, was published in Dudgdale's *Antiquities of Warwickshire* (Fig 33). It stood in the chapel itself and was joined by her son's monument erected about 1613 by Thomas's wife Elizabeth. They were still in the same position in 1830, but by 1909 only Thomas's monument had been moved to St Andrews Chapel in the second north aisle.[86] The monument was destroyed in the November 1940 blitz.

Katherine had held Caludon Castle for life as part of her jointure, and after her death it was made over to Elizabeth, her daughter-in-law, the tradition that the manor form part of the wife's marriage settlement by now well established.[87] Katherine's death coincided with legal action relating to events that took place at Caludon. Cyprian Wood, groom to Lady Katherine's chamber was accused by Henry Berkeley of misappropriating money and stealing linen. Wood was given £100 a few days before Katherine's death. Whatever was the intended use of the money, Wood appears to have kept it for himself. He was eventually brought to account and paid 'what was found by them [auditors] to remaine unissued in her lifetime.'[88] His lord had been particularly distressed not by the theft, but the fact that Wood had also brazenly made off with two trunks of good quality cloth, a plan he had devised with one of Katherine's gentlewomen. This bungled operation had an element of silent comedy about it. The linen had been placed in one of the brew house coolers which Wood was then to ferry across the Caludon mere at night in a boat (Fig 34).

> The bunghole fell open, and soe the ferry boat being heavy laden bagan to sinke ere it was two yards from the shore; wherof this lord [Henry] had early notice by such as lay in waite to have intercepted them; And soe saved his linnens and other things therein.[89]

Fig 34 *The temporarily flooded former mere or pool 2007; the photograph emphasises the picturesque nature of the view across the water to the castle, perhaps enjoyed as far back as the late sixteenth century from a banqueting house situated on the north bank*

In June 1595, a year before Katherine's death, a rental of Caludon was compiled.[90] It did not include any description of the castle, but there was significant difference between the rental made twenty years earlier in 1575 when much of the demesne land was being leased (see above).[91] By 1595 a large part of the land immediately around Caludon had been taken into the 'lords hands'. It included not only, as might be expected, the 'Scyte of the manor' and the park divided into three parts, but also the demesne fields, such as *Ashmore, Litle feyld, Michelfeyld now divided into the groundes called Stubbyfeyldes, and Newhewen [Pertridge feyldes and Crabtree feylde excepted]*, all names familiar from earlier medieval surveys (Fig 19). A field that lay to the north east of the castle was mentioned for the first time – *new close or le Slaughterhouse close.* The rental also made reference to the ancient fields taken into the park that had belonged to the Earl of Chester, *Lake medowe and Stoake hooke alias Caldwell.* The directly managed lord's lands stretched farther afield to *Sowe Waste alias Morgayns Waste, Deadmore,* Henley mill and Sowe mill, *Cocksales* and near to it *Potters greene.* The remainder of the Caludon estate consisted of rents paid by free tenants in Wyken, Chilvers Coton, Astley, Exhall, Foleshill, Stoke and Marston Jabet. Land was also held by indenture and 'at will' in Stoke, Sowe, Wyken, Binley, Astley and also in Caludon.[92] The Coventry houses had been sold with the estate in Stivichall in 1579-80 to Arthur Gregory.[93] A rental of 1600 recorded much the same situation, but by 1605 much of the demesne had been leased again, leaving only the castle (*fortelettus*), the park, some closes to the north-east, *Lake Medowe, Stoke hoke, Stublefield Grove, deadmore, Newhewen, Potters greene, Sowe wast* in the lord's hands.[94]

Thomas Berkeley continued the profligate lifestyle of his father, 'profuse in expence beyond his ordinary means; for the support of which excesse he sold (without the consent of his father)' his reversionary interests in a number of manors and some other estates that his father agreed to sell.[95] A huge sum of money was raised, but it was insufficient to clear the debts. In the first fourteen years of their marriage they spent £1500 yearly above the annuity of £600 which they had been granted upon their marriage in 1596.[96] All efforts, including agreements with John Smyth, to restrain spending failed and in 1600, 1608 and 1610 Thomas travelled the Continent, visiting Paris, Rome, Naples and Venice. After he returned for the last time from the Continent he spent the summer at Berkeley Castle with his father and then in hope of better health at Nibley, Smyth's house. He returned to his wife and father at Caludon at the end of September 1611 and died there at the age of thirty six, predeceasing his father by two years.[97] He was never to inherit his father's title or lands, albeit recently severely depleted. He was buried with his mother in St Michaels's church, Coventry.

Lord Henry maintained the lavish lifestyle, but with a diminished enthusiasm and spirit. In early 1598, at the age of 64, he married for a second time. His new wife was Jane, the widow of Sir Roger Townsend and the sister of John Stanhope, the 1st Baron Stanhope of Harrington. Her father, Sir Michael Stanhope, had been executed in 1552 for plotting to assassinate the Duke of Northumberland. The motivation for the wedding was almost certainly financial. Jane was past child bearing age and so it was not to provide a further heir and the union was not a result of a love match. As a married couple the two appear not have had any interests in common and it is doubtful whether they even actively lived together.

> For as they never bedded togeather that any of their attendants could observe, whereby they
> might have become one flesh; soe were themselves and their families for the most part as farre
> asunder as Barbican in London, and Callowdon by Coventry.[98]

Smyth has little to say about Henry's last years at Caludon following his marriage to Jane. Fortunately a continuous run of accounts for Caludon Castle has survived for the period 1592-1605, which includes the last few years of Katherine's life. Such is their detail that they deserve separate treatment and to which the next chapter is devoted. Henry was most concerned about his two grandchildren, George and Theophila, teenagers, who had been left orphans and in dire straits by the death of their father intestate and in huge debt.[99] He secured a wardship, in his mind beneficial to his grandson (an opinion not shared by George's mother, Elizabeth), by placing him in the care of his brother-in- law, the Earl of Northampton. He also arranged for the marriage of his granddaughter to Sir Robert Coke, 'his further care for her... was likewise comfortably taken off'.[100] Death finally dispatched Lord Henry in a most banal way at Caludon Castle, aged 80. On 26 November 1613 having:

> taken the liking to the tast of small custards then served to his table, hee willed that some of
> them bee reserved for his supper; whereupon feeding, surfeited, so that the same not well
> digesting, he grew distempered in the night following, sicknes by degrees increasing upon him
> until that day fortnight after...at five of the clock in the morning the...26th November 1613,
> rendered back his spirit to him that gave it.[101]

As if to play down this ignominious cause of death, probably caused by salmonella poisoning, Smyth dramatically describes how Henry's last words, 'Come, Come, Lord Jesus,' gradually faded to a single barely audible 'T' sound. Although Caludon had been his favoured residence, he had requested in his will that his body be returned to the family's home at Berkeley Castle. The funeral train set off on 21st December and wove slowly via Warwick, Chipping Campden and Tetbury, arriving at Berkeley on Christmas Eve. His body remained for a few months in the family chapel in the castle awaiting the completion of his monument in the parish church of St Mary the Virgin adjacent. The impressive tomb can be still seen today in the family mausoleum attached to the chancel (Figs 35, 36 and 37). Henry's recumbent effigy in alabaster lies next to Katherine's, both considered by Smyth to be a close likeness, but only Henry's remains 'were laid thereunder.'[102] Katherine, as described above, was buried in St Michael's church, Coventry, but it is not known whether her remains were subsequently disturbed.

The estates, which take three pages to list in Smyth's chronicle of the Berkeleys at the death of Thomas VI, in one generation had been reduced by a third to pay off immense debts.[103] This fact alone explains why Caludon was to be sold by the next generation of Berkeleys. The death of Henry marks the beginning of the slow decline of Caludon, which led eventually to its complete demolition, except for a solitary fragment. The zenith of Caludon, reached in the second half of the sixteenth century, proved to be short lived. Caludon had been granted to Elizabeth Berkeley, now widow of Thomas, as part of her marriage settlement dated 1597. Their daughter, Theophila, was born in 1596, and son, George, in 1601 at Thomas's house near London. The young George would not have expected to have inherited the Berkeley estates in 1613, but for the premature death of his father in 1611. His parents, only in possession of an annuity from Henry Berkeley had 'noe houses wherin to settle themselves' and were forced to live with friends or rent a home.[104] George consequently moved several times in his early years, eventually settling at Caludon. His education was entrusted to Dr. Philemon Holland of Coventry, a celebrated translator of Greek texts and a man who was regarded as one of England's foremost scholars. Since translating the words of Pliny, Plutarch, and Suetonius was not a lucrative business, he paid his way by teaching wealthy sons of the aristocracy. It would appear that George attended the Free Grammar School (the former medieval hospital of St John in Bishop Street) where Holland taught for a year. In November 1613 Caludon had witnessed the last death of a Berkeley to have lived there and George stayed no longer than a month afterwards. In December 1613 he moved to London with his mother where, shifting between several of her houses, his education continued.[105]

On 7 December 1616 Elizabeth Berkeley leased Caludon Castle to Thomas Lygon 'of Callowdon', presumably already living there. Thomas had been a receiver to Henry Lord Berkeley and he may have moved into Caludon soon after it had been vacated by the Berkeleys.[106] The lease was granted for only a term of five years from March 1617 (to March 1622) at a rent of £100 per annum, describing the castle as 'her Mansion or Manor Howse called Callowdon House' and included the park, estimated to be 220 acres in size and *Lake Meadow* at 16 acres. Thomas could avail himself of twenty loads of firewood yearly collected from the park, but Elizabeth Berkeley reserved its timber and trees for herself. Under the terms of the lease Lygon was also responsible

Fig 35 *The impressive Berkeley mausoleum in Berkeley Church, Glos, dominated by the recumbent effigies of Lord Henry and Lady Katherine 2011*

for maintaining all the buildings, keeping them 'dry and tenentable' and the pales, fences and mounds (the boundary banks) of the park.

The expiration of the lease in 1622 coincided with George Berkeley's coming of age and it appears that Thomas continued to live at Caludon for a few more years. He married Elizabeth Pratt at Sowe church on 18 August 1623 and their daughter Joan was baptised at the same church on 3 April 1625.[107] In both cases the register entry confirms that the Lygons were from 'Caledon'. Thomas in fact died in the following year and was buried at Sowe on 20 December 1626, when he was described as 'of Stoke'.

Evidence has emerged that another family may have lived at Caludon at this time, it being a large enough house to share, as will be seen in the next chapter. An obscure reference in the diary of the English College in Rome written in 1639 by a newly arrived student, Henry Shirley reveals that he was born in Caludon (*in arce Calydoniensis*).[108] His year of birth was approximately 1622. The Shirley family did not appear by chance as tenants at Caludon for Henry's father, Sir Thomas Shirley, was a well-known and respected antiquarian and genealogist. His father, Sir George Shirley, had married Frances, one of the daughters of Henry and Katherine Berkeley (Fig 24).[109] Frances was born in Yate (Glos) but in June 1565, aged about four, was brought to Caludon 'in a litter', where she presumably lived throughout her childhood. She married George Shirley of Astwell, Northamptonshire, on 29 February 1586. It is now known that Thomas, their third son and future antiquarian, was probably born at Caludon in 1593. He was baptised on 22 June 1593 'in the Great Chamber at Calladowne.'[110]

Frances was a steadfast adherent of Catholic faith, probably inherited from her mother Katherine. Frances died in 1595 imploring that her three young children, including Thomas, 'be instructed and brought up in the fear of God and true, Catholick religion.'[111] It can be assumed that these instructions were carried out as Sir George, their father, was recorded as dying 'in the bosome of his mother, the Roman Catholic Church.'[112] The year of his death, 1622, is of particular significance as Sir George Shirley's oldest son, Henry inherited the main Shirley estate at this date, whilst Thomas, had succeeded to a smaller portion, including Bottolph (Bottle) Bridge in Huntingdonshire. Although Henry owned Ettington in Warwickshire, he did not live there, for the principal seat was at Staunton Harold, Leicestershire. His brother, Thomas, married Mary Harpur (Harper) about 1622, 'one of the most devout Catholics of her generation', and it appears that the antiquarian set up his first home at Caludon, with Henry, his eldest son, born in the same castle as his father nearly thirty years earlier.[113] Thomas was also knighted in the same year of 1622.

It is possible that the newly-knighted Thomas Shirley, in search of a home commensurate with his status, had heard that the Caludon was available through his family connections. The house was quite large enough to share with the Lygons for a few years. Thomas would also have been attracted to Caludon as an ancient seat being an avid collector of manuscripts and a lover of antiquities. George Berkeley may also have been happy to grant an informal tenancy to his cousin for he had no desire to live at the castle. As late as 1630-1 William Burton, the author of the *Description of Leicestershire*, had offered Sir Thomas the opportunity of writing the equivalent history of Warwickshire, eventually taken over by William Dugdale.[114] Thomas declined as he was deeply

Fig 36 *Close up of the effigies of Lord Henry and Lady Katherine Berkeley 2011; only Lord Henry is buried in the Berkeley mausoleum as Katherine was interred in St Michael's church, Coventry, now the old cathedral.*

Fig 37 *Inscription tablet above Lord Henry's tomb 2011*

engaged in his own family research and is renowned for producing in 1632 an enormous Shirley family tree measuring 11ft. 9 in. by 29 ft. 2 in.[115] This knowledge of local history and genealogy would have been most conveniently gained whilst a county resident, but we know that he could not have lived at Caludon later than the year 1626 (see below).

The connection between Catholicism and Caludon was re-awakened by the tenancy of the Shirley family. The religious stance of the Berkeley family is more difficult to interpret, ostensibly adherents of the Protestant faith. But George Berkeley and his mother, Elizabeth, were about to make a decision that would consolidate the association of Caludon with the old faith for almost the next two centuries.

Elizabeth Berkeley, describing herself as of Cranford, Middlesex, probably dealt with Caludon as part of her jointure after the death of her husband, Thomas, in 1611.[116] Smyth completes his biographies of the individual Berkeleys in about 1618, probably adding details as late as the early 1620s. He leaves the Lady Elizabeth 'at her new purchase at Cranford, 12 miles from London, amongst her thousands of books.'[117] It is for this reason that Smyth provides no further information on Caludon and the evidence for its sale must be sought elsewhere.

The remainder of the Berkeley estates were destined to fall to George, her son, when he reached his majority in 1622. In the meantime his inheritance was being managed as a wardship by his 'rapacious' great uncle, the Earl of Northampton, who died without heirs in 1614.[118] Lady Berkeley took the opportunity to regain control of her son's affairs with swift and skilful negotiation. In the previous year she had also managed to marry off George to one of her relatives, Elizabeth Stanhope. George was only thirteen and a half years in age, his child bride a mere nine years old.[119] Putting aside any scruples regarding this premature union, the marriage introduced a degree of stability into the rapidly sinking Berkeley financial position. The infant bride brought with her a number of manors in Suffolk and Middlesex, which provided an annual income of £1,500.

Henry's profligacy and his numerous and expensive legal suites had left George with barely 11,000 acres, mostly in Gloucestershire and a yearly income of only £1,200. Although this was immense wealth to the vast majority of the population, it was not enough to maintain the dignity of the Berkeleys without severe retrenchment. This continued, however, to prove difficult.

In March 1626 the Lady Elizabeth of Cranford granted new leases of Caludon demesne and outlying parts of the manor.[120] Six months later in September 1626 Elizabeth granted a new lease of Caludon Castle and park to Francis Wright, a butcher of Coventry, more accurately described as a grazier.[121] Francis would have been as much involved in fattening cattle on the pasture fields around Coventry, before bringing them into the city to be slaughtered and sold as meat. Some graziers became wealthy from their combining farming and butchery.[122] The lease confirms that the castle was more commonly called 'Calloughdon Manor House' and that it was already in the occupation of Francis Wright. The land attached to the house included 'the impaled ground' roughly 240 acres in area, 'now commonlie called Calloughdon Parke,' *Lake Meadowe*, measured at 13 acres and *Ashmore*, c.76 acres (Fig 19). One of the most interesting features of the lease was the reference to the mining of coal, a right reserved by Lady Berkeley:

> Reserving all manner of Delfes [pits] of Coles and Cole Mynes within the said premises and if any coles, cole delfes or cole mynes shall fortune to be there found with booringe or searching then with like free liberty to sinke convenient pittes for drawinge of water and getting of the said coles and to make such sitches, [channels], slowes [channels], and other convenient passages for the conveying awaie of water from the said pittes and also to drawe uppe, stacke, fetch, and carrie away the said coles.

The exposed measures of the Coventry coalfield appeared in a narrow line from Tamworth to Hawkesbury and the seam lay below the ground a few hundred yards to the east of the castle. Farther to the north on the seam itself, the coal could be found exposed on surface and only needed shallow pits to extract it, although the ingress of water was a problem frequently encountered. Beighton's map of Knightlow Hundred clearly shows the necklace of coal mines stretching from Griff to Hawkesbury in 1730.[123] There is no evidence, however, that coal was ever in fact mined in the immediate vicinity of Caludon Castle, but Smyth recalled an incident when Henry Berkeley was hunting hare 'not farre from his manor of Callowdon'. In the last moment his horse, a trusty gelding called Brimsley, spotted an old coal pit hidden by bushes and threw himself onto his side, thereby saving himself and his rider, his master, from a potentially fatal accident.[124]

In 1628 Lady Elizabeth made five further leases of outlying land at Caludon, but it seems that Francis Wright did not take up his lease of Caludon House and Park for very long.[125] The lease was surrendered, perhaps before June 1629 when Elizabeth Berkeley and her son, George, mortgaged the whole of the manor of Caludon for £3000 to Paul Bayning, Viscount Bayning of Sudbury, Suffolk.[126] To redeem the mortgage and recover the property, the sum of £3240 had to be paid by 16 June 1630. It is not clear how George had become party to his mother's estate, held as part of her jointure, and only two days later on 15 June 1629, George agreed to convey Caludon manor to his mother for a sum of £5600.[127] The large sums of money being borrowed and exchanged in 1629 reflected the calamitous financial predicament in which the Berkeleys found themselves and foreshadowed the sale of Caludon two years later.

Fortunately the deeds of the sale of Caludon to Thomas Morgan of Heyford in Northamptonshire have been discovered and they contain the great number needed to convey the manor with adequate guarantees and security of title.[128] The main sale was completed on 14 June 1631, when for the sum of £8200 the 'Mannor of Callowdon alias Callowghdowne' and the 'Scite capitall messuage and Manor house…and all that parke or impaled ground called Callowdon Parke' and all the other houses and land and rents in the surrounding villages and hamlets and farther afield were conveyed by Lady Elizabeth and George Berkeley to the new owner. This conveyance marks a historic break in continuity, as the Morgan family had no connection with the Segrave, Mowbray and Berkeley lines, which had possessed Caludon for four hundred years. The Morgans were, however, Catholics, heralding almost two centuries of ownership by various families who were all to adhere the old faith, some to suffer the consequences of their recusancy through fines and confiscations.

The other title deeds reveal that the large sum of £8200 received in two instalments from Thomas Morgan, would still not clear the massive Berkeley debts. Elizabeth and George had failed to pay back the £3000 mortgage to Viscount Bayning and this was redeemed by Thomas Morgan himself. Two days after the main conveyance the Berkeleys became bound to Thomas Morgan for the sum of £10,000 and the document reveals another £20,000 owed to other parties, including Viscount Bayning.[129]

The 16 June 1631 conveyance also explains why there is relatively little material on Caludon in the estate papers at Berkeley castle. Thomas Morgan had insisted that all the deeds relating to Caludon be transferred to him, to reassure him that his title was secure, and it is clear that a systematic trawl of what was already a substantial archive at the time took place. These papers, dating back to the thirteenth century, in turn were passed to the Cliffords when they obtained Caludon in the early eighteenth century. In view of the subsequent history of Berkeley Castle and the preservation and recoding of its valuable family and estate archive, it could be concluded that if the early Caludon material had remained there, it is unlikely that they would have been thrown out or destroyed.

The Berkeleys had reached a nadir in their fortunes in the 1620s and 1630s and Lord George lived on in increasing penury, losing Berkeley Castle during the Civil War. He died during the years of the Parliamentary Commonwealth in 1658. Elizabeth, his mother, had continued to live at Cranford near London and probably died there in 1635. Caludon's story, however, was about to transfer from the dynastic entanglements of the Berkeleys and join a new network of aristocratic connections and religious alliances.

Chapter 3 – NOTES

1   Extensive notes on the Berkeley family can be found on the A2A (Access to Archives) web site relating to the Berkeley Castle archive, compiled in meticulous detail by David Smith, the archivist.

2   Sir John Maclean (ed) *The Lives of the Berkeleys. Lords of the Honour, Castle and Manor of Berkeley in the County of Gloucester from 1086 to 1618* by John Smyth of Nibley, (published 1883 in three volumes) (subsequently Smyth). This is the principal source for the history of the Berkeleys until the early seventeenth century and is a pioneering work of archival research.. It was written by their trusted and able administrator and steward (from 1596) and is an erudite and scholarly work, revealing considerable information on Caludon based on sources that have subsequently been lost. Some authors who have written on Caludon using Smyth as a main source have introduced errors and misinterpreted his eloquent and intelligent commentary. His work should be consulted first in all instances.

3   Smyth, Vol 2, 173

4   VCH Warwick, Vol 8, 121

5   op. cit., Berkeley, BCM/D/1/1/20, 1467

6   Clifford W (E) 1/7, 1 June 1486

7   Clifford W (E) 1/7, 18 July 1588

8   Humphrey Talbot had been a feoffee of Elizabeth Mowbray's, nee Talbot's, jointure of 1467, see note 4 above; Smyth, Vol 2,118, 131,

9   Smyth, Vol 2, 131

10 Clifford W (E) 1/20, Final concord 6 Henry VII; Ethel Stokes, Frederick C Wellstood (eds), *Warwickshire Feet of Fines* [1345-1509], vol III, Dugdale Society, Vol 18 (1943) no 2742, p. 203; John Skille appears in other Berkeley final concords of 1491 in relation to land in Leicestershire, TNA CP 25/1/126/80, nos 5-6

11 Clifford W (E) 1/20; published in op. cit. *Warwickshire Feet of Fines*, no 2742, p. 206

12 Smyth, Vol 2, 131,

13 Smyth, Vol 2, 171

14 Smyth, Vol 2, 153-192; Thomas Try was grandson of William Try, who married Isabel, only daughter of James Berkeley and sister of William.and Maurice

15 Smyth, Vol 2, 172-176, 187

16 Smyth, Vol 2, 174-176

17 Smyth, Vol 2, 91

18 Smyth, Vol 2, 271

19 Smyth, Vol 2, 176

20 Smyth, Vol 2, 194-195

21 Smyth, Vol 2, 196-199

22 Smyth, Vol 2, 199; Thomas Dudley Fosbroke, Berkeley Manuscripts Abstracts and Extracts, (1821) 174

23 Smyth, Vol 2, 208

24 Smyth, Vol 2, 207

25 Smyth, Vol 2, 271

26 Smyth, Vol 2, 201

27 Clifford W (E) 1/4, 1528; Inquisition post mortem of Isabel Berkeley

28 Also Smyth, Vol 2, 271

29 CA PA24/1

30 Smyth, Vol 2, 225-227

31 Smyth, Vol 2, 227

32 Smyth, Vol 2, 221-222

33 Smyth, Vol 2, 253

34 Smyth, Vol 2, 271-272

35 Smyth, Vol 2, 272

36 ibid.

37 ibid; TNA Stac 2/31/17

38 Smyth, Vol 2, 272

39 Smyth, Vol 2, 273

40 Smyth, Vol 2, 253

41 Smyth, Vol 2, 254

42 Smyth, Vol 2, 253

43 Smyth, Vol 2, 271-2

44 *Letters & Papers, Foreign and Domestic, Henry VIII*, Vol 7, 1 Nov 1534, no 1359, 516

45 *Letters & Papers, Foreign and Domestic, Henry VIII*, Vol 9, 7 Aug 1535, no 44, 12

46 According to Smyth, Vol 2, 268, the wardship of Thomas was eventually granted to Robert Earl of Sussex, who then granted to Lady Anne

47 Smyth, Vol 2, 274-275

48 ibid.

49 Elizabeth Hodges, *Some Ancient English Homes and their Associations Personal, Archaeological and Historic*, (1895) 134

50 Smyth, Vol 2, 285

51 Smyth, Vol 2, 280

52 Smyth, Vol 2, 284

53 ibid.

54 Smyth, Vol 2, 286

55 Smyth, Vol 2, 356-362

56 Smyth, Vol 2, 281

57 Smyth, Vol 2, 363

58 Smyth, Vol 2, 285

59 Smyth, Vol 2, 339

60 Berkeley Castle, GBU ff.12-1,; Gloucester Record Office, microfiche 1474/205

61 Smyth, Vol 2, 287

62 Smyth, Vol 2, 292-3

63 Smyth, Vol 2, 384-5; Frederick Colville, *The Worthies of Warwickshire – who lived between 1500 and 1800*, (1869) 33

64 Smyth, Vol 2, 382

65 Smyth, Vol 2, 394-5

Chapter 3 – NOTES

66 The Elizabethan Garden at Kenilworth Castle, English Heritage (2013)

67 Smyth, Vol 2, 394

68 Smyth, Vol 2, 362

69 Smyth, Vol 2,363, 379-380

70 Smyth, Vol 2, 394-395

71 Smyth, Vol 2, 362

72 ibid.

73 Smyth, Vol 2, 395

74 Horace Howard Furness (ed), *A Midsummer Night's Dream, A New Variorum Edition* (1895)

75 Harold F Brooks (ed), *A Midsummer Night's Dream*, Arden Shakespeare (1979) xxi-cxlii, lvii

76 David Wiles, *Shakespeare's Almanack: A Midsummer Night's Dream, Marriage and the Elizabethan Calendar*, (1993)

77 Helen Hackett, Shakespeare and Elizabeth A Meeting of Two Myths, (2009) 124

78 ibid.

79 Smyth, Vol 2, 387

80 Smyth, Vol 2, 386

81 Smyth, Vol 2, 385

82 Smyth, Vol 2 383, 385

83 Smyth, Vol 2, 387

84 Smyth, Vol 2, 387-391

85 ibid.

86 Dudgdale, Vol 1 (1730) 168; *Gentleman's Magazine*, (Oct 1816) 312; William Reader, *Description of St Michael's Church Coventry, with the inscriptions, etc.*,(1830) 31; Frederick Woodhouse, The Churches of Coventry, (1909.

87 Smyth, Vol 2, 396-397

88 Smyth, Vol 2, 355

89 ibid,

90 Clifford, W(E) 1/30

91 op. cit., Berkeley GBU 13, Glos R O, microfiche 1474/205

92 Confusingly *Partridge feilde* formerly *Stubbyfeilde* and *les Crabree feyldes* formerly *michelfeyld* were let out on lease, in contradiction to the earlier part of the rental

93 Smyth, Vol 2, 359

94 Berkeley, GBU 63, Glos RO, microfiche 1474/235

95 Smyth, Vol 2, 397

96 A revision of original grant of £600 from Henry to Thomas Berkeley has been found: Clifford W(L) 1/7, 20 Oct 1601

97 Smyth, Vol 2, 399

98 Smyth, Vol 2, 393

99 Smyth, Vol 2 405

100 ibid.

101 Smyth, Vol 2, 406

102 Smyth, Vol 2, 409

103 Smyth, Vol 2, 259-261, 409-410

104 Smyth, Vol 2, 426-427

105 Smyth, Vol 2, 427

106 Smyth, Vol 2, 184

107 Sowe Parish Registers, Smyth Vol 2, 184

108 Anthony Kerry (ed), 'The Responsa Scholorum of the English College, Rome,' *Catholic Record Society*, Vol 55,(1963) 46

109 Smyth, Vol 2, 403-4

110 Sowe Parish Registers; Sir Thomas's birth has traditionally been placed around 1590, based on his being aged five at his mother's death as related in one source, see Sir Thomas Shirley, Dictionary of National Biography. It is possible, however, that his baptism was delayed three years

111 Richard Cust, 'Catholicism, Antiquarianism and Gentry Honour: the Writings of Sir Thomas Shirley,' *Midland History*, Vol XXIII, (1998) 40-70, see also E P Shirley, *Stemmata Shirleiana* (1873) 83-84

112 op. cit, Cust, 44; Shirley Association Genealogical Research website

113 op. cit., Cust 44

114 Jan Broadway, 'Unreliable Witness; Sir William Dugdale and the Perils of Autobiography,' in *William Dugdale, Historian 1605-1686*, edited by Christopher Dyer and Catherine Richardson (2009) 39; also Richard Cust, 'William Dugdale and the Honour Politics of Stuart Warwickshire,' 95-96

115 The original is lodged in Leicestershire and Rutland Record Office, 26B53/2681

116 Clifford, W (E) 1/4

117 Smyth, Vol 2, 437

118 George Berkeley (1601-1658), Dictionary of National Biography

119 Smyth, Vol 2, 427-8

120 Clifford, W (E) 1/6

121 ibid.,

122 Francis Wright, 'grasier of Coventry', had his will proved in 1647 at the prestigious Prerogative Court of Canterbury, TNA Prob 11/201

123 J C Mitcheson, *The Warwickshire Coalfield, in Birmingham and its Regional Setting A Scientific Survey*, (1950) 289-302, Dugdale, (1730) map between pp. 2-3

124 Smyth, Vol 2, 380

125 Clifford, W (E) 1/6

126 ibid.

127 ibid.: Clifford, W (E) 1/4 Fine Trinity term 1629

128 Clifford, P4 [Preston]

129 Clifford P4, 18 June 1631, 20 June 1631

CHAPTER 4

Life at Caludon with the Berkeleys
1592-1605

With the almost complete demolition of the buildings on and around the moat at Caludon Castle in the mid eighteenth century, it has proved difficult to reconstruct their appearance. The drawings by Pete Urmston of Caludon based on the ground plan discovered by the geophysical surveys, however, provide a good impression of how the castle may have looked in the third quarter of the sixteenth century (Figs 26, 29 and 30). By contrast, for the period around the turn of the seventeenth century, after the Berkeleys had radically rebuilt and refurbished Caludon, one of their favourite residences, there is abundant evidence of day-to-day life and events at the castle. Accounts have come to light that provide much detail on the running of the household and the management of the estate, but this book-keeping has produced more than a meticulous financial record. Many aspects of the Berkeleys' personal life are revealed by the items and services that they purchased.

Charity

The Berkeley family expenditure on luxury items is not unexpected, but we also discover that outgoings included charitable donations. Henry Berkeley was known for his profligacy, experienced by many as generosity, inspiring both loyalty and affection in those who benefitted. Smyth himself drew attention to Henry's local charitable gifts.[1]

> three daies in the weeke wherein the poore of the 4. 5. and six country parishes and villages next adjoyning to Callowdon were relieved.

Each pauper received:

> a messe of wholesome pottage with a piece of beoffe or mutton therein halfe a cheate loaf,[2] and a kan of beer.[2]

Smyth estimated that Henry paid out between eight and ten shillings a day from his own purse 'for private Almes' in small coins in addition to the food relief. On Maundy Thursdays 'many poore men and women were clothed by the liberality of this lord and his first wife [Katherine].' Over twenty pounds was given at Christmas, Easter and Whitsun.

to two or three of the cheifest inhabitants of those villages, and of Gosford street at Coventry, to be distributed amongst the poore according to their discretions.[3]

The household expenses reveal that the ad hoc, daily relief was also distributed at the castle gates. In March 1595 a 'lame boy' was given 4d, along with '2 poore men at your Lords gates.'[4] These acts of 'noblesse oblige' appear generous when seen in isolation and the recipients were undoubtedly grateful for them, the difference often between life and death for a pauper at this time. Many of Berkeley's peers in fact did not share his sense of obligation and were oblivious or indifferent to the poverty of their tenants. A note of caution must, however, be sounded for when the amount of charitable donations is compared with other items of expenditure in the accounts, the generosity does not appear to be so impressive. At Easter 1593, 39s was donated to the local poor 'at the gate'. In May 1593, 19s 9d was paid for 'Reynishe wine' and in the following February, 35s for a pair of pink silk stockings.[5] In January 1595 Berkeley paid out 36s 6d for 'white whine for my lady' and in August, 43s for crimson velvet and another 43s 8d for green velvet to repair two chairs. In January 1597, £20 was given as a down payment for a new coach.

Luxury goods

Not unexpectedly, a major category of expenditure was paid for the Berkeleys' personal items and belongings such as wearing apparel and furniture and the cloth required for it: a hose and doublet made for 'Master' [Thomas] Berkeley cost 6s 9d, (March 1595), '1 oz and 1 quarter of black fatten silk' was needed to make a pair of 'backhose' (2s 6d), '13 yardes and a half of bone lace' was required for '6 bandes', which together with six pairs of cuffs cost 19s 6d (May 1595). Expensive cloth was also used in upholstery and decorating bedding: In July 1595 Humfrey Kindon made a down bed, which consumed '24 yards of white fustian cloth at 3s 2d a yard', '3 dosen of blewe and white binding lace to mend the bed (18d)' and 'Crimsen and White silke laces to lace the seames of the bed' (15s 3d). In the following month '18oz of Crimsen silk and gould fringe at 5s the oz' was used to decorate chairs, totalling £4 12s 6d. These expensive items, beyond the financial reach of the servants and workmen who toiled at Caludon, convey an impression of the sumptuousness of the décor and fittings in the castle. There were at least two Arras tapestries, one in the hall and the other in 'my Ladies [Katherine's] chamber.'[6] These needed to be cleaned and repaired (April, July 1596). A painter was paid 12d for 'laying coulers [colours] in the great chamber,' (Jan 1594). The rich fabrics of the Berkeleys' dress matched this luxurious environment. Other expenditure extended the display of opulent colour and texture into the garden, with the extra cache of rarity and curiosity. Three peacocks cost 4s 6d in November 1595.

We also catch a glimpse of the Berkeleys' more personal possessions, some of which they may have valued amidst a surfeit of luxury: Henry's watch was mended for 9s (Aug 1595), his two crossbows provided with new strings, arrows and bolts (1s 8d) and a looking glass purchased for 2s (July 1595). After Lady Katherine died in 1596 a bill was settled with 'Tuck the gouldesmith for two ringes sett in my Ladies time' (June 1597).

Essential items

The accounts also record the more mundane purchases that the running of a noble family's household required. These included a new cart (wayne) with its fittings (25s 6d, Aug 1595), locks for doors to Master [Thomas] Berkeley's study (8d, March 1595) and the schoolhouse (6d, Aug 1596). 100 loads of 'stone Cole', each costing 3s, were delivered in May 1595, presumably from the local coal pits, but despite their geographical proximity this was still expensive fuel in the late sixteenth century (£17 20d). Charcoal was, however, even more expensive at 14s a load and only three loads were supplied, perhaps to heat braziers.

Labourers and Craftsmen

The Caludon accounts are comprehensive, listing items of expenditure in a wide variety of categories including payments to hired workers. These provide an insight into the comparative cost of labour and service in the late Tudor and early Stuart period. For example, in February 1594 a barber was paid 2s 6d for cutting Henry Berkeley's hair and, by contrast, Thomas Truelove and Henry Bushell were paid 2s for two days 'threshing in Calowdon Barne.' The sum of 6d a day was apparently the 'going rate' for basic labouring, for 2s was received by Thomas Newcom for '4 daies ditching the hoppyard,' (April 1595).The 'goodwife Ascue' was paid a shilling week for seven weeks for the unpleasant task of emptying the closet stool (toilet) (May 1604). The more skilled work of William Howe, a carpenter, was rewarded with 4s 6d for five days work making a cheese press at Henley (June 1595). At the top of the craftsman's scale Humfrey Kindon was paid 16s 6d for 'dressing Mr Berkeleys rapier,' (Sept 1595). It is evident that Caludon in its heyday was an economic magnet, providing work for local people at all levels of skill. Tradesmen from the immediate parishes and further afield in Coventry supplied the house with all manner of goods, from food, medicines, barrels, locks, coal and fabric. The death of Henry Berkeley in 1613, and the subsequent departure of the remainder of his family must have severely affected the livelihoods of the local population that had come to rely on Caludon for part or possibly all of their income.

Repairs and Maintenance

The accounts record payments made to repair and maintain the Caludon buildings and for work done outside in the courts and fields. Through them we obtain a selective list of the rooms and buildings that were in existence not long after the Berkeleys had substantially rebuilt and renovated them. Some idea of the appearance of the interiors can also be gained. It is clear that the maintenance of the freshly restored Caludon buildings was still a major drain on resources, demonstrating how difficult it would have been for the succeeding grazier-tenants to continue this level of expenditure.

Much of the work was done by local craftsmen. In January 1594/5 John Sarge[n]son, a well-known Coventry mason repaired the stairs that led to the great chamber (6 days, 6s 6d) for which '40 foote' of stone was consumed (Fig 38).[7] In June 1593 a painter mended the walls and pasted them with paper in Master [Thomas] Berkeley's study. The Arras tapestries in both the hall and in

Katherine's chamber were dressed about the time of her funeral (April and June 1596). The hall tapestry was taken down, re-lined with canvas and re-hung on tenter hooks. Even though glass was expensive, a modernised house of the size of Caludon would be expected to have a goodly number of glazed windows. In July 1596 Hoskins, the glazier, scoured and mended the glass windows about the house.

Moving from works of art and craftsmanship to the disposal of human waste, Henry's 'Closet stole' (WC) was mended for two shillings in June 1595. It is tempting to think that the reference to a sweep cleaning out the chimneys in April 1593 included the one that survives in the present ruined wall. The existence of an armoury is known from the lamp black and oil which was purchased to maintain its contents. This room may have been in the main part of the house or in a separate building.

Frustratingly there was relatively little work done to the family apartments, perhaps because of their recent refurbishment and most items related to the service buildings. January 1595/6 was a busy time:

> To William Howe Carpenter for 3 daies work in setting the bellowes
> and setting his Anfield [Anvil] and other things...3s 4d
> To Thomas Truelove, Thomas Astyn and Henry Buswell
> for painting the Smithy House...4s 6d
> To Robert Seabridge Tiler for 3 daies in the sealing the Clock House
> with lathes and heare [hair] mortar at 1d the day 2 6d
> To William Howe Carpenter for 5 dayes work in making needful
> thinges in the kitchen and mending the wheele Barrowes at 10d 4s 2d
> to William Coxe Carpenter for mending of the plump [pump]...2s
> To Robert Eliot mason for mending the kitchin and squilery [scullery]
> paving and for mending of ovens for 5 daies at 12d..5s
> To Thomas Truelove, Thomas Astin Henry Buswell for 8 daies worke
> in the paling the woodyard 4s
> more to them for 10 daies worke in paling of the great garden...5s
> To William Howe Carpenter for one daies worke in the
> mending of the manger and work in the strawe house 10d

Another important service room which required considerable work was the brew house. It appears to have been located near the bridge (April 1605). In May 1593 Thomas Cheyney, a cooper, made five hoops for the great mash vat (20s). This was followed in May 1595 by more coopery:

> Paid the Cowper for 3 great hoopes for the great ycking [sic] fatt [vat] 24s
> for 8 hoopes for a mashe fate [vat] 32s
> for settinge in 3 new staves in the mashing fate [vat]..10d
> for 3 hoppes for the long Coler in the slaughterhouse 3s

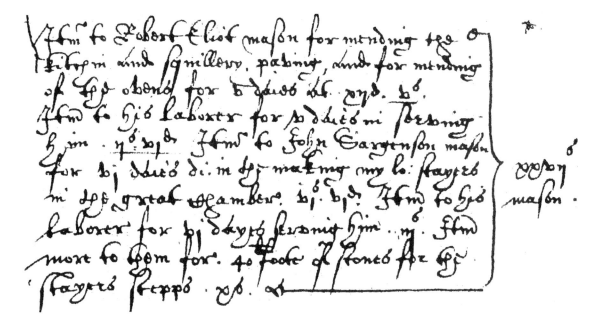

Fig 38 *Extract from the Berkeley accounts of Caludon Castle January 1594/95*

Other service buildings in which repairs were carried out included: the pigeon house, laundry and tallow store house (June 1593), straw house (January 1593/4), candle house and bakehouse (Dec 1595), dairy house, barn and granary (July 1596) the keepers lodge and schoolhouse (Aug 1596).

There is information on the spaces and courtyards, which were either situated around the main building complex on the moated platform or outside of the moat. There are several mentions of gardens, including the 'great garden', which was fenced in January 1594/5, an 'Upper garden' and an 'old garden' (Aug 1596). If any of these were located on the moat, they would most likely have been on the west side, between the hall and chamber ranges and west arm of the moat water. Here seclusion from the busy main courtyard entered from the gatehouse on east could be guaranteed and is the location chosen for the bird's-eye views (Fig 29). Next to the pigeon house was a courtyard fenced with palings in June 1593. There was a hop yard, essential to keep the brewery supplied, but location unknown. In June 1593 it was 'dressed', and in April 1595 - ditched. The moat itself received some attention with posts and rails constructed around the internal circuit (Oct 1595). Steps were cut into the bank, probably on the north side in order to reach a boat and cross to the banqueting house (Nov 1595). Close by a number of new channels were dug in the same month to avoid the pool overflowing.

The accounts record work done farther afield on the demesne and in the park. The park was railed in July 1595 and the same workmen were transferred to mow *Lake Meadow* and *Hungerlie Meadow*. Further mowing took place in the same month on *Stokehoke* [Stoke Hook], *Ashmore meadow* and *Slaughterhouse Close* (Fig 19). The carpenter, William Howe, erected more park paling and mended all the gates. The mown hay was then gathered into ricks and by the following

November the hayricks were fenced. In the same month a rabbit warren in the park was secured by erecting a 'new haye (fenced enclosure) for coneys' to prevent their escape. Rabbit meat was an important source of protein along with fish from the pool; a casting net was made in June 1593.

The servant household

The Caludon household, consisting mainly of servants and retainers, was extensive and hierarchically organised, a necessary display of aristocratic status. The more servants that could be maintained and the greater their differentiation, the higher was the prestige that the family enjoyed, despite the huge expenditure required. The Berkeleys were no exception and the costs of running their household contributed to their disastrous financial situation and the Caludon accounts are illuminating in this respect.

At the top of the pecking order stood the household steward. He was the principal administrator and it is thanks to the preservation of his records that this chapter has been written. The steward did not compile the accounts, however; this was left to a clerk or 'receiver', whose clear hand appears throughout the full run of accounts from 1592 to 1605. The steward's position was crucial and one which required a man of both great diplomatic and bureaucratic skill, and, above all, trustworthiness. Henry Berkeley was blessed with the intelligent, perspicacious and loyal John Smyth, who was his household steward from the death of Katherine in April 1596 to the arrival of John Creswell about a year later. John Smyth then took up the apparently more lucrative office of steward of the Hundred and Liberty of Berkeley. He remembered:[8]

> At the first coming of John Creswell his steward of household, giving him [Henry Berkeley] authority of displacing whomsoever he found in his house disorderly, hee by special words exempted his Cookes Huntesmen and faulkeners; which intimated to the observation of all his family then present his inbred inclination to his sports, and to hospitality, which was generally applauded.

Creswell could not have savoured dealing with the potential insubordination or misbehaviour of staff serving Henry in his favourite pursuits, feasting and hunting, but he was paid a handsome wage as recompense. In October 1604 the steward received £10 for half a year, making his annual salary £20, a substantial sum. A half-year payment to John Smyth appears below Creswell's in the account, but for significantly less - 33s 4d. By this time Smyth was also acting as the family solicitor, 'preparing cases... and expediting the administration of the numerous Berkeley lawsuits.'[9] He may have been paid from separate accounts for these duties, which had burgeoned and left little time to devote to the Vale of Berkeley estates.

It is probable that the steward would have lived at Caludon and maintained his office or 'counting house' there, for this was where the household resided for much of this period. Next below in the household hierarchy was normally the gentleman usher, who dealt with the day-to-day running of the household, organising the staff and dealing with visitors and guests. His role would have combined that of secretary, butler, and confidant and he was likely to have been on fairly intimate terms with Lord Henry. In 1604 a John Wheeler occupied this position for which he was paid the same as John Smyth – 33s 4d. Their names and that of John Creswell were prefixed by 'Mr,' denoting their status as gentlemen or squires, an important social distinction.

If rank is judged by the level of wages alone, however, then John Wheeler's position was more ambiguous, as there were other officials at Caludon who were more highly paid. An example was the position of 'Clerk of the Kitchen', occupied by John Prowting, who received 40s per half year, compared to Mr John Wheeler's - 33s 4d. He would have been responsible for maintaining the kitchen accounts and overseeing deliveries, leaving the cook, Hugh Fowler, who was paid even more - £3 6s 8d per half year, to concentrate on running the kitchen and deciding menus. This level of payment reflects the value that was placed on his work by Henry Berkeley. It is ironic that Henry was to die of food poisoning, but in the pre-ice house and fridge age this was an unavoidable occurrence. Another office of comparable status was held by John Freeman, who was Yeoman of the Horse. He received no payment 'because he hath a ground in Gloucester for his wages', presumably given to him by the Berkeleys. The keeping of the stables was an important and onerous duty, with horses needed in particular for Henry's other favourite pastime, hunting. Veterinary science was in its infancy, hence the administering of two 'drinks' of unknown fluid to a bay horse named 'Harry', perhaps Henry's favourite hunting horse and the bleeding of eighteen horses for 3s (May 1595). It is interesting that John Watson, the brewer, was paid the same as the gentleman usher, John Wheeler. Ale with its alcohol content, although weak, was valued as much for its lack of contaminants as for its intoxicating effects.

Humfrey Ellis was yeoman of the great chamber at Caludon and paid 40s, equal to the brewer and the clerk of the kitchen and more than the gentleman usher. The great chamber, presumably located in the main chamber range of which the ruin is a fragment, was distinguished from the 'lords chamber', a more private room, which was overseen by the groom, Robert Kinge (26s 8d). He would look after Henry Berkeley, brush and clean his clothes and generally be in his attendance whilst Henry was in occupation of his private apartment. The salary of Thomas Pinkerman, the falconer, set at 40s, reflected Henry's enduring passion for hunting at Caludon and farther afield. The list of staff given in October 1604 concluded with the following men and their half yearly wages:

Ralph Heath, for his wages and bord for keeping Callowdon House £3 10s

Roger Segar, keeper of Callowdon Parke 26s 8s

Richard Cole, Usher and Slaughterman 26s 8d

John Borlson, Cator [caterer] 26s 8d

Barnaby Knott, footman for 1 quarter 20s

Thomas Stratton ....[no information]

John Burnell ....[no information]

The groome of the kitchin, for 1 quarter..7s 6d

The keeper's boy 10s

It is interesting that there is a Keeper of both Caludon House, as it was called at the time, and a Keeper of Caludon Park. It is likely that Ralph Heath was responsible for the repair and maintenance of the main house in the same way that Roger Segar looked after the park, ensuring that its encircling pale was kept secure, timber and brushwood felled and transported away, the deer protected from poachers and hunting parties organised. Richard Cole was both an usher and a slaughter man, the latter duty taking time only when venison was needed for the Lord's Table.

It is difficult to estimate the size of Henry Berkeley's household from these accounts, as the great majority of servants were not formally waged, receiving board and lodging and other allowances in kind. These included grooms, resident farriers, huntsmen and porters as well as numerous footmen, postillians, kitchen and scullery maids, under-cooks and attendants. Many years earlier in the 1560s when Henry and Katherine travelled between Caludon, London and Berkeley, they were seldom attended by fewer that one hundred and fifty servants:[10]

> In their tawny cloth coats in summer, with the badge of the white Lyon rampant imbroidered on the left sleeve; And in coats of white frize with crimsen tafetty in the winter. This lord allowing only cloth, buttons, and badge; amongst whom many were gentlemen and Esquires of remarkable families and discent, and of alliance to this house.

Henry's household was likely to have been much smaller, once he became a widower in 1596.

The badges marked the servants with the Berkeley insignia. This was regarded by the family as essential to reflect their wealth and high status, but the marking was also as a means by which the servants could distinguish between themselves in their own rigid 'downstairs' hierarchy. In May 1595 'Harrison's wife' was paid £9 10s for:

gentlemens badges	10 at 5s	50s
yeomans badges	20 at 4s	£5
gromes badges	12 at 3s 4d	40s

The forty-two badges which were made could be interpreted as the number of servants in each of the Caludon ranks, but there is a possibility that an extra number was ordered for future use.

The duties of each of the servant offices were strictly defined, including the behaviour that was expected. Smyth, fortunately, provided a copy of the extensive rules of conduct.[11] These had been compiled with the help of previous household stewards and other officers and approved by Henry and Katherine. It begins with the rules for the gentlemen. For example, no gentlemen should 'come into the great chamber without his cloake or livery coate'. They could not be absent from mealtimes without permission and when called to the dresser (presumably to serve food) they should 'behave themselves decently without noise or uncivill behaviour.' When the gentlemen rode out on any journey they were arranged in pairs ahead of Henry Berkeley and had to avoid 'lewd speech or other rudeness.'

The yeomen likewise were required to attend in the hall at all times, such as meals, and could not be absent without licence. They could not 'lye out any night' and had to be in their lodgings by nine o'clock. They had no right to enter the buttery, pantry, cellar, kitchen or scullery without good cause. These rooms would have been situated at the opposite end of the hall to the great chamber and were full of tempting provisions and goods. There appears to have been a separate dining chamber for the yeomen who were required to:

> strew the rushes; to take out all spotts as shall happen in the carpetts, chaires, or stooles; to dust the cushions; In the winter to have fire in the chimney, and in the sommer flowers in the windows;...And they shall suffer no doggs in the dyneing chamber.

Food and Entertainment

Fortunately the accounts record not only the purchase of material objects, but also indirectly reveal the events which took place within the walls of Caludon, given an invaluable additional perspective by Smyth. The Berkeleys were hospitable, known for lavish entertainments at which music, singing and dancing, as well as acting, played an important part. They shared their pleasures with their guests, invited, depending on the occasion, from all levels of society. Smyth, in fact, highlighted a facet of Henry Berkeley's character which could not have been gleaned from the Caludon accounts. He was clearly impressed by Henry's sociability and lack of snobbishness and aloofness, unusual for a man of his social standing.

> Such was the humanity of this lord [Henry].That in times of Christmas and other festivalls when his neighbour Townships were invited and feasted in his hall, hee would in the midst of their dinner rise from his own, and, going to each of their tables, cheerfully bid them welcome; And his further order was, having guests of honor of remarkable ranke that filled his own table, to seat himself at the lower end; And when such guests filled but half his bord, and a meaner degree the rest of his table, then to seat himself the last of the first rank and the first of the latter, which commonly was about the midst of his longe table neare the salt; This I tell his posterity, the better to knowe the practice of that time, and the posture of this their noble ancestor beloved by all good men.[12]

It would not be difficult to imagine this scene taking place in the great hall at Caludon, the Lord's table at the upper end, but Henry happy to sit himself on occasions at the lower end, presumably near the porch and its draughty cross-passage. With his top table occupied by guests of both 'first' and 'mean' rank, he would position himself at their junction rather than in the midst of his social peers. The reference to 'near the salt' is interesting, as social status was usually reflected by how far away one sat from the salt, an expensive commodity kept in an elaborate cellar on the top table.

The food provided at these feasts was lavish and plentiful; roasted boar, peacock (served with its tail display intact), brawn, frumenty (boiled wheat with porridge) fruits, jellies, blancmange and all the wines and ales which could be mustered. The kitchen at Caludon was probably stocked with the produce of its own demesne, and tenant farms, but it also purchased from farther afield, through local suppliers. So we find '3 barrells of white hearinge at 34s the barrel and '2 Cades of red

Fig 39 *A contemporary engraving of musicians from the title page* of Giardino Novo belissimo…Primo libro, *published in 1605; this ensemble may closely resemble John Dowland's Consorte performing at Caludon Castle. It is possible that the lutenist is, in fact, John Dowland playing at the court of of the Danish-Norwegian King Christian IV*

hearinge at 16s,'1 cade of sprats' (5s) and three dozen salted eels purchased from Walker, a fishmonger of Coventry (May 1595).[13] Mutton was purchased from Derby Fair, but from more exotic climes and therefore expensive, came 30 lemons and 50 oranges supplied by a John Harbert for 5s 4d (April 1605). In June 1596 a wide array of spices and delicacies was acquired for 18s 3d.

> pepper, sugar, largde ginger, powder sugar, Currander, mace, rose, water, prunes, large mace, cloves, nutmege, rise [rice], raisins, allomons

A year earlier a pound of carroway seeds was supplied at a cost of 16d. Many spices, owing to the long distances they travelled from their growing areas, were costly, but to the aristocracy who could afford them, spices were an intrinsically desirous commodity. Nevertheless, as today, spices were primarily sought to give food extra and exotic flavour and it is a myth that they were used in earlier times to mask the taste of rotten meat. The Lord Henry's dog may not have had spices added to his meat, but it was well fed with horse flesh, a carcass, costing 14d, transported to Caludon in March 1595/6 for an extra 6d. In the month before two strikes of barley, costing 6s, were also intended as dog feed.

Henry was an enthusiastic patron of the arts especially dance and drama, and Caludon frequently hosted musicians and bands of actors. Both Henry and Katherine were themselves musically trained and Lady Katherine was a particular lover of the lute. Smyth remarked that:[14]

> At the lute shee played admirably, and in her private chamber would often singe thereto, to the ravishment of the hearers.

This was a skill that they wished to impart to their son, Thomas, and in November 1595, when he was twenty years of age, 'Mills the Lute player' was employed for three weeks to teach 'Master Berkeley to play on the Lute' for which Mills was paid 15s.[15] Even in the years following Katherine's death in 1596 Henry still employed players to perform before him at Caludon.

The accounts are, in fact, an important source for late Tudor and early Stuart court entertainers - musicians, dancers and actors (Fig 39). Peter Greenfield analysed nearly a hundred payments or 'rewards', as they were called, made to them.[16] Published in 1983, this is the first known occasion that the accounts have been used as a historical source. Unfortunately Greenfield did not have access at the time to the middle volume in the sequence (GBB 108), which recorded in January 1598/9 the engagement of the services of John Dowland, England's pre-eminent lute player. This was reported more recently by Mike Ashley, a lutenist himself and member of the Lachrimae Consort, a group of players specialising in Elizabethan music (Fig 40).[17] Dowland was both an

Fig 40 *The Lachrimae Consort performing in St. Mary's Church, Walsgrave in 2007*

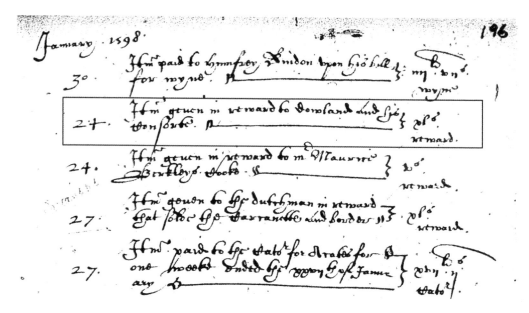

Fig 41 *Extract from Berkeley accounts at Caludon Castle Jan 1598/9: payment to John Dowland and his Consort outlined in red*

extraordinary lute player and a song writer of great reputation. He recently achieved widespread popularity when the pop singer, Sting, produced an album of his songs and learnt to play the lute for that purpose. In his day Dowland was, however, the most famous lute player in Europe and his melancholy songs such as *Flow my Tears, Come Heavy Sleep* and *I Saw My Lady Weep* are amongst the finest songs written in the English language.[18] Dowland was a Catholic, which may explain why he performed personally for the Berkeleys when in fact he was supposed to be in Denmark in the employ of King Christian IV. It is possible that he returned to England on leave, perhaps at the behest of Lord Hunsdon, the father-in-law of Henry's son Thomas, who knew Dowland from his diplomatic post at the Langrave of Hessen. 40s was paid in January 1598/9 to Dowland and his 'Consorte' (a group of players), probably for performing at Caludon at Christmas (Fig 41). This in itself is interesting, for it is the only known reference to Dowland playing with a consort; it has always been assumed that he was a brilliant solo lute player and writer of magnificent songs.[19]

John Dowland was the most famous name to appear in the Caludon accounts, but they are full of payments to other individual performers and groups: musicians, trumpeters, dancers (one a sword dancer), bearwards, fools and morris dancers. Anonymous musicians were paid £3 for playing at Christmas 1592 (Jan 1592/3). Two years later the cost of hiring a group of unnamed musicians was £4 and taberer (a drummer), 10s (Jan 1594/5). In December 1595 musicians performed in 'ye lord [Henry Berkeley's] chamber' and a group of 'singars of Coventry' were rewarded with 3s 4d and a blind harper given 2s. Throughout the 1590s there are regular payments to musicians for performing at Christmas, undoubtedly the major festival in the year to be celebrated in this way.

Troupes of actors regularly visited Caludon, making it one of the cultural centres of Warwickshire during this period. In December 1593 a company known as the 'Earl of Derby's players' performed at Caludon and in the following July another company, the Queen's players, was paid 12s for their appearance. Christmas 1600 was particularly hectic artistically with the arrival of three groups: Lord Dudley's, Lord Huntingdon's and, once again, the Queen's players. After 1600 the number of visiting acting companies declines sharply, but musicians remain popular.[20] Other kinds of performers replaced the actors, such as the fools of Lord Dudley (June 1604) and of Lord Bedford (Jan 1603) and a Morris dancer, who came from Kenilworth (May 1605).

In contrast to the sparkling and lively entertainments that were staged regularly at Caludon, the accounts record a much more solemn occasion. The sombre but spectacular funeral of Lady Katherine Berkeley that took place in 1596, has already been described in a previous chapter, but we now know of some of the preparations that were made for this event. At Caludon a total of £33 18s 8d was paid out for:

> three weekes work against the funeral for matting my Lordes study, covering and sowing the tent and taking it down againe and dressing feathers and filling the bedes and mending chayres and stools.

Henry Berkeley's study had been prepared to receive Katherine's body after it had been 'opened up and preserved' by David Astley and Henry Hickmen (paid £7 7s 2d, April 1596). Katherine was laid out under a canopy or 'tent', around which, presumably, chairs were arranged for the numerous mourners that came to pay their respects. Some visitors stayed overnight, and the more important for longer, and feather beds had to be repaired to cope with the demand. Three shillings were given to the 'Ringers of Sowe' [church] for ringing a doleful peel in Lady Katherine's memory (April 1596).

The financial accounts of a great historic house could at first glance be regarded as dry and uninteresting, not worthy of attention except for scholars of abstruse historical detail and minutiae. This chapter, it is hoped, has demonstrated how rich a source such documents can be and how their analysis can enliven the history of any time or place where the facts are sparse and the physical remains insubstantial. It is no longer so difficult to imagine what life was like at Caludon Castle (or Caludon House as it was called at this time) at one of its high points in its history - the turn of the seventeenth century.

These three volumes of accounts are a goldmine awaiting the extraction of yet more interesting revelations and justify a publication entirely devoted to the life of Lord Henry Berkeley at Caludon.

Chapter 4 – NOTES

1   Smyth, Vol 2, 368
2   Cheat is wheaten bread of the second quality
3   Smyth, Vol 2, 369
4   The original Caludon accounts are to be found at
    Berkeley Castle, BCM /GBB107-109 (General
    Books Bound). Microfiche copies are at Gloucester
    Record Office, for the years 1592-94, (GBB107)
    microfiches 1478/167; 1594-1600 (GBB108)
    microfiches 1478/171-80; 1600-1605 (GBB109)
    microfiches 1478/181-5. Subsequent quotes from
    these accounts will not be individually referenced to
    prevent repetition.
5   'Rhennish' wine was a sweetish wine from the
    Rheinhessen region of Germany
6   Arras, France, a major centre for the production of
    fine wool tapestries.
7   VCH Warwick, Vol 8, 293; George Demidowicz,
    *A History of the Bluecoat School and Lych Gate
    Cottages*, Coventry, (2000) 22
8   Smyth Vol 1, iv, Vol 2, 378, Vol 2, 364,
9   Jan Broadway, 'John Smyth of Nibley: A Jacobean
    Man-of-Business and his service to the Berkeley
    Family, *Midland History*, Vol 24, (1999) 84

10 Smyth, Vol 2, 285-286
11 Smyth, Vol 2, 364-367
12 Smyth, Vol 2, 381
13 A cade consisted of 500 herring or 1000 sprats
14 Smyth, Vol 2, 383
15 Another 15s was paid to Mills in January 1595/6.
16 Peter A Greenfield, 'Entertainments of Henry, Lord
    Berkeley, 1593-4 and 1600-1605,' *Records of Early
    English Drama*, Vol 8, no 1, (1983) 12-24.
17 Michael J Ashley, 'Who sent Dowland to Coventry
    in 1598?' *The Lute Society Magazine*, no 82 (July
    2007); *Coventry Evening Telegraph*, 27 March 2007.
    The Lachrimae Consort in fact performed in
    Walsgrave church on 30 March 2007 to celebrate the
    link between John Dowland and Caludon Castle.
18 Mike Ashley pers. com.
19 ibid.
20 op. cit., Greenwood

CHAPTER 5

The Morgan and Preston Lordships and their Tenants
1631-1685

Fig 42
Morgan coat of arms

After the grandeur and cultural splendour of the era of Lord Henry Berkeley, arguably the most flamboyant but profligate of its Lords of the manor, Caludon Castle descended rapidly from being the principal seat of an aristocratic domain to an oversized home farm of an extensive farming estate, surrounded by a number of small and dispersed holdings. The seventeenth century was not kind to the fabric of the once imposing castle, but it appears to have survived the century albeit in a decayed form. It has been long assumed that it was brought to its present form of a single fragment of upstanding wall as a result of being besieged and captured during the Civil War, but there is no evidence that any such action took place at the castle and it was inhabited long after the war had ended.[1] This is not to deny that the new owners of Caludon escaped the ravages of the Civil War unscathed, but these were not to be so dramatically expressed through the condition of the castle as hitherto imagined.

The new owners of Caludon, the Morgan family, unlike the Segraves, Mowbrays and Berkeleys, could claim no great lineage. Their recorded history begins in the mid sixteenth century with roots in Northamptonshire. Likewise they did not occupy the highest levels of the aristocracy, but were of the 'middling sort', part of the gentry class that had originally acquired its wealth in trade, law and estate administration. At the earliest opportunity this was invested in land and property, particularly in the countryside. Francis Morgan, the founder of the Heyford (Northants) branch of the family, was appointed recorder of Northampton in 1553 and shortly before his death in 1558 became a judge.[2] His son and heir, Thomas, added to his father's already extensive Northamptonshire estate by acquiring a half share (moiety) of land in Weston-under-Wetherley, creating a foothold in Warwickshire.[3] Thomas married Mary, the daughter of Sir Edward Saunders, the co-owner of Weston, thereby uniting this manor under his ownership. The estate was enlarged in 1586 when Thomas Morgan purchased the neighbouring manor of Wappenbury from Constance Fennys.[4]

Thomas made a will in 1588, although he did not die until 1603. He settled the bulk of his estates on his wife, his younger brother Anthony Morgan of Aynho and his niece Bridget, Anthony's

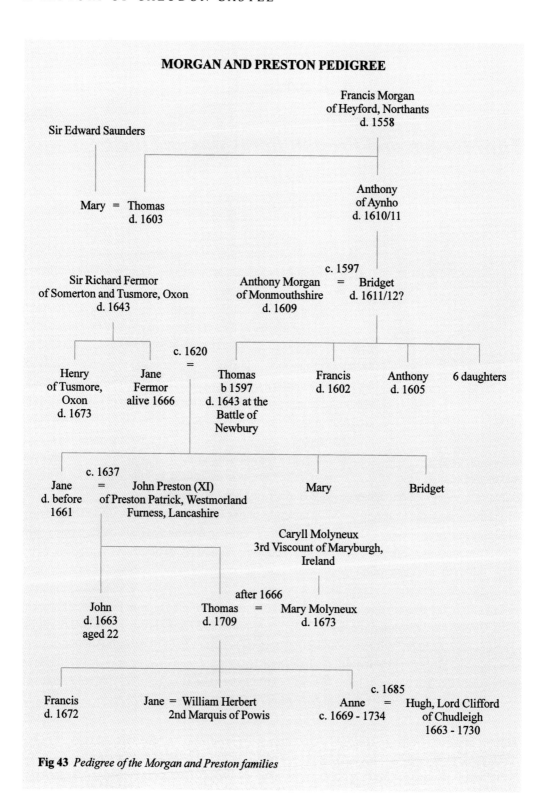

MORGAN AND PRESTON PEDIGREE

Fig 43 *Pedigree of the Morgan and Preston families*

daughter (Fig 43). His other two daughters had died in childhood.[5] In 1599, after the marriage of Bridget to another Anthony Morgan of the more distant Llanfihangel-Llantarnam in Monmouthshire, the succession was confirmed.[6] Anthony's life interest in his brother's estates expired when he died in 1611.[7] Bridget's husband, Anthony Morgan, had died in 1609 and according to the Rev Serjeantson she quickly re-married, her second husband being another Morgan, Sir William of Tredegar. Bridget was supposed to have died in 1626 having provided Sir William with two children, but other records contradict Serjeantson's conclusion, indicating that she was probably dead by 1611-2.[8] Her first and probably only marriage had produced three sons and several daughters. Thomas the eldest son was a minor aged about fourteen and so his deceased parents' estates were taken into wardship by the Crown and only returned when he reached the age of twenty-one in 1619.[9] It was this Thomas who purchased the manor and castle of Caludon from the Berkeley family in 1631.

The recorded facts of Thomas Morgan's life are few but telling. It is known that he attended Christchurch College, Oxford matriculating on 30 Oct 1612, when only fourteen. He obtained his BA two years later in July 1614 and continued his education at the Inner Temple in London.[10] Serjeantson recounts an amusing story presumably from Thomas's early wardship. In order to remove him from the influence of many of his friends who were Catholics, he was placed under the tuition of John Preston of Queen's College, Cambridge, a strict Calvinist.[11] Thomas had been invited to take the part of a young girl in a comedy to be performed in front of James I, who was visiting the college, much to the displeasure of John Preston. The boy's guardians, un-named, did not object, calculating that it might advance his career to catch the eye of James. In fact the King and the whole of the court much enjoyed the performance and 'the manner of the young gentleman'.

John Preston's tuition and guidance did not seem to have had the desired effect and his early years before being orphaned were likely to have exerted the strongest influence on the development of his religious beliefs. Within three to four years of becoming Lord of Caludon, Morgan was cited for recusancy, that is remaining a member of the Catholic or a dissenting faith and refusing to acknowledge the authority and teachings of the Church of England.[12] Laws designed to extract fines from Catholics were placed on the statute book from 1558 as well as measures to criminalise their faith. With the growth of the 'Puritan' sect within the church at the beginning of the seventeenth century, Roman Catholics came under even more scrutiny. The Morgans, along with many other Warwickshire families, were simply not prepared to forego or repudiate their religion. Surveys from the period reveal that the county had one of the highest proportion of Catholics in England. Eighteen of the 288 gentry families recorded in the early 1640s had a recusant as their head.[13] The Morgans of Weston-under-Wetherley were among those in Warwickshire who remained loyal to the 'old religion', as were the Smiths of Wootton Wawen and the Sheldons of Weston. These families formed a close knit group, strengthened by intermarriage and friendship.[14] In the face of growing anti-Catholic feeling this would only have been expected. Thomas Morgan made William Sheldon an overseer of his will and undertook correspondence with other Catholics in Northamptonshire and beyond.

On estates where Catholics were the lords, Catholic rites and rituals remained strong and often flourished among their tenants and labourers. This was true of the Sheldons' estates, the Bishops' lands in Brailes and the Morgans' own properties in Warwickshire at Weston-under-Wetherley and Wappenbury. There is, however, no direct evidence for Catholicism persisting at Caludon. The Shirleys were tenants from only about 1622 to 1626 and we have no other names until the 1660s. The Morgans appear never to have occupied the castle after they acquired it in 1631. In the same year, by coincidence, the meetings of the Justices of the Peace of Kineton Hundred in Warwickshire were reported to have been entirely taken up with complaints against Catholics. They are described in vivid language as 'so cunning and confident in declining, subterfuging and withstanding all our warrents.'[15] It was no doubt this sort of complaint which eventually resulted in Morgan's charges only a few years after taking ownership of Caludon.

Fig 44 *Preston coat of arms*

Thomas Morgan had married Jane, eldest daughter of Sir Richard Fermor of Somerton, county Oxford, in about 1620, soon after his coming of age. At least three daughters were the result of the union, Bridget and Mary, who died unmarried, and Jane, who survived them. In 1637 Jane married the Catholic, John Preston of Preston Patrick and Under Levens Hall in Westmorland and of the manor of Furness in Lancashire. This event marks the next change in ownership of Caludon (Fig 44). With Thomas having no male heirs, he had probably arranged that Caludon and all his other estates would at least eventually pass to another Catholic family, ensuring continuity in this respect. Probably earlier in the same year Thomas had created a complex family settlement of all his Warwickshire estates, including Caludon, so that they would in turn pass through all members of the family and all possible heirs and their descendants (a so-called entailed estate, not free to be sold by anyone inheriting).[16] At this time all his daughters were alive.

The country was soon to be convulsed by greater events which were to sweep up and consume both old and new owners of Caludon. Many of the conflicts that had simmered for years erupted finally as the Civil War. Charles I's sympathy with the Catholic cause was a major factor, exacerbated by his marriage to the Catholic Henrietta Maria, daughter of Henry IV of France. When the conflict finally broke out in 1642 many of the Catholic aristocracy and gentry eagerly joined the Royalist side, hoping that the laws that had impoverished them would soon be repealed. Thomas Morgan took up arms on behalf of his King, receiving a commission as colonel, and he died at the first battle of Newbury, fought on 20 September 1643 at Wash Common just outside the Berkshire town. In his widow Jane's own words many years later, 'Thomas Morgan ingaged himself for the late Kinge's Majesty in the unhappy Warrs as a Collonell under the Prince Regent...in the Battayle of Newbury... in 1643 was slayne.'[17] The battle was the result of an attempt by the Earl of Essex to relieve the besieged Parliamentarian city of Gloucester. After succeeding in his goal, Essex then set off to return his army to London but was intercepted by Charles' army which had been billeted in Newbury. The King was the first to appear on the field but Essex made better use of the site and occupied high ground at Round Hill. The Cavaliers, mindful of their opponent's superior position, attacked the hill but at a heavy expense and many of their number were killed. Like many Civil War battles the intensity of the fighting was initially high but rapidly waned and although there was no clear cut victor, Charles was forced to withdraw through a lack of ammunition.

It is not known how Thomas Morgan died in the battle and to which regiment he belonged, but his death left the family estates in a precarious position. His only heir was his daughter Jane, wife of John Preston, who had also joined the Royalist cause. The two families had been close for a number of years before the Civil War, drawn together by their common circumstances. The Morgans could trace their ancestry back to the reign of Edward III when Sir John Preston, of Preston Patrick, represented Westmorland in Parliament.[18] Eleven generations separated Sir John [I] from the Sir John [XI], who married Jane Morgan in 1637.[19] His father, also Sir John [X], settled the manors of Preston Patrick, Nether Levens and Holme on the issue of the marriage of John [XI] with Jane. The family had also acquired the Lordship of the manor of Furness in Lancashire. Although the Preston family had rendered loyal service to the Crown, they had neither sufficient wealth nor influence to be raised to the peerage. It was only through the creation of the title of Baronet by James I that this class of gentry could be offered a hereditary honour.[20] When the King planted his standard and summoned his loyal subjects in 1642, Preston responded with great energy and, raising a regiment at his own expense, placed himself at his monarch's service. He was probably involved in the battle of Lindal Close which took place on 1 October 1643 between Furness Royalists and a force of Parliamentarians. This ended in an ignominious defeat by the Royalists, many of whom were captured with minimal Parliamentarian casualties. Undeterred by this setback, in the summer of 1644, Preston brought the remains of his cavalry force to Furness where he joined an army led by Sir John Maney. Another skirmish took place at nearby Hawcoat, besieged and taken by the Royalists, who took 200 prisoners. Sir John Preston, however, had his horse killed from under him and received a blow to the head, according to the diarist, Sir Henry Slingsby, possibly delivered by the foot soldiers running past whilst he lay on the ground.[21] He remained speechless and 'in a swoon' for many days afterwards and it took another six months for him to recover fully. Jane Morgan, his mother-in-law, confirmed in 1661 that Sir John had served the king 'in the late Warrs… was wounded in the sayde service and not long after dyed.'[22]

John Preston had been rewarded for his actions in defending the Royalist cause in Westmoreland. He was raised to the honour of baronet on 1 April 1644, but was destined not to enjoy his title for very long, probably dying of his wound sometime in 1645. Given his involvement in the war against Parliament, it is no surprise to find that all his estates, including Caludon and that of his wife's family, were confiscated and declared forfeit. An Ordinance (authoritative command or decree) was duly published on 5 January 1645 naming a number of trustees:[23]

> An Ordinance of the Lords and Commons in Parliament Assembled for the Assuring and Setling of the Mannors, Lands, Tenements and Heriditaments hereafter mentioned upon Oliver St John Esquire, his Majesties Solicitor General, Sir Benjamin Rudyard, Knight, John Carew Esquire, Francis Rous, Esquire, Anthony Niccols Esquire, and Alexander Pym, son and Heir of John Pym Esquire, Decease Persons named for Performances in certain Trusts hereafter Mentioned.

The forfeited estates of Morgan and Preston were used to erect a trust in which the profits and rents from the manors would be used to 'provide for the present necessary maintenance of…Alexander Pym, Charles Pym, his Brother, and Katherine Pym, his younger Sister.' The trustees were given the power to sell parts of the estate in order to pay for debts accrued by John Pym their father, now deceased, who 'with all faithfulness and industry, served the Common-wealth, even to the impairing of his Health and Estate.' The ordinance makes plain that the land was seized because Thomas Morgan and John Preston were considered by Parliament to be:

> notorious Papists and active Recusants and this they did take up Armes against this present Parliament, and by their so doing, did endeavour to the utmost of their powers to overthrow the True Protestant Religion and Lawes Established in this Kingdom.

Morgan was listed as being dead, but Preston was still alive and 'in Armes against the Parliament.' Thomas's widow, Jane Morgan, their daughter Jane Preston and another daughter, Mary, had been left in nominal control of the Morgan/Preston lands. These were divided between the Preston lands of the northern counties, including Furness, and the Morgan manors in Warwickshire and in Northamptonshire, Caludon being specifically mentioned (Calledown). The forfeiture removed all their assets and transferred them to the Parliamentary trust.

Pym had been the leading Puritan politician of the age and had been a fervent opponent of Roman Catholicism. He sat in Parliament until it was dissolved by Charles I in 1629. When Parliament was recalled in 1640, Pym quickly established a reputation as a leading opponent of the King. During the Long Parliament, which first convened in September 1640, Pym became one of the leaders of the opposition and demanded the King's arrest when Charles entered the chamber in January 1642. The war had only been in progress a year at the time of his death in 1643, but in that time as head of the Committee of Safety he had successfully raised funds for Parliament's army. He was succeeded by his eldest son, Alexander, who inherited the family manor at Brymore in Somerset and then became a trustee of the Morgan/Preston estates.

There appears to be some doubt as to the extent to which the Pym family benefited by this order.[24] In July 1648 it was reported that Morgan's tenants had refused to pay their rents to the sequestrators, but instead paid them to Anthony Morgan, a recusant.[25] This was likely to have been Thomas's brother. It was ordered that that the tenants' goods and estates be seized and sold. Despite this threat the tenants were still refusing to pay rent and their arrears in October. In January 1649 Jane, widow of Thomas Morgan, appealed against the ruling claiming that in 1637 her husband had conveyed certain lands to her and her three daughters. It was likely that she was invoking the 1637 family settlement mentioned above. She had in fact managed to recover some of the lands from the Parliamentary trustees, and had lodged further suits for the remainder. In April 1649 Alexander Pym petitioned for the continued execution of the Ordinance, complaining that the Northamptonshire tenants were a year in arrears and that the profits of the remainder of the estate had been retained by the tenants as a result of Mrs Morgan's suits. Despite the fact that her own petition was dismissed, the matter dragged on for at least another two years with a surprising outcome. On 17 June 1651 the original Ordinance was rescinded:[26]

> Resolved, That the Commissioners for Compounding be authorized and required to take off
> the Seizure from the Estate of Thomas Morgan, of Heyford in the County of Northampton,
> Esquire, a Papist and Delinquent, who died in Arms against the Parliament; and of John
> Preston, of Furness in the County of Lancaster, Esquire, a Papist and Delinquent.

The Pyms must have objected for on 23 July 1651 leave was granted to speak against the lifting of the order given a month earlier. Further orders were issued to obtain the trustees' accounts in order to establish how much rent had been received and the magnitude of any underpayment. The trustees were in the meantime allowed to retain the estates until all the tenant arrears were paid.[27]

How the matter was finally resolved is not known, but it is of significance that on 3 August 1654 Mary Morgan, daughter of Thomas Morgan, deceased, (and sister of Jane Morgan, by now widow of John Preston), granted the Warwickshire and Northamptonshire estates, including Caludon, to Henry Fermor of Tusmore, her uncle on her mother's side (see below).[28] The Fermors were a prominent Oxfordshire Catholic family. She had previously granted the same estates in 1650 to a William Bellamy, also of Tusmore. It is probable that these conveyances were not true sales but transfers to trusted people to protect the family interest from potential confiscation by the state. Caludon was described using the familiar wording of earlier deeds:

> The mannor of Callowdon alias Calloughdon …and all that Scite Capital Messuage and
> Mansion House and all that parke or impaled ground…[29]

On its own this description does not provide evidence that Caludon Castle had survived the war for there is a tendency for property deeds to repeat a formula for many decades if it is adequate enough. New material has, however, been recently found that confirms that the castle, or most of it, was standing on the accession of Charles II to the throne in 1660.

Whilst two of the owners of Caludon, Thomas Morgan and Sir John Preston, had been swept up by national events and lost their lives as a consequence, the violence and destruction of Civil War appears largely to have by-passed the castle. Well over a century ago the war was given as the cause for the state that we find Caludon in today, tentatively repeated by the authoritative Victoria County History as late 1969.[30] The first version of the myth appears to have been published in the trade magazine, *The Builder*, in 1883 and Christine Hodges writing in 1895 directly quoted from it:[31]

> It is impossible to say which party was responsible for the destruction of Caludon and when it
> actually took place as no account seems extant. Tradition says that it was 'besieged, the
> opposing force gathering at a place called "Campfield"', but it is silent as to whether the 'force'
> was composed of Royalists, or whether it was battered down by Parliamentarians themselves
> lest it should be used against them when Charles lay siege to Coventry.

No account of the attack has subsequently been found for the simple reason that neither side laid siege to the castle nor reduced it to rubble. In fact William Dugdale, the great antiquarian, in his

Antiquities of Warwickshire, published after the cessation of hostilities in 1656, noted only that the chapel was ruinous.[32] He would very likely have recorded the castle's destruction, if it had taken place. The chapel had probably reached its parlous state as a result of neglect, as its owners had not resided there from at least 1613.

The only hint of violence in this period comes from the Morgan/Preston tenants, who refused to pay their rents to the Parliamentary trustees acting for Alexander Pym. He complained 'that they came in a hostile manner with threatening speeches, forcing your petitioners to forbear…putting us and other well-affected persons in danger of our lives.'[33]

It is not known, however, whether the Caludon tenants were specifically involved in these disturbances or if, generally, the resistance was due to their loyalty to their landlords or to their religion. Certainly Coventry was strongly Parliamentarian and repulsed an attack from the King himself in 1642. The Parliamentary sentiment was also strong in the surrounding district, but whether this was a true reflection of the population's opinions or merely those of their masters is open to debate. We do not know how widespread the tenants' rent strike was on the Morgan/Preston estates. It is perfectly reasonable to imagine that Caludon tenants would wish to avoid the attention of the local Parliamentary authorities by paying Pym's trustees promptly. Coventry had been administered throughout the war by a capable and resolute Parliamentary committee, which had managed 'out of this chaos to create a military and financial organisation that was, by Civil War standards, efficient.'[34] The committee was responsible for gathering money from properties which had been sequestrated. Since they were also authorised to gather supplies from the local area no doubt the committee were aware of Caludon, its 'recusant' owners and its forfeiture to Pym's trustees.

In about 1661 Sir John Preston jnr, whose father, Sir John, had died of his wounds in 1645, submitted a bill to the Chancery court. This has not survived but the answers to the charges of one of the defendants, his grandmother, Jane Morgan, provide much detail on the tangled financial affairs of the Morgan-Preston family in the years previously.[35] The confiscation by Parliament for the benefit of the Pym family was confirmed, the young Sir John Preston, 'left destitute of mayntenance and lyvelyhood.' Jane Morgan claimed that 'out of the tender care shee had of him did maytayne him in those sadd and distracted times.' She had tried to recover the estates 'by long and tedious attendance upon the Committtee of the Lords and Commons' without success. In the meantime the estate woods were being cut down and 'all thinges [were] runninge into decaye and ruin.' She then turned for help to Francis Bagshawe, her nephew, another defendant named in the bill who, according to Jane, worked indefatigably, expending his own money in the cause of restoring the family estates. He was helped by Edward Cooke, another defendant, and they managed to negotiate the purchase of the estates in July 1654 for the sum of £7600, which was paid by loans and taking out of bonds. Jane could not understand why her grandson was 'so little sensible of the great paynes care and engagement of...Francis Bagshawe' and why he would resent any payment of compensation as reward for all his endeavours. The estates were handed over to Jane to administer on behalf of her grandson as 'if it had been her own' and for the 'good' of Sir John, who had returned from France in 1654. It is possible that his mother Jane jnr, neé Morgan, had died

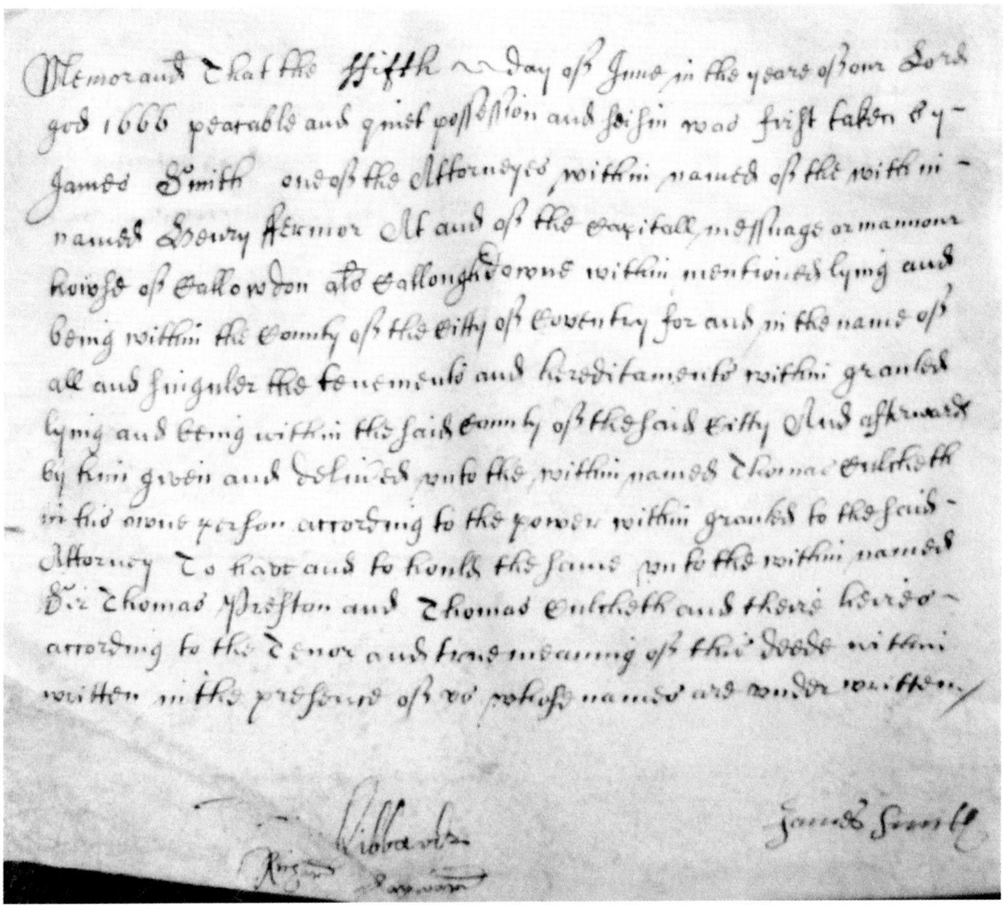
Memorand That the ffifth day of June in the yeare of our Lord
god 1666 peaceable and quiet possession and seisin was first taken by
James Smith one of the Attorneyes within named of the within
named Henry ffermor Esq and of the Capitall messuage or mannor
house of Callowdon als Callowghdon within mentioned lying and
being within the County of the Citty of Coventry for and in the name of
all and singuler the tenements and hereditaments within granted
lying and being within the said County of the said Citty And afterwards
by him given and delivered unto the within named Thomas Culcheth
in his owne person according to the power within granted to the said
Attorney To have and to hold the same unto the within named
Sir Thomas Preston and Thomas Culcheth and their heires
according to the Tenor and true meaning of the deede within
written in the presence of us whose names are under written

Gibbard
Ric Hayward
James Smith

Fig 45 *Endorsement of the 1666 Caludon deed with signatures of Richard Hayward and Timothy Gibbard, the Clifford tenants*

abroad, as she is not mentioned in the evidence given by Jane snr, her mother. The latter referred to the 1654 conveyance to Henry Fermor (see above), who 'doth make a clayme to parte of the estate.' It appears that he had contributed £1000 as part of the purchase price, a probable explanation of the 1654 deed. As Henry was anxious to have the loan repaid, it was agreed that this should be achieved by selling timber from 'Callowdon Woods.' Convoluted arguments over this sale were one of the causes leading to the Chancery case. Jane contended that she did not wish 'young thriving oaks' wasted especially those that 'grew neare ye Park Pale falling whereof would endanger ye breaking of ye said pale and some were ornament to ye parke.' Whether this complex intra-family dispute was settled amicably is not known.

Eventually on 18 December 1665 Henry Fermor with his wife, Ursula, returned the mortgaged estates to the Morgan/Preston family.[36] The purchaser was Thomas Preston, who was required to pay £800 for the re-conveyance. He was Jane Preston's second son, having become heir owing to the death of his elder brother, Sir John Preston in 1663.[37] An endorsement to the deed reveals that six months later on 5 June 1666 actual possession of Caludon was obtained by Thomas Preston's attorney, Thomas Culcheth 'of the Capital messuage or mannour howse of Callowdon alias Calloughdowne', repeating the formulaic description of previous deeds.

Of significance are the two signatures attached to the endorsement, that of Timothy Gibbard (various spellings) and Richard Hayward (Fig 45). They were in fact the joint tenants of Caludon Castle and its park and demesne lands. It is not known, however, when they took up their joint tenancy. In January 1662 Timothy Gibbert was already being described as being of Caludon and Richard Hayward as a 'grazier of Caloughdan.'[38] The hearth tax assessment of the mid 1660s confirms their occupation of the castle.[39] Richard Hayward was assessed at six hearths and Timothy Gibbard at eight hearths in 1664-5 whilst the 1666 returns adjusted these figures to six with three decayed for Hayward and six with five decayed for Tymothy Gibberts. The house was perhaps too big for one local tenant to take on, but, most importantly, there is now no doubt that it still existed after the Civil War, although parts had been abandoned, shut up or were not in use. There were altogether about twenty hearths at Caludon, but not all would have been used simply to heat a room since a number would have been located in the service buildings for cooking, baking, and brewing. An unknown number of rooms can be added as not all were heated. Caludon Castle had certainly suffered as a result of absentee landlordism, particularly during the Civil War, and probably presented in part a dilapidated appearance with 40% of the hearths not in use. It was, however, home to two prosperous families as will be seen from their inventories described below.

It is probable that Sir Thomas Preston had not agreed the leases to these tenants of Caludon. As a second son, he very likely did not expect to inherit the main estate and chose to become a priest. On succeeding to the title after the decease of his brother in 1663, he obtained dispensation from the Pope to renounce his orders and marry.[40] This course of action was to ensure that there would be heirs to whom he could bequeath his extensive estates, He married twice, the name of his first wife remaining unrecorded.[41] His second wife was Mary, the daughter of Caryll Molyneux, 3rd Viscount Molyneux of Maryburgh, Ireland, his father's old Civil War commander, probably marrying her after 1666 as she was not mentioned in the deed of this year (see above). Molyneux had also fallen foul of Parliament during the Civil War and had exiled himself to Ireland.

Having abandoned his vocation for the sake of an heir, it at first appeared that the reluctantly undertaken union would be successful in its principal aim. Unfortunately Francis, their only son, died in childhood in September 1672, followed by his mother in June 1673.[42] Two daughters, Mary and Anne, lived into adulthood to become Thomas's heirs. Ultimately the estate was divided and lost through their respective marriages, the Preston male line finally extinguished after surviving at least three centuries.

The death of Thomas's wife and son was a devastating double blow, which induced him to 'renounce the world and embrace a religious life.'[43] He travelled to Flanders and entered the Society of Jesus (Jesuits) at Watten on 28 June 1674, using the alias, Saville. He remained a scholastic, refusing to take holy orders on account of his having been married twice and remained at Watten until his death on 27 May 1709.

GIBBARD (GIBBERD) PEDIGREE

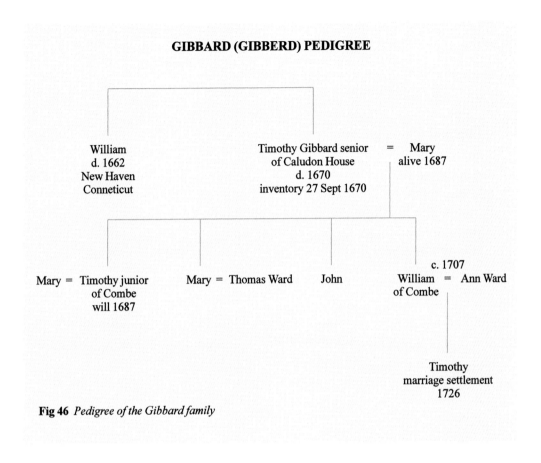

Fig 46 *Pedigree of the Gibbard family*

The fate of his infant daughters after his removal to Flanders is unknown. He had presumably arranged for their care through guardians and trustees, the latter perhaps the same as those that appear on documents of 1685 relating to the marriage settlements of Mary and Anne.[44] About this year Mary, the elder (c.20), married William Herbert, 2nd Marquess of Powis and her sister Anne (c.14), married Hugh, Lord Clifford. Both marriages were with families boasting a long and durable Catholic lineage. The net result of these highly complex arrangements was for the Northamptonshire estates to pass to Mary and the Marquesses of Powis and the Warwickshire estates to transfer to Anne and ultimately the Barons Clifford of Chudleigh in Devon. The Clifford ownership of Caludon belongs to the next chapter, but first we must return to the castle and its tenants, far removed from the religious and personal dramas that had shaken the Preston owners. New and revealing information has come to light following the discovery of their names.

Timothy Gibbard's brother, William, had emigrated to America and set up his home in New Haven, Connecticut. His will, dated 6 Aug 1662, appointed his brother Timothy 'of Calladownehouse near Coventry' as overseer of his estate in England (Fig 46).[45] In 1663-4 both Timothy senior and junior were mentioned in a will.[46] Timothy Gibbard, senior 'of Caledon house' was buried at Binley church on 25 August 1670 and his inventory was made on 27 September (Fig 47).[47]

For the first time we have a list of some of rooms within the castle, with their contents and value. The rooms were as follows:

Hall *
Wardrobe
Darye
Cellars
Dynring Room
Servantes Chamber
Room next that Chamber
Long Chamber
Maides Chamber
Green Chamber*
Wooll Chamber
Corne Chamber
*rooms with fireplace equipment

This is an unusual inventory as it is split between two sites, Caludon Castle itself and a house on the Coombe Abbey estate. The rooms here were:

Darye Howse
Kitchin
Cellar
Kitchin Chamber
Dary Chamber
Chamber over the hall
Servantes Chamber
Parlour Chamber
Cockloft.

Timothy Gibbard was described as a gentleman, late of 'Caloughdon', but it is clear that he was not merely a man of leisure but a prosperous grazier with an inventory valued at over £2000. His main wealth was tied up in his livestock, thirty seven oxen (beastes) and hundreds of sheep, although he also grew wheat, barley and peas. The majority of his animals in September 1670 were kept at Coombe, there being only two oxen, eight cows, thirty sheep, fifteen lambs and two hogs at Caludon. Timothy was running two households, one at Caludon and the other at what was later to be called Coombefields Farm, near the border of Coombe fields with Stretton under Fosse.[48] The Coombe household was a more modest set-up with only one room, the chamber of the hall, with the comfortable furnishings of a feather bed, curtains, a coverlet and bolsters. Otherwise it appears to have accommodated servants and farm staff responsible for running the Coombe farm of about 320 acres.

The puzzling fact about Gibbard's part of Caludon Castle was the absence of a kitchen; his co-tenant, Richard Hayward, had a kitchen and back kitchen in 1680 (see below) and it is possible that some arrangement had been made between them to share the cooking facilities. The kitchen at Coombe, without fireplace equipment, did not appear to be geared up for cooking, except for a pot hanger. Caludon certainly contained the most expensively furnished rooms, the Green Chamber in particular with a bedstead with valances (deep frills of drapery hanging from the canopy and from the mattress to the floor), feather bolsters, pillows, a red a counterpane, two 'great' chairs, curtains, a red rug and a considerable amount of bed and table linen (total value £43 6s 8d). The room had a fireplace and its name indicates the principal or original colour scheme of the furnishings, but with the addition of red, a fashionable combination in the second half of the seventeenth century. The hall was also heated with a large table, stools and chairs, and interestingly was the room where two guns were kept. A large curtain on a rod hung at the window and there was a screen, perhaps in the position of an original screen passage, running through the room at the 'lower' end.

It is difficult to reconstruct the plan of Caludon Castle based on this inventory. Only part of the building was appraised and large manor houses and castles are the least predictable in their layout, particularly if modified for a divided tenancy. It is possible that one tenant occupied the north south 'hall range' and the other the east-west chamber block and their ancillary buildings. (see Chapter 8 and Figs 26, 29 and 30). It would appear that any original large medieval hall, open to the roof, had long been floored over, perhaps in the Berkeley period. The lack of

Fig 47 *First part of the inventory of Timothy Gibbard 1670*

fireplace equipment in certain rooms does not imply that there was means of heating within them, but that the hearths were not in use at the time. According to the hearth tax returns, between six and eight of Timothy Gibbard's rooms had hearths a few years earlier, and twelve are listed in the inventory, many of which would not have been heated (e.g., the wool chamber, corn chamber and wardrobe). Empty rooms or rooms without the belongings of the deceased would not appear in the inventory. The confirmation that Caludon had cellars has significant implications on the preservation of the building today below ground. It is likely that the cellars remain intact (less the floor over, originally supported by a stone vault or on timber joists) and that on demolition, rubble was thrown in to fill the cellars. This broken masonry could, therefore, hold much evidence of the building materials and architectural style of the castle in its latter days.

In 1668, two years before the inventory was compiled, a detailed survey of Caludon manor was completed, which listed every field individually with acreages in Caludon itself and its outlying parts, including the scattered strips in the open fields of Sowe and Foleshill (Fig 48).[49] At the head of the survey appeared:

> The Mannor house Banqueting house, Motte Fishpond Little Court and gardens containe
> 5a[cres] 0r[oods] 2p[erches]

'Mr Gibbard' and' Mr Heyward' shared *great Court, little close, great parke, Lake meadow, Ashmore meadow, Long Ashmore*, whilst Timothy had exclusive use of the *Little court* and Richard – *Slaughter house close*. Other tenants held the other former demesne lands of *Stublefeild, Pattridge field, Newhewen*, and *Crabtree field*, names familiar from earlier surveys (Fig 19). Although it was not explicit, presumably Gibbard and Heyward were sharing the accommodation of the deteriorating castle. It appears that after Timothy Gibbard senior died the family moved out of Caludon and set up home in Coombe Fields. Timothy junior 'of Combe' died in 1686 and left a will proved in the following year, which mentioned his mother, Mary, widow of Timothy senior.

There is another undated survey of Caludon, but it must have been made after 1670, as it only records Richard Hayward:[50]

> The Mannor house Courts Garden Fish poole the Great Court set all to Mr Richard Haward

Richard also exclusively rented the fields around the castle, including the park; The wood Yard, The Slaughter house Close, The litle Parke, The great Parke and The Lake Meadow for which he paid altogether £86 6s per annum (Fig 19). The rent income for the whole of Caludon and its outlying parts was £414 14s 4d (Fig 49).

Richard like his former co-tenant was also a grazier, as confirmed by his will written in his own scribbly hand on 25 March 1680 (Fig 50).[51] Fortunately his friends and neighbours also compiled an inventory, which, though not as detailed as Timothy Gibbard's of ten years earlier, at least gives a list of rooms and a summary value of their content. They were as follows:

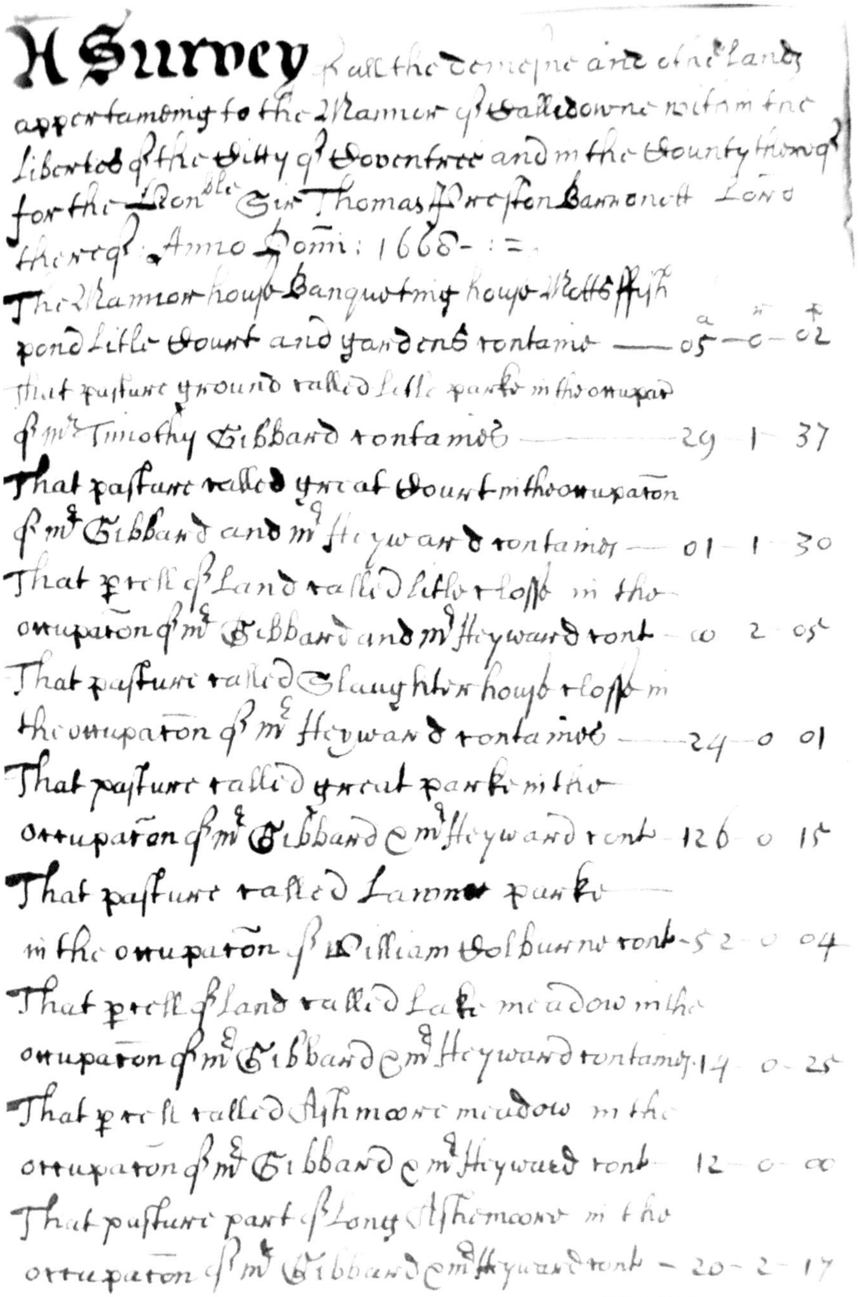

A Survey of all the Demeqne and other Lands appertaininge to the Manner of Caludowne within the Liberties of the Citty of Coventree and in the County thereof for the Honoble Sir Thomas Preston Barronett Lord thereof Anno Domi: 1668 - : =

The Manner house Banquetting house & little fish pond little Court and yardens containe — 05 - 0 - 02

That pasture ground called little parke in the occupac̅on of mr Timothy Gibbard containes — 29 - 1 - 37

That pasture called great Court in the occupac̅on of mr Gibbard and mr Heyward containes — 01 - 1 - 30

That peece of Land called litle close in the occupac̅on of mr Gibbard and mr Heyward cont — 0 - 2 - 05

That pasture called Slaughter house close in the occupac̅on of mr Heyward containes — 24 - 0 - 01

That pasture called great parke in the occupac̅on of mr Gibbard & mr Heyward cont — 126 - 0 - 15

That pasture called Lawne parke in the occupac̅on of William Colburne cont — 52 - 0 - 04

That peece of land called Lake meadow in the occupac̅on of mr Gibbard & mr Heyward containes — 14 - 0 - 25

That peece called Ashmoore meadow in the occupac̅on of mr Gibbard & mr Heyward cont — 12 - 0 - 00

That pasture part of Long Ashmoore in the occupac̅on of mr Gibbard & mr Heyward cont — 20 - 2 - 17

Fig 48 *The first page of the survey of the Caludon estate 1668; note that the banqueting house and fish pond or mere are still in existence*

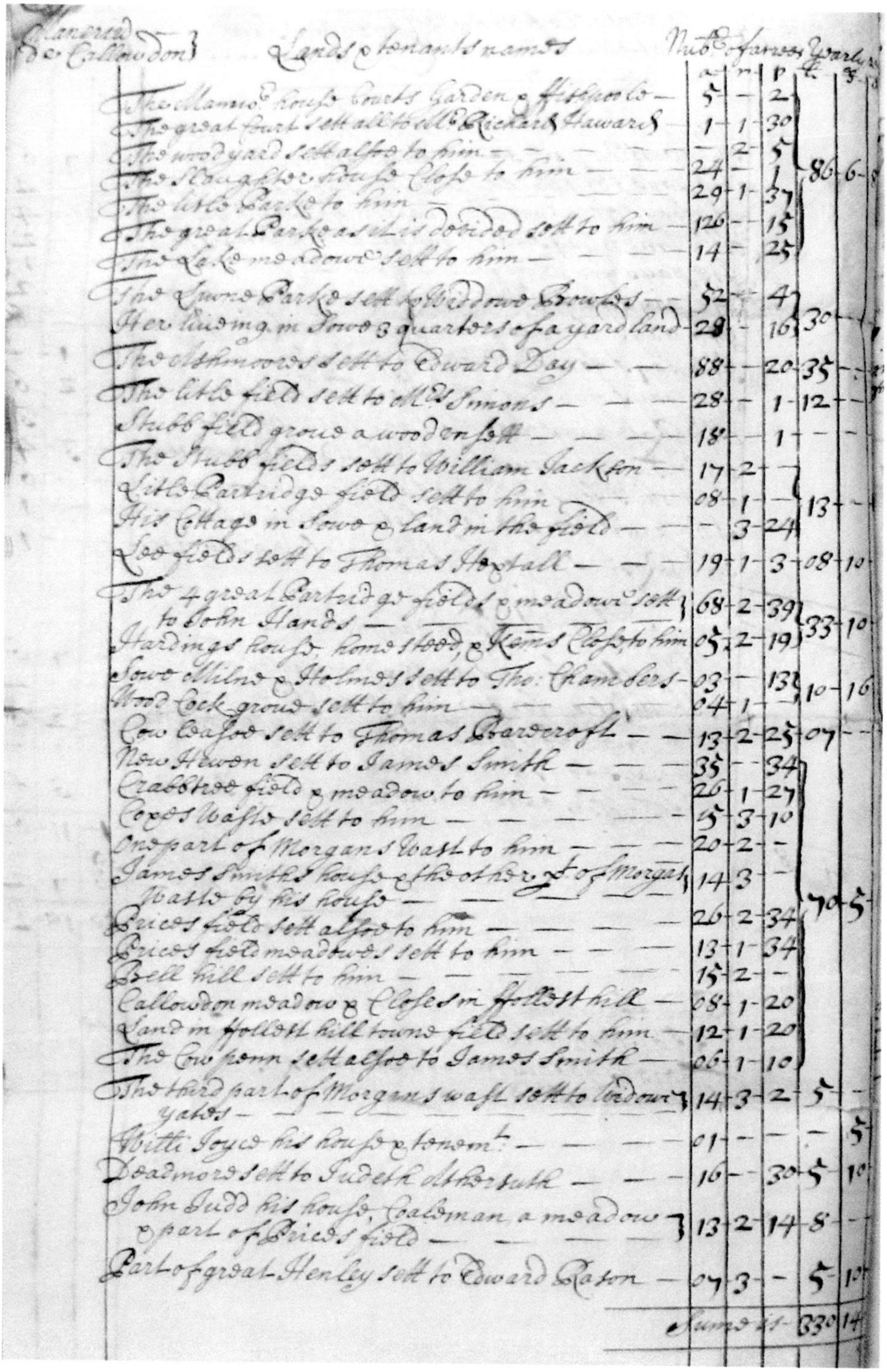

Mannor de Callowdon	Lands & tenants names	a	r	p	li	s
	The Mannor house Courts Garden & ffishpoole	5	-	2		
	The great Court sett all to Mr Richard Haward	1	1	30		
	The wood yard sett alsoe to him	-	2	5		
	The Slaughter house Close to him	24	-	1	86	6
	The little Parke to him	29	1	37		
	The great Parke as it is devided sett to him	126	-	15		
	The Lake meadow sett to him	14	-	25		
	The Lune Parke sett to Widdow Bowles	52	-	4		
	Her living in Towne 3 quarters of a yard land	28	-	16	30	
	The Ashmoores sett to Edward Day	88	-	20	35	-
	The little field sett to Mrs Simons	28	-	1	12	-
	Stubb field growe a wooden sett	18	-	1	-	-
	The Stubb fields sett to William Jackson	17	2	-		
	Little Partridge field sett to him	08	1	-	13	-
	His Cottage in Towne & land in the field	-	3	24		
	Lee fields sett to Thomas Horstall	19	1	3	08	10
	The 4 great Partridge fields & meadow sett to John Hands	68	2	39		
	Hardings house, home stead, & Kems Close to him	05	2	19	33	10
	Sowe Milne & Holmes sett to Tho: Chambers	03	-	13		
	Wood Cock grove sett to him	04	1	-	10	16
	Cow Pasture sett to Thomas Bardcroft	13	2	25	07	-
	New Heven sett to James Smith	35	-	34		
	Crabtree field & meadow to him	26	1	27		
	Coxes Waste sett to him	5	3	10		
	One part of Morgans Wast to him	20	2	-		
	James Smiths house & the other ⅓ of Morgans Waste by his house	14	3	-		
	Prices field sett alsoe to him	26	2	34	70	5
	Prices field meadowes sett to him	13	1	34		
	Bell hill sett to him	15	2	-		
	Callowdon meadow & Closes in ffollett hill	08	1	20		
	Land in ffollett hill towne field sett to him	12	1	20		
	The Cow penn sett alsoe to James Smith	06	1	10		
	The third part of Morgans wast sett to Widdow Yates	14	3	2	5	-
	Willi Joyce his house & tenemt	01	-	-	-	5
	Deadmore sett to Judeth Atherstuth	16	-	30	5	10
	John Judd his house, Coalman a meadow & part of Prices field	13	2	14	8	-
	Part of great Henley sett to Edward Paton	07	3	-	5	10
	Summe li				330	14

Fig 49 *A survey of the Caludon estate, after 1670*

Manerium de Callowdon	Lands & tenants names	This Enfarees Yearly			a	r	p	l	s	d

The other p.t of great Henley sett to — 23 3 —
ffrancis Perkins —
Henley miln meadowes sett to him — 06 1 —
Henley old miln & miln holme to him — — 1 14 32 —
Henley house Orchard garden & other 2 3 4
mans meadowe sett to him — 5 2 30
The loops yard & meadow sett to him 8 2 — 6
Part of litle Henley to Tho: Welton 8 2 — 6
The other p.t of litle Henley sett to 8 2 22 8 6 8
Joseph Longworth —
Wm Stoores his house & Backside & 14 3 10
ffallow fordsadle — 07 2 4 15
Great Copalls sett alsoo to him 4 1 22
Litle Copalls sett also to him — 2 2 26
Tho: Esser his house & backside — 1 13 4
Part of Maymets meadow in his posses- 1 3 —
tion —
Inner Sowe Waste sett to Moses Norma 67 2 16 19
& Thomas Met —
The outward Waste lyes comon — 61 1 —
There are 6 small houses standing 1 0 24
on Sowe Waste —
Elioner Pratts house & the Close in Stoke 1 1 14 8 8
Bettridge house & Close in Copall — 4 — 1 10
The hedge Rowe soo called a pice of — 1 8
ground not certainely knowne & in
the possession of one Clarke —

Sume is 84 — 4
brought from y other 330 14 —

The totall of Callowdon 414 14 4
rents are —

8 8
14 14 4

Hall

Matted Chamber

Green Chamber

Passage Room

Wenscoate Chamber

Hall Chamber

Back Kitching

Kitching

It is evident that Richard had taken over Timothy Gibbard's Green Chamber of 1670. The hall may not be the same room as had been occupied by Timothy, and it is reasonable to assume that this list mostly represents Richard's original division of the castle. We therefore have nineteen rooms listed in two inventories, which is close to the twenty hearths assessed in 1666. It must be emphasised, however, that these are not equivalent figures, as a number of rooms had no hearths at all and not all rooms with fireplaces had contents to enter on the inventory. On the basis of the hearth tax count, Caludon in the mid seventeenth century belonged to the second division of house size in Warwickshire. The first division contained seventeen houses, the largest ranging from seventy rooms (Stoneleigh Abbey) to twenty-five (Billesley Hall).[52] There were twenty houses in Caludon's league, defined by having between twenty and twenty-two hearths, the membership now having to be increased by one to include Caludon, as it was not originally recognised in recently published hearth tax analysis.[53] There is no doubt that in the Berkeley heyday there were in excess of twenty hearths and that in this period it would have ranked amongst the largest of houses in Warwickshire.

Richard Hayward left an inventory valued nearly as high as Timothy Gibbard's of a decade earlier - £1846 4s 8d. It also demonstrated where the wealth of a grazier was concentrated. 108 oxen were worth £573 and 225 sheep - £165. His thirty-one cows and six heifers were valued at £150. He possessed at his death a staggeringly high amount of cash, £363 3s, and was owed nearly £500. By comparison the contents of all his rooms, including his wearing apparel, only amounted to about £70. The overall impression is that his rooms were considerably more sparsely furnished than his former co-tenant, his Green Chamber having only £5 2s of furnishings compared to Gibbard's - £43 6s 8d. For a man of considerable wealth, this grazier did not wish to display it with sumptuous furnishings. It also appears that he had remained in his part of the house, only taking over the Green Chamber when Timothy Gibbard died. The hall that appears in each of the inventories was probably not the same room.

Richard Hayward's younger son, Richard junior is better known than his father, owing to his active participation in the political administration of Coventry (Fig 50). He did not take up farming, excluded from the inheritance of Caludon, but became a Coventry ironmonger, dealing with articles made from metal rather than producing and forging iron. This undoubtedly made him enough money to be accepted into the Coventry political oligarchy. In 1672 he was appointed as Sheriff, by 1680 was a member of the Council and elected as mayor in the following year.[54] He was a J.P. in 1684 and alderman for Earl St in 1688. Although brought up at Caludon, when he died in 1689

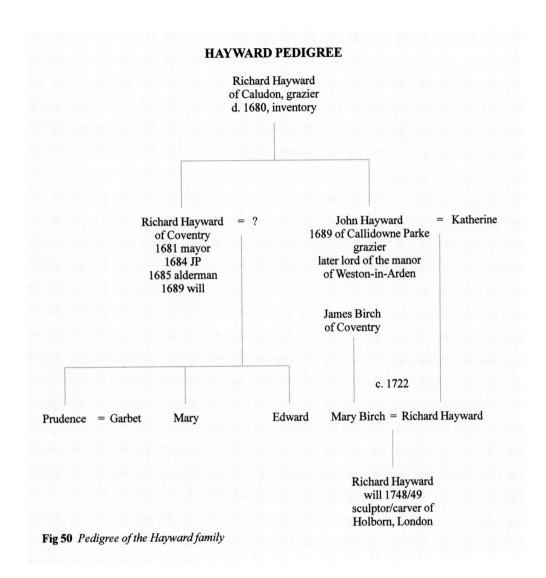

HAYWARD PEDIGREE

Fig 50 *Pedigree of the Hayward family*

he had been a resident of Coventry for a considerable time. In his will he described himself as an alderman of the city of Coventry.[55] Fortunately he mentioned his elder brother John Hayward of 'Callidowne Parke' whom he made one of his executors. John very likely had taken up residence on his father's death in 1680 and presumably continued his father's business as a grazier. He eventually made sufficient money to become the lord of the manor of Weston in Arden, acquiring it in about 1696 or 1710.[56] The Weston estate lies to the north-east of Coventry and east of Bedworth, not a great distance from Caludon, and it is possible that Richard moved from the castle when he acquired Weston. The status of the tenants of Caludon suggests that the castle, though in part run down and shabby, had retained sufficient grandeur and presence to be still regarded as a home fit for men of their standing. The next century, however, was to witness its final decay and demolition.

Chapter 5 – NOTES

1   VCH Warwick, Vol 8, 121
2   R M Serjeantson, *Chapels of Kingsthorpe and Upton*, (1904)189-190; Serjeantson's work on St Peter's church is the most convenient single source for the history of the Caludon Morgans and the Preston family that followed, but it does contain some errors (subsequently: Serjeantson).
3   *Calendar of Patent Rolls Philip and Mary 4 & 5, 1557-8,* (1939) 267
4   VCH Warwick Vol 6, 250
5   Searjeantson, 194
6   VCH Warwick, Vol 6, 248-251; TNA C142/281/84
7   Searjeantson, 196
8   Searjeantson, 197-198; inquisitions post mortem for Bridget Morgan of Warks and Northants, 24 March 1611 - 23 March 1612, TNA C142/427/126; C142/320/72;WARD7/35/68; Clifford W(E) 1/24; copies of inquisitions post mortem for Bridget Morgan, 1617-19, 1620-21. It is very likely that the Rev Serjeantson was relying on another family genealogy, *Some Account of the Family of Middlemore*, by W P W Phillimore and W F Carter, (1901) which suggests in the extensive note on pp. 66-67 that Lady Morgan died in the second year of reign of Charles I [1625-6]
9   Clifford W(E) 1/24, livery granted to Thomas Morgan in 1619
10 Oxford University Alumni website, 1500-1714, part of ancestry.co.uk
11 Serjeantson, 199
12 VCH Warwick, Vol 6, 248-251
13 Ann Hughes, *Politics, Society and Civil War in Warwickshire*, 1620-1660, Cambridge, (1987) 62-63
14 ibid.
15 ibid., 64
16 Clifford P4, 25 October 1637
17 TNA, C6/156/12, 1661
18 Joseph Nicolson, *The History and Antiquities of the Counties of Westmoreland and Cumberland*, Vol 1 (1777) 239
19 ibid., 239-241
20 John Burke, *A genealogical and heraldic history of the extinct and dormant baronetcies of England, Ireland and Scotland*, London (1841) 425-428; *A genealogical and heraldic history of the commoners of Great Britain and Ireland*, (1834) 480
21 Rev Daniel Parsons (ed), *The diary of Sir Henry Slingsby*, (1836) 125; Serjeantson, 201
22 TNA C6/156/128
23 Clifford P2
24 Notes and Queries, 9th S VII, 9 March 1901, 181-182;
25 *Calendar of the Proceedings of the Committee for the Advance of Money: Part 1 1642-45,* (1888) 304-314, see Alex. Pym, Son and Heir, and other Children of John Pym, deceased.
26 House of Commons Journal, 1648-1652, Vol 6 (1802) 587-589
27 ibid., 607
28 Clifford P1
29 ibid.
30 *The Builder*, 4 Aug 1883, 142-3; Hodges, 151-2 VCH Warwick, Vol 8, 121
31 Hodges, 151-2
32 Dugdale, (1730) 128
33 op. cit., Hughes, 269 quoting from TNA SP24/69
34 op. cit., Hughes, 181
35 op. cit., TNA, C6/156/128
36 Clifford P1
37 Will of Sir John Preston, TNA Prob 11/311/16; he wished that a debt of £850 owed to Master Francis Bagshawe, his cousin, be paid out of his estates.
38 SBTRO, ER2/74;Warwick RO, CR285/132
39 TNA E179/259/10, Michaelmas 1664 - Michaelmas 1665, copy in Warwick RO Z366/2; Tom Arkell with Nat Alcock (eds), *Warwickshire Hearth Tax Returns: Michaelmas 1670*, Dugdale Society Vol XLIII (2010) 446; the Coventry returns are for 1666. Caludon Castle is comparable in same size to about nineteen houses in Warwickshire, but was not counted in the publication not having been recognised as a joint tenancy. Furthermore it appeared at the end of the Sowe assessment, as Caludon was not assessed separately, ibid., 124-125, Map 11, 154. Fletchampstead Hall with 22 hearths was similarly divided between tenants.
40 op.cit., Burke (1841) 428; Charles Starle Besterling; *William Preston of Newcastle-upon -Tyne, England: and Philadelphia, Pennsylvania, and allied families,* (1934) 19
41 Serjeantson, 203
42 op. cit., Burke, (1841) 428; *Family Search* web site
43 J P Smith (ed), *Lancashire Registers III Northern Part*, Catholic Record Society Vol XX (1916) 2-3, Serjeantson, 203
44 Clifford, P1, 22 May 1685; Clifford 3; Abstracts, Warwickshire 9/1-4; they were likely to have been Caryll, Lord Viscount Molyneux, Francis Lord Carrington and Robert Dalton. The names of those who actually took care of the children have escaped the record.
45 *The New England Historical and Genealogical Register*, Vol 81, (1924) 124
46 Frederick Arthur Crisp (ed), *Sepulchral Memorials of Bobbingworth, Essex, with genealogical notes and pedigrees*, (1888)

Chapter 5 – NOTES

47 TNA Prob 4/3443

48 The inventory refers to Grindon Hill at Coombe which can be identified with the ridge that rises northwards to the present M6 motorway. The Gibbard tenancy of a large farm in Coombe Fields can be traced back to 1622 when Master Gibbert shared it with a Master Holbatch. In 1652 Timothy Gibberd held the farm on his own consisting of 273 acres at Grindon Hill, the cottage there only containing two rooms, and another two fields making 320 acres altogether, Craven Collection, Bodleian Library, Oxford. It is not known whether Timothy had taken up a tenancy at Caludon by this time. In the 1923 sale particulars of the Combe Abbey estate Coombefields Farm consisted of 257 acres (CA).

49 Warwick RO CR1097/87, 1668 survey by Richard Johnson

50 Clifford, P1, 'A Rental and Survey of Sir Thomas Prestons estate (for one whole yeare) lying within the County of Warwick…'

51 Lichfield Record Office, Richard Hayward will and inventory, proved 19 April 1680.

52 op. cit., Arkell and Alcock, 123-125 and Table 26

53 See note 36 above

54 There are numerous references to Richard Hayward at Coventry Archives, see Persons/8/619 index

55 TNA Prob11/396

56 VCH Warwick, Vol 6, 48-67; John Nichols, *Bibliotheca Topographica Britannica*, (1780) Vol 8; *Gentleman's Magazine*, Vol 65 (1789) 253

CHAPTER 6

The Clifford Lordship and their Tenants
1685-1822

Fig 51
Clifford coat of arms

The marriage settlements of 1685 effectively transferred Sir Thomas Preston's Warwickshire estates, including Caludon, to Hugh, 2nd Baron Clifford of Chudleigh, Devon, his son-in-law, although Anne Preston retained a life interest if she outlived her husband.[1] The self-exiled Jesuit, Sir Thomas, had ensured that his mother's estates would at least descend to well-established Catholic families after the death of his male heir in 1672.

The Clifford family of Ugbrooke is a cadet branch of the great medieval family which came to England at the Norman Conquest. It can trace its lineage back to Sir Lewis Clifford, a brother of Thomas, 6th Baron Clifford, who settled in Devon during the fourteenth century.[2] In 1552 Sir Piers Courtney died and left Ugbrooke to his daughter, Anne, who married Anthony Clifford of Borscombe. Their grandson, Sir Thomas Clifford (1630-1673) was one of the most trusted advisors to Charles II (Fig 52). After the collapse of the Republic, he emerged as a leader of the Royalist faction in Devon and urged that Charles II be returned to England and placed on the throne. He was in fact both a Royalist and devoted Anglican (although he changed to become a Roman Catholic after the passing of the Test Act) and 'wished to reconcile his church with that of Rome by a process of negotiation and compromise'.[3] He was closely involved in negotiating the secret treaty of Dover (1670) signed with France, which, in exchange for a formal declaration of Charles II as Catholic, was to assist the English in an attack on the Dutch. Although the treaty came to nothing, his efforts had been rewarded with official duties in the household and treasury, an able, loyal and articulate servant of the King. He had gradually moved much closer to the Church of Rome, particularly during his growing friendship with the future James II (Duke of York). The planned war against the Dutch in fact destroyed his career. There were insufficient funds to conduct war without help from Parliament, which insisted that in return a statute be passed, (the Test Act), requiring those engaged in public office to profess to the Church of England. Latest opinion considers that Thomas Clifford was not exposed as a Catholic by the Act but 'forced to make a conversion', being slightly inclined to Rome.[4] He resigned as Lord High

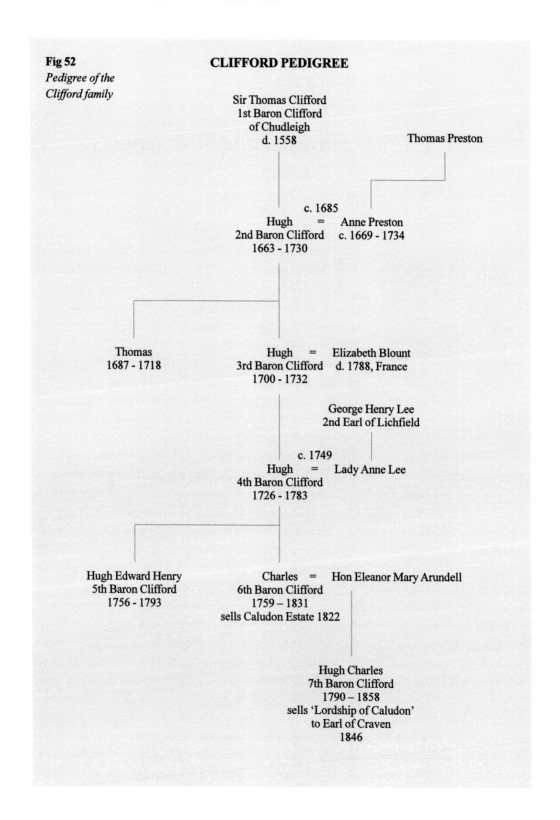

Fig 52
*Pedigree of the
Clifford family*

CLIFFORD PEDIGREE

Sir Thomas Clifford
1st Baron Clifford
of Chudleigh
d. 1558

Thomas Preston

c. 1685
Hugh   =   Anne Preston
2nd Baron Clifford   c. 1669 - 1734
1663 - 1730

Thomas
1687 - 1718

Hugh   =   Elizabeth Blount
3rd Baron Clifford   d. 1788, France
1700 - 1732

George Henry Lee
2nd Earl of Lichfield

c. 1749
Hugh   =   Lady Anne Lee
4th Baron Clifford
1726 - 1783

Hugh Edward Henry
5th Baron Clifford
1756 - 1793

Charles   =   Hon Eleanor Mary Arundell
6th Baron Clifford
1759 – 1831
sells Caludon Estate 1822

Hugh Charles
7th Baron Clifford
1790 – 1858
sells 'Lordship of Caludon'
to Earl of Craven
1846

Fig 53 *Portrait of Hugh,*
2nd Lord Clifford (1663-1730)

Treasurer in June 1673 and only then did he practice his Catholic faith openly. He died a few months later on 17 October 1673. Charles II had, however, rewarded him with the title of Baron Clifford of Chudleigh on 22 April 1672.

The collision of religion and politics at national level had played a major part in the conversion of Thomas, the first Baron Clifford of Chudleigh, to Catholicism. The 'foundation of one of England's most remarkable Catholic families' was 'perhaps his most enduring achievement.'[5] Thomas's conversion soon had repercussions on inter-family alliances and unions, which would bring Caludon to the Cliffords. The next Clifford generation was considered suitable for a match with the Catholic heiress Anne Preston and presumably, vice-versa. It was to the first Baron's son and heir, Hugh Clifford, that Caludon would eventually pass, through his marriage to Anne in 1685 (Figs 53 and 54).

He was born at Ugbrooke in 1663 and educated at Windsor and Eton. In recognition of the loyal service performed by Hugh's father, the King personally donated £300 to Hugh's schooling after Thomas' death. Since he was openly known to be a Catholic, Hugh was unable to seek a public or political career. On the accession of the Catholic James II in 1685 Hugh was generously received at court, but only through courtesy, with no prospect of advancement. In lieu of any office or position in the new administration he dedicated himself to the arts and his private life. The defeat and deposition of James II during the 'Glorious Revolution' of 1688 wrecked any chance of a political career. The Protestant settlement made on the accession of William and Mary ensured that Catholic peers would be barred from state service.

The marriage settlements of 1685 had assigned the Preston estates to Hugh and his wife, Anne, for their lives and to their heirs and successors.[6] Hugh died on 12 Oct 1730, outlived by Anne so that Caludon reverted to her possession for the last four years of her life (Fig 54). She died in July 1734 aged about 62 (will 13 September 1733).

There is no surviving evidence of the management of Caludon during Hugh Clifford's ownership, (1685-1730) estate rentals, accounts and correspondence not having survived. In 1715 the Caludon estate was valued at £458 2s 0d, compared to Wappenbury and all the remaining parts of the Warwickshire estates at £598 17s 10.[7] These figures suggest that Caludon manor had remained a valuable landed property, but it was its land rather than buildings that contributed to the vast majority of its wealth. There was no

Fig 54 *Portrait of Anne,*
2nd Lady Clifford (1669-1734)

Fig 55 *The first part of the survey of the Caludon estate 1731*

prospect of the castle returning to the favoured position it enjoyed in the Berkeley period, with the
main Clifford seat well-established at Ugbrooke in Devon. Furthermore well over a half century of
neglect had taken its toll, and the castle must have looked shabby and old-fashioned. No significant
modernisation or new construction had probably taken place in nearly a century.

The last known tenant was John Hayward in 1689 and it is not until 1731 that we have a record
of the next occupier. The later Dowager Anne Clifford, as a Catholic, was required to register her
Caludon estate under the Acts of 1715 and 1717 with the Coventry Clerk of the Peace. Fortunately
the detailed rental has survived, filed in the Quarter Session records.[8] The first item on the rental
reads (Fig 55):

> Joshua Jeacocks holds as Tenant at Will from the said Ann lady Dowager Clifford All that
> mannor house called Callowdonhouse and all the Stables thereunto belonging togeather with
> all other His buildings Outhouses Courts Gardens Orchards … And all those several Closes or
> inclosed grounds of arable meadow and pasture ground called… Great Park the Lake Meadow
> the Little Park the Slaughter House Close and the Stubble field…and the yearly reserved Rent
> is………………………… £140 0s 0d

GODDARD PEDIGREE (GODDARDS FARM)

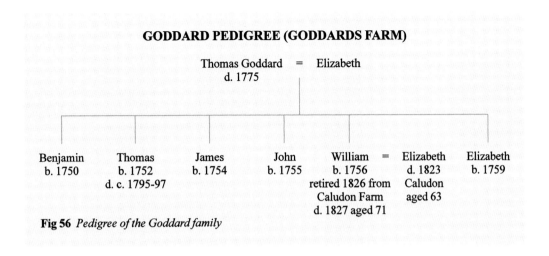

Thomas Goddard = Elizabeth
d. 1775

Benjamin	Thomas	James	John	William	=	Elizabeth	Elizabeth
b. 1750	b. 1752	b. 1754	b. 1755	b. 1756		d. 1823	b. 1759
	d. c. 1795-97			retired 1826 from		Caludon	
				Caludon Farm		aged 63	
				d. 1827 aged 71			

Fig 56 *Pedigree of the Goddard family*

Joshua Jeacocks paid another £30 separately for the *Lawne Parke*. He farmed, except for *Stubble field*, a compact holding immediately around the castle, stretching from the road to Sowe (Ansty Road) to include the whole of the former medieval park (Fig 19). The former demesne was held by Joseph Ash (five closes called *Ashmore*, west of the *Lawne Parke*, and a pasture called *Woodcock Close*), whilst Thomas Smith (*partridge fields*) and Richard Swain (the *Newhewn, Crabtree field and Crabtree Meadow*) tenanted that part of the demesne situated north of the Ansty Road. Joseph Ash's land also contained a house, probably of recent construction, which can be identified as 'the Hermitage' on early editions of Ordnance Survey maps. The timber-framed barn at the rear of shops on Longfellow Road was destroyed by fire in the early 1990s. The row of shops facing the road appears at first sight to be of twentieth-century construction, but their roofs are constructed from ancient re-used timbers. The remainder of the manor consisted of the already familiar scatter of holdings in Wyken, 'Walsgrove upon Sowe', Foleshill and Exhall, including the valuable Sowe and Henley mills.

A Joshua Jeacocks married Mary Benfoy in St Michael's church, Coventry on 5 March 1716.[9] They were both from Weston (-under-Wetherley) another Preston/Clifford estate. A possible reason for their marriage having taken place away from their home parish was Joshua's new tenancy of Caludon, the estate situated in a detached part of the parish of St Michael's. In 1723 Joshua 'from Caludown' buried his infant son at Sowe church. In 1726 'Ann daughter of Joshua and Mary Jeacock from Caludown' was baptized at the same church.[10] In 1842 a Joshua Jeacocks, yeoman, was recorded at Willenhall, with his daughter, Elizabeth.[11] This Joshua was one of the many sons of Thomas Jeacock of Cubbington. Another son, Abraham, a clerk, left a will in 1738 leaving money to the son and six daughters of Joshua.[12] In 1746, administration of Abraham's will was granted to Judith, another daughter of Joshua, both of them of 'Winnal,' (Willenhall) in the County of the City of Coventry. It is possible that Joshua Jeacock of Willenhall was the same Joshua that leased Caludon in 1731. If so, he had left Caludon but not moved far. A Joshua Jeacock, widower, was buried at Binley church in 1763.[13]

The next recorded tenant of Caludon was Thomas Goddard (Fig 56). The 1748 land tax roll records a 'Mr Goddard for Callodon Farm.' He was assessed at £32 8s 0d, a considerable sum

(Fig 57).[14] This is the first documented instance of Caludon being called a farm and strongly suggests that new buildings had been constructed, considerably smaller and more compact than the rambling, ramshackle castle buildings that they probably replaced. The demolition of the old buildings at Caludon has, therefore, been narrowed down to the years between 1731 and 1748. There is every reason to believe that material from the old castle was re-used in the farm building. In fact it is possible that more survived from the old buildings than the one ancient medieval wall. As discussed later, the castle stable block may have been converted into the farm house, leaving the stalls on the ground floor (see Fig 92 and Chapter 7).

Circumstantial evidence also supports the suggested dating. Elsewhere on the Clifford Warwickshire estates the demolition of another old but substantial house took place around this time. Weston-under-Wetherley Hall, an exuberantly timber framed manor house, was probably demolished before 1730.[15] Beighton's map of Warwickshire, surveyed in 1725, using a drawing rather than a geometrical symbol to mark the position of large houses and castles in the county, interestingly omits Weston Hall, but marks Caludon Castle (Fig 58).[16] Weston Hall was the principal seat of the Morgans in Warwickshire, having twenty hearths in 1666 when occupied by the widow Jane Morgan.[17] Her great granddaughter, Anne Preston, who married Hugh Clifford, was apparently born in the house and 'had the greatest regard for it.'[18] Whilst Weston was held by her husband 'unknown to her and to her infinite regret it was pulled down to the Ground.' This must have taken place before Hugh Clifford died in 1730, for the Warwickshire estates then passed to Anne for the remainder of her life (d.1734).

The recording of Caludon on Beighton's map with its distinctive, miniscule drawing is further evidence that it had survived well into the eighteenth century (Fig 58). Furthermore, Beighton would probably not have used a picture to represent a new more lowly farmhouse. As at Caludon, a new farm, Weston Hall Farm, was constructed to replace the old house and the close parallels with Caludon suggest that the events were connected.

The Cliffords were absentee landlords of both houses, ancient seats that were too big for local tenants to occupy and upkeep. The Lady Dowager Anne Clifford outlived both her husband, Hugh, the second Baron, and her two sons, Thomas, (1687-1718) and Hugh (3rd Baron, 1700-1732), to whom the title had descended after the death of his elder brother. She retired to France but held Caludon until she died in 1734, the next in line to inherit being Hugh, the fourth Baron who was only five years of age (1726-1783). It seems likely that his minority provided the opportunity for his trustees and estate stewards to rid themselves of their second over-sized and difficult to let house in Warwickshire. His mother, the Lady Dowager Elizabeth, had left for France at her husband, the third Baron's death, where she died in 1788.[19] Although a notable spendthrift, obstreperous, and interfering even from afar, many of the day-to-day decisions on the management of the Clifford estates must have been made without her knowledge.

The farm at Caludon was a viable concern, with a large acreage (c.250 acres) of good pasture land. The new farmhouse was established at the east end of the moated platform, near to the site of the old gatehouse (Fig 59). The eastern arm of the moat may already have been filled in by this time, or was used as a convenient dump for demolition rubble. The farm buildings themselves were

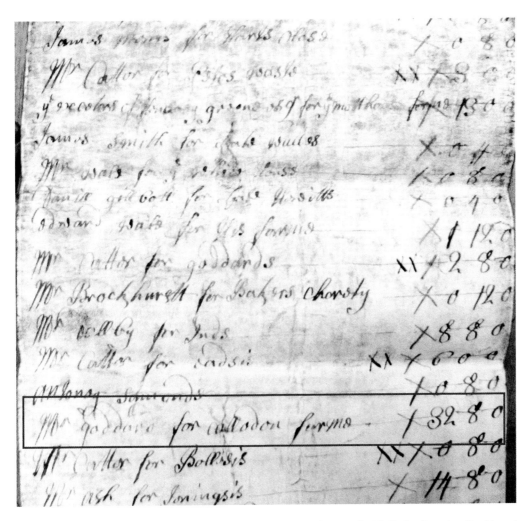

Fig 57 *Extract from a land tax roll for Caludon 1748; Mr Goddard's entry for 'Callodon farme' outlined in red*

placed slightly farther to the east where the driveway from the main road across the dam terminated (Fig 60).

In the year after Thomas Goddard was first recorded at Caludon Farm (1748), Hugh the fourth Baron, recently come of age, married Lady Anne Lee, daughter of George, the second Earl of Lichfield.[20] A marriage settlement assigned Caludon to Hugh Clifford for life and it is evident from a surviving letter, dated 31 October 1749, that Hugh was 'desirous of having Callowdon not to be Included' in the settlement.[21] From henceforth it was no longer to be regarded as part of a wife's jointure. Fortunately the letter also gives a list of Caludon tenants, confirming that Thomas Goddard paid £150 per annum for 'Callowdon Farme,' the whole rent roll amounting to £546 1s 8d.

It is not known how long Thomas Goddard had been a tenant at Caludon prior to 1748, but there is a possibility that he was the first to occupy the new farmhouse. Land tax records provide our only

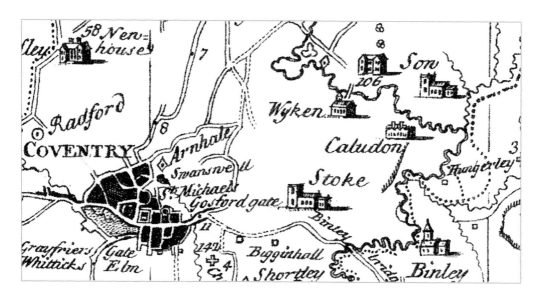

Fig 58 *Extract from Henry Beighton's map of Knightlow Hundred 1730*

Fig 59 *The site of the former Caludon Castle farmhouse 2013; the buildings stood on the moat platform to the right with the filled in ditch to the left. The viewpoint is similar to that in Fig 109*

138

source for the tenants of Caludon for the rest of the eighteenth century as no other Caludon rentals have survived for this period.[22] The tenants were as follows:

'Callowdon/Callodine Farm'
1748-1775 ....Mr Thomas Goddard
1775-1780 .... Mrs Elizabeth Goddard
1780-1795 ....Thomas Goddard
1798-1815 ....William Goddard[23]

The records demonstrate that the Goddard family remained tenants of the Cliffords until the estate was put up for sale in 1815 (Fig 56). 'Thomas Goddard of Calidon house, Grazier', died in 1775 leaving a will.[24] In his own right he owned freehold property in Frankton, Warks, and held a copyhold estate in Burbage (Leics), but did not mention his Caludon lease. His eldest son was Benjamin, born in 1750, to whom he left his heavily mortgaged Frankton estate.[25] A younger son, Thomas, baptised in 1752, was registered as 'son of Thomas Goddard and Elizabeth his wife from

Fig 60 *The site of the former Caludon farm buildings, which stretched from the car on the new car park on the left into the children's playground on the right; the posts roughly divide the former site into two*

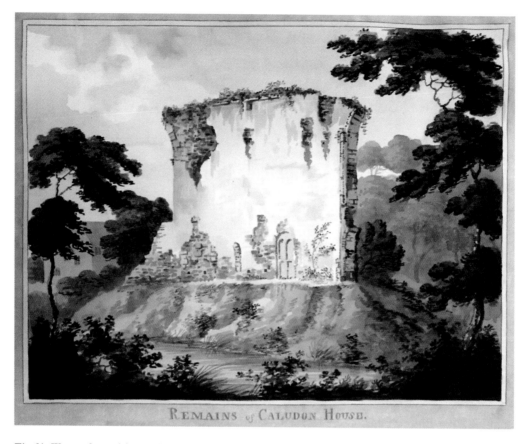

REMAINS of CALUDON HOUSE.

Fig 61 *Watercolour of the castle ruin c.1800, the earliest known view from the north side*

Caledown.' He was followed by James (b.1754) John (b.1755) William (b.1756) and a daughter, Elizabeth, baptised in 1759.[26]

Elizabeth Goddard, Thomas's widow, took over the lease of Caludon, the amount of land held having been reduced, perhaps in the few years before her husband's death (assessment decreased from £32 8s in 1756 to £24 6s by 1772).[27] She subsequently restored her holding to its original size, her assessment increased to £32 8s by 1780. Elizabeth's date of death is not known, but by 1784 her son, Thomas junior, had taken over the lease and preserved it at this size until at least 1792. He was alive in 1795 in which year he paid a reduced amount of £22 13s 4d. This is the amount that his younger brother, William, paid in 1798 when he had taken over the lease, possibly after the death of Thomas junior.

From 1817 to 1822 rentals are extant for Caludon. They confirm that Willam Goddard was still the tenant, paying an annual rent of £289 6s 8d and in addition land tax of £25 13s 4d. These figures remained constant to his last appearance on the rental of 1821-2. The Goddard rent is not recorded in the following rental as a consequence of the sale of Caludon.

It was very likely that the first known drawings of the ruined Caludon Castle wall were made during William Goddard's tenancy or perhaps shortly after (Figs 61, 62 and 63). The watercolour of the south elevation (Fig 62) clearly shows a third undercroft window with its tracery intact on the east side of the ruin and a pile of rubble in the foreground, presumably from the demolished castle, partly obscures it. The engraving was probably based upon it (Fig 63). In the main body of the ruin itself the tracery of the two upper windows also survives, stabilised by an infill of masonry, which was plastered on the north side to obscure the windows completely.

The affairs of the Clifford family in faraway Devon might have seemed of little consequence to the three generations of Goddard tenants. The stability of this family tenancy would have been appreciated by the Clifford stewards as long as the rents were paid promptly and in full and the farm kept in good order. We can only guess how quickly the Goddards became aware of the death and succession of the Lords Clifford. By coincidence there were three changes of landlord during the long Goddard tenancy. The fourth Baron, Hugh, died in 1783, having helped repair the family finances following the profligacy of his mother from whom he had inherited £20,000 of debt.[28] He was succeeded by his eldest son, Hugh (1756-1793), the fifth Baron, who suffered from ill health and in fact died in Munich on his return from Europe in search of a cure. The title then passed to

Fig 62 *Watercolour of the castle ruin c.1800, the earliest known view from the south side*

Fig 63 *Engraving of the south side of the ruined wall published by George Eld c.1820?*

his younger brother, Charles, the sixth Baron (1759-1831) (Fig 64). All three had been brought up as Catholics and married staunchly Catholic wives, leading to highly complex and impenetrable family settlements.[29] The Caludon estates were 'entailed' by a series of these arrangements, that is only able to pass through a succession of named heirs and future unborn descendants, effectively preventing their sale by any member of the defined family line. With the arrival of the new century the decision was made to break with this tradition. In 1811 the estate was 'disentailed', a normal legalistic practice, but, instead of usually being followed by a new entailing settlement, in 1814 Charles, the sixth Baron and his son and heir, Hugh Charles, formally agreed to sell or exchange their

Fig 64 *Portrait of Charles, 6th Lord Clifford (1759-1831)*

Warwickshire estates including Caludon. The normal incentive for land sales was financial - to obtain cash to pay off debts and losses, but the explanation here may be more straightforward. In the Clifford accounts there is a document that compares the income received from the sale of the Warwickshire estates in 1817, with the expenditure on the purchase of estates near Ugbrooke in Devon.[30] The simple conclusion was that a geographical consolidation of the Clifford estates had been the prime purpose, with the shedding of the distant Warwickshire lands in exchange for land more conveniently located nearby.

Advertisements for the sale of the Caludon estate were placed in the local press in late 1814 (Fig 65).[31] Sale particulars had already been prepared and on 30 January 1815 an auction took place at the King's Head Inn, Coventry (Figs 66 and 67).

> Particulars of the Manor, or Reputed manor, of Callowden, and Divers Valuable Farms & Estates Near the City Of Coventry To Be Sold by Auction, In Lots, At the King's Head Inn, in Coventry, on Monday the 30th Day of January, 1815, the sale to begin at eleven o'clock in the forenoon.

The printed particulars provide the first reliable large-scale map of Caludon manor, which clearly shows that it was composed mainly of a single irregularly shaped block of land, stretching from the southern extremity of Caludon Park in the south (near Stoke House) via land in Wyken to Foleshill parish at the junction of Bell Green Road and Henley Road in the north (Fig 68). There were two detached blocks of Sowe land at Lentons Lane and Potters Green and a few small isolated plots in Exhall, Stoke and Foleshill. Altogether the estate measured nearly 1100 acres and was divided into twenty-two lots for sale.

Lot XVIII corresponded with Caludon Farm: 'The Manor, or Reputed Manor, or Lordship of Callowden and Callowden Farm.' It was described as a:

> ...capital and truly eligible Estate, &c, comprising an excellent Farm House, suited for the residence of a genteel Family, with convenient attached and detached Buildings, of every description, in the most excellent Repair and Condition, and Lands not only of the first quality, but in the highest state of Cultivation, is now held by Mr. Willam Goddard, for a Term whereof 7 Years will be unexpired at Lady-day, 1815.

The plan clearly shows the farmhouse located on the eastern flank of the moated platform with its buildings lying farther to the east, not yet forming the 'U' shape complex of later years (Fig 69). By their shading they could be mistaken for water. Three sides of the earlier Caludon moat to the south were also depicted. Twenty six fields measured 206a 0r 29p with another 27a 0r 7p straddling the boundary with Wyken to the north-east of the farm. Essentially it still consisted of the castle site and land immediately surrounding it with its former deer park. The ancient demesne lands were divided between Lot XVII (late Whittingham's Farm – the Hermitage) and Lot XX (New Farm) and some of their fields still preserved names traceable from the medieval period: *Little and Great Ash*

WARWICKSHIRE.

Valuable and most desirable

FREEHOLD ESTATES, MANOR, &c.
FOR SALE.

TO BE SOLD BY AUCTION,

At the KING's HEAD INN, at Coventry, sometime in the ensuing month of November (of which timely notice will be given in this Paper),

THE MANOR or LORDSHIP of CALLOW-DEN, with divers highly cultivated and well-apportioned Farms, situate in the several Parishes of St. Michael's, Foleshill, Wyken, and Sow, and comprising together 1050 acres, or thereabouts, of rich arable, meadow, and pasture Land, lying, for the most part, contiguous to the populous City of Coventry, and in the several tenures or occupations of Messrs. Sumners, Goddard, Atkins, Cater, Inge, Stairum, Cantrell, and the Widow Jackson.

The whole will be divided into Lots.

The Tenants will shew the Lands in their several occupations; and other information may be had by applying (if by letter, free of postage) to Mr. Knight, Solicitor, Axminster, Devon; or of Mr. Burcham, Connisby, near Horncastle, by whom printed particulars of the property will shortly be prepared and circulated.

October 1, 1814.

Fig 65 *Advertisement for the sale of the Caludon estate,* Coventry Mercury, *7 November 1814*

8

LOT XVIII.

The MANOR, or Reputed Manor, or Lordship

OF

CALLOWDEN,

AND

CALLOWDEN FARM.

Refer. to Plan	Names of Closes					Quality.	In St. Michaels A. R. P.	In Wyken A. R. P.
1	Underwood Hill	—	—	—	—	Pasture	12 3 13	
2	Binley Hill	—	—	—	—	Ditto	14 3 8	
3	Deer Pen	—	—	—	—	Meadow	4 1 8	
4	Lake Meadow	—	—	—	—	Ditto	14 2 16	
5	Fen Hill	—	—	—	—	Pasture	11 2 15	
6	Lake Meadow	—	—	—	—	Meadow	5 2 29	
7	Park	—	—	—	—	Pasture	17 3 1	
8	Cow Close	—	—	—	—	Ditto	14 2 37	3 2 5
9	Cow Close	—	—	—	—	Arable	2 3 6	5 1 32
10	Slaughter House Close	—	—	—	—	Ditto	2 1 20	6 3 20
11	Ditto	—	—	—	—	Pasture	2 1 23	11 0 30
12	Summer House Lawn	—	—	—	—	Arable	13 1 26	
13	Old Pool	—	—	—	—	Pasture	3 2 3	
14	Farm Yard, Barn, Stables, and Outbuildings				—	—	0 2 5	
15	Farm House, Yard, Garden and Moat			—	—	—	1 2 30	
16	Orchard	—	—	—	—	—	0 2 21	
17	Scullery Close	—	—	—	—	Meadow	6 0 3	
18	Pond Close	—	—	—	—	Pasture	0 1 23	
19	Booth Hill	—	—	—	—	Arable	7 2 6	
20	Sheep Pen Close	—	—	—	—	Pasture	8 1 34	
21	Benley Hill	—	—	—	—	Ditto	15 2 20	
22	Three Cornered Lawn	—	—	—	—	Arable	9 0 25	
23	Marl Pit	—	—	—	—	Pasture	7 1 34	
24	The Lawn	—	—	—	—	Arable	10 2 0	
25	Shoulder of Mutton	—	—	—	—	—	5 2 10	
26	Clover Close	—	—	—	—	Arable	11 3 13	

The above capital and truly eligible Estate, &c. comprising an excellent Farm House, suited for the residence of a genteel Family, with convenient attached and detached Buildings, of every description, in most excellent Repair and Condition, and Lands not only of the first quality, but in the highest state of Cultivation, is now held by Mr. William Goddard, for a Term whereof 7 Years will be unexpired at Lady-day, 1815.

206 0 29	27 0 7
27 0 7	
233 0 36	

This Lot is Tithe free, subject (as to such parts thereof, as are situated within the Parish of St. Michaels,) to the payment of the sum of 6s. per Annum, to the Corporation of the City of Coventry, in lieu thereof. This payment also exempts other Lands not above comprised, from the like payment of Tithe, but is henceforth to be borne exclusively by the Proprietor of this Lot.

Fig 66 *Extract from the sale particulars for Caludon (Callowden) Farm 1815*

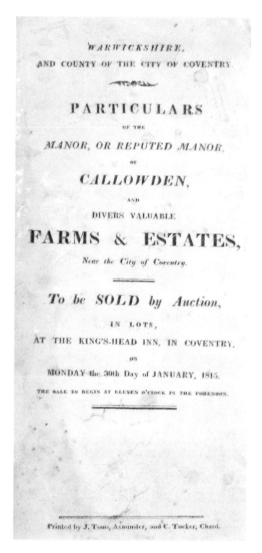

Fig 67 *Title page from the sale particulars for Caludon (Callowden) Farm 1815*

Moor, Far, Middle and Near Little Field, Great and Little Stubble Field, Partridge Meadow and Field and Crabtree Field (Fig 19).

Only about half of the twenty two lots were disposed of by 1817, fetching £13,662, but Caludon Farm did not find a buyer until 1822.[33] The purchaser was the Rev. John Brown of Trinity College Cambridge, who also acquired the lot at Potters Green in Sowe. Caludon Farm was valued at £12,000 and it is possible that £13,500 was actually received (Fig 70).[34] The conveyance was carried out on 13 and 14 September 1822.[35]

Fortunately some of the correspondence relating to this sale has survived, which indicates that the Rev John Brown had expected to purchase the Lordship of Caludon as well as the farm and land itself.[36] His brother, William Wale Brown, acting on his behalf, had travelled to the offices of Mr H Knight, Lord Clifford's steward and agent in Axminster, Devon, where the printed sale particulars were inspected (Fig 71). According to the Rev John Brown, his brother made an offer for Caludon based upon the description in the particulars. There is no doubt that the Caludon Farm lot was headed, 'The Manor, or Reputed Manor, or Lordship of Callowden and Callowden Farm' (see above and Fig 66). The Browns had assumed that the Manor or Lordship had been included in the sale. By this time the concept of the Manor of Caludon, principally an entitlement to certain rights, such as the holding of a manorial court and the collecting of fines levied by it, was in reality obsolete. On the other hand, the Lordship also bestowed the authority on the owner to reserve the minerals in the soil, which with the coal seams close by had potential monetary value. In addition, the title of 'Lord of the Manor' was still attractive as a status symbol. The Rev Brown was dismayed to hear that his purchase had not included the manor or lordship and wrote to Hugh Clifford on 30 August 1822 expressing his dissatisfaction over it being omitted. He understood from his own solicitor that the Manor was not 'of any pecuniary value; but it is still an appendage to the property, which I would wish to have.' Mr Knight, embarrassed by the Rev Brown's direct approach to Lord

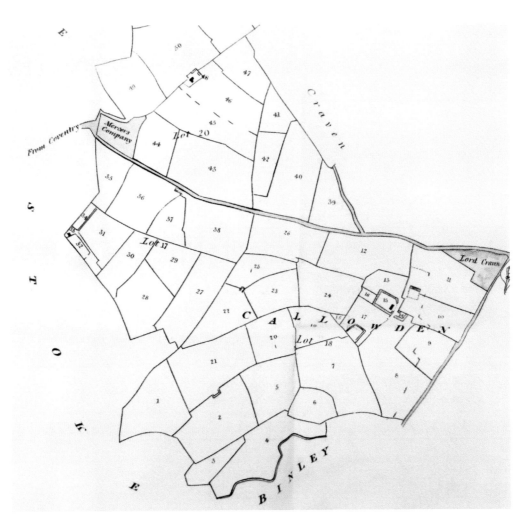

Fig 68 *Extract from a plan of Caludon Farm accompanying sale particulars 1815; the road that passes from right to left is the present Ansty Road*

Fig 69 *Detail from the sale particulars plan showing Caludon Farm, its moat and the upper moat 1815; confusingly the 'L'-shaped farm buildings near no '14' are shaded in a similar way to the water*

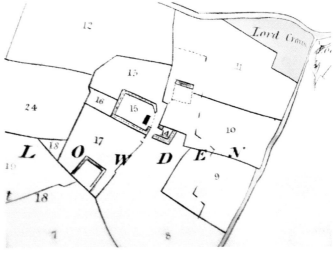

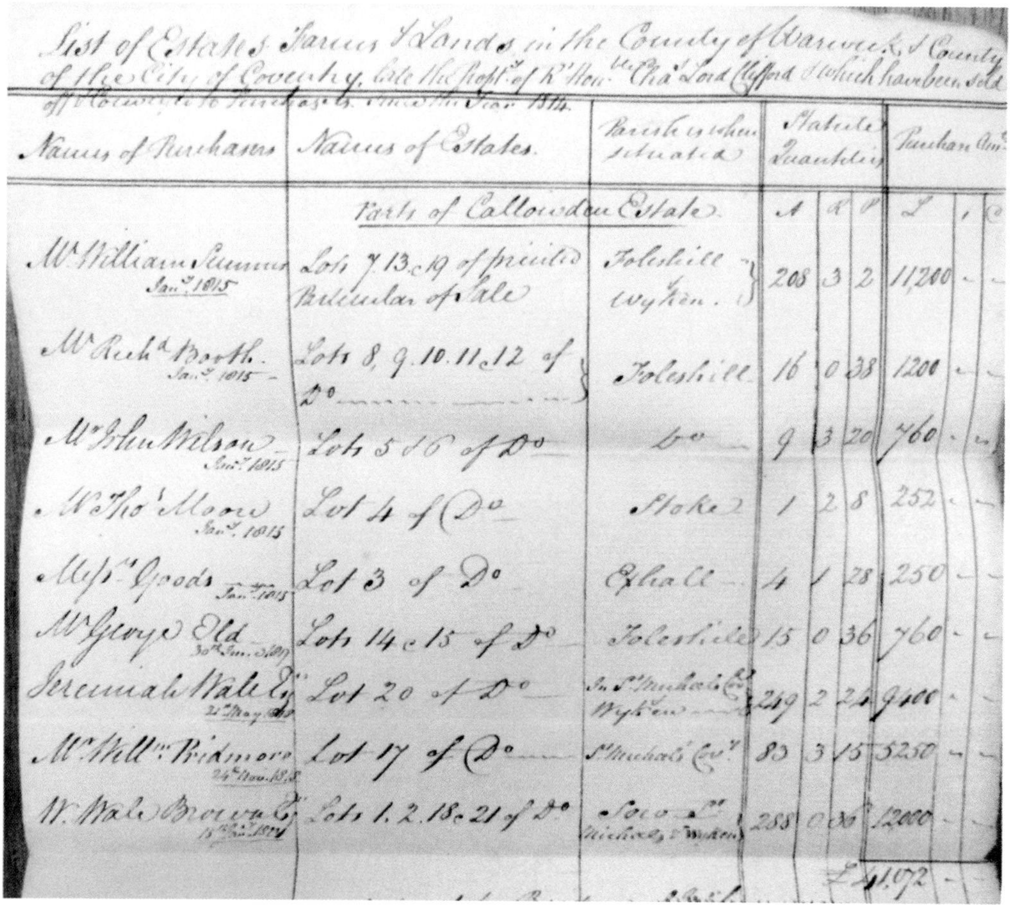

Fig 70 *Document summarising the sale of the Caludon Estate 1822*

Clifford, explained to his master the background to the sale in a letter dated 5 September 1822. It reveals that, after some prior negotiation and hesitation, a price for 'Goddards Farm' had been agreed with William Wale Brown in the Axminster office. William demanded that a contract be immediately prepared so that he could return with it by the next stagecoach to Bristol. Despite Mr Knight's expressing reservations about such haste, the contract was prepared with the proviso that it should be inspected in detail on William Wale Brown's return home and referred to his own solicitor, Mr Wilmott of Coventry. Mr Knight claimed that he had subsequently heard nothing more from the Browns or their solicitor, particularly in relation to the issue of the lordship. It is evident from Mr Knight's letter that the Lordship at this time was still in fact in receipt a small amount of fee farm rents (chief rents); he additionally drew attention to the financial potential of coal deposits in the area of Potters Green: 'many small spots of Land in the Neighbourhood of Skinners Farm [Potters Green] where Coal is Suspected to abound.' No reply was apparently penned to the Rev Brown, who wrote again to Lord Clifford on 11 September, 1822 expressing once again his

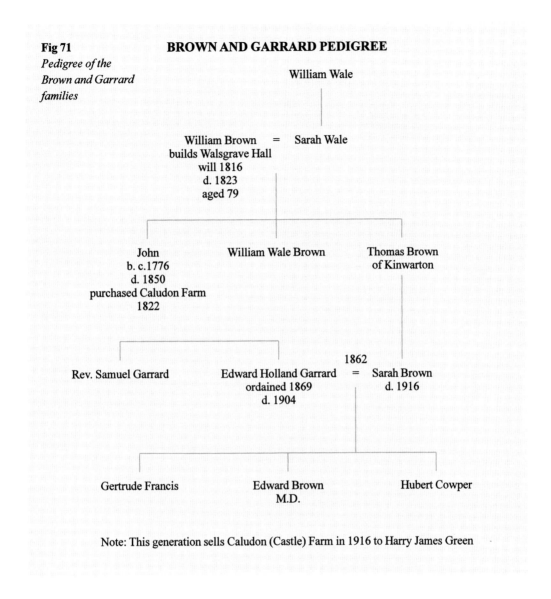

Fig 71
Pedigree of the
Brown and Garrard
families

BROWN AND GARRARD PEDIGREE

William Wale

William Brown = Sarah Wale
builds Walsgrave Hall
will 1816
d. 1823
aged 79

John
b. c.1776
d. 1850
purchased Caludon Farm
1822

William Wale Brown

Thomas Brown
of Kinwarton

Rev. Samuel Garrard

1862
Edward Holland Garrard = Sarah Brown
ordained 1869   d. 1916
d. 1904

Gertrude Francis

Edward Brown
M.D.

Hubert Cowper

Note: This generation sells Caludon (Castle) Farm in 1916 to Harry James Green

disappointment over the omission of the Lordship from the sale, which he stressed had occurred through no fault of his own. Although he considered that it had no financial value, John Brown was willing to pay extra if this could be agreed. The correspondence ceases with this letter and it is clear from later documentation that John Brown was unsuccessful in acquiring the Lordship of Caludon, as will be shown in the next chapter.

The purchaser of Caludon Farm was a Warwickshire man by birth. John Brown was son of William Brown, originally of Hartshill, who married Sarah Wale, daughter of William Wale, at Grendon (Warks) in 1775 (Fig 71). In the mid eighteenth century William Wale was the largest freeholder in Sowe after the Craven family.[37] William Brown, his son-in-law, eventually settled in

Sowe and built Walsgrave Hall on the site of a former Coventry Priory house. John Brown, born about 1776, entered Cambridge University in 1796, obtaining his MA in 1802.[38] He spent most of his life at Trinity College (Fellow, 1801-48, Tutor, 1807-24, Senior Dean, 1809-16, 1824, 1828, Vice-master, 1830-42), although for a short time he was vicar of Bottisham in Cambridgshire (1828). His acquisition of Caludon Farm was partly financed by his father's bequest to him of £4000, which was to be paid out of the Sowe and Kinwarton estates that the same will had granted to his brothers, William Wale Brown and Thomas Brown.[39] Their father's will was made in 1816, William Brown eventually dying in March 1823, six months after the Caludon sale was completed. John's brother, William Wale Brown, did not leave Warwickshire and remained a resident of Sowe. He had probably informed John far away in Cambridge that Caludon was up for sale. For the first time in its history a man of local birth was to be owner of Caludon, but it was now much reduced in size from the estate that had been built up during the medieval period.

Chapter 6 – NOTES

1 Clifford 3, Abstracts Warwickshire, 9/1-4
2 Hugh Clifford, The House of Clifford; from Before the Conquest, (1987)
3 Thomas Clifford, first Baron Clifford of Chudleigh (1630-1673), Dictionary of National Biography
4 ibid.
5 ibid
6 op. cit., Clifford 3, Abstracts Warwickshire, 9/1-4; Warwick RO CR2582/20/3
7 *Names of Catholics, Nonjurors and others , who refused to take the oath to his late King George.* (printed 1745, reprinted 1862) 11, 121: Rev Edgar Estcourt and John Payne (eds), *The English Catholic Nonjurors of 1715*, [1885] 25, 274; Caludon was listed under Coventry as its lands were mainly contained with the County of the City of Coventry. Caludon itself formed a detached part of St Michael's parish, all of which was contained within the County of Coventry.
8 Coventry RO, BA/E/B/22/6
9 St Michael's Parish Registers
10 Sowe Parish Registers
11 CA PA 2560/1/36-7
12 W F Carter and E A B Barnard, *The Records of King Edward School Birmingham*, Vol III, (1933) Dugdale Society Vol XII, 202-206, BCL Archives, 373946; Abraham was recorded as matriculating from Trinity College Oxford in March 1690/1, son of Thomas of 'Collington'. The latter is probably a corruption of Cubbington, the village immediately west of Weston-under-Wetherley, where the Jeacock family were well established in the seventeenth century.
13 Binley Parish Registers, 21 Nov 1763
14 Clifford, W (L) 1/9, Land Tax Assessment for Caludon, 1748
15 Geoffrey Tyack, *Warwickshire Country Houses*, (1994) 268-270
16 Dugdale (1730), Map of Knightlow Hundred, between pp 2-3
17 op. cit., Arkell and Alcock, 125, 284
18 Thomas Ward, *Manuscript Collections for the Continuation of the History and Antiquities of Warwickshire*, (1830) 173v-174v, BL Add. Ms. 29264; copy in Warwick RO.
19 op. cit., Clifford (1987) 161-162
20 The marriage took place 17 Dec 1739, op. cit, Cockayne, *The Complete Peerage*; the date given in op. cit., Clifford (1987) 163 is probably incorrect.
21 op. cit., Warwick Record Office, CR2582/20/3, CR3899/1; Clifford 3 Abstracts, Warwickshire, 9/1-4; TNA IR23 /91/9 f 39v
22 Coventry RO , BA/E/2/77/33-38; PA95/55/1-7; Clifford W (L) 1/9
23 Clifford III/6/4
24 Lichfield RO, Thomas Goddard's will, 14 Feb 1775, proved 10 Jan 1776; buried at Sowe church 16 March 1775.
25 Sowe Parish Registers; BCL Archives, 377039
26 Sowe Parish Registers, 8? Aug 1752, 4 April 1756, 3 Sept 1759
27 See note 18; The land totals for each assessment district were fixed and most changes that occur in an individual's charge were mostly the result of reducing or increasing the size of property.
28 op. cit. Clifford (1987) 161-2
29 See note 6
30 Clifford, III/6/3d
31 Coventry Mercury, 1 Oct 1814, 14 Nov 1814
32 Clifford 3/2 Sales Catalogues; W (L) 1/7
33 Clifford W(L) 1/9; III/6/3d
34 Clifford III/6/3d
35 SBTRO, ER/91/4
36 Clifford, III/6/3d, letters 30 Aug 1822, 5 Sept 1822, 11 Sept 1822.
37 VCH, Warwick, Vol 8, 106
38 Cambridge University Alumni, 1261-1900, ancestry.co.uk site; Grendon Parish Registers
39 TNA Prob 11/1668

From Manor to Municipal Park
Caludon 1822 to 2013

The Rev. John Brown purchased Caludon House and its farm in September 1822, seven years after it had first been advertised for sale.[1] Goddard's Farm, as it was also called, contained the moated castle site, the earlier moat and much of the former medieval deer park lying to the south. It also included the land lying to the north and east of the farm so that its northern and eastern boundaries were the present Ansty Road and Clifford Bridge Road respectively. The ancient demesne lands to the west also took some time to sell, the likely purchasers of New Farm (Lot XX, 205 acres), being Thomas and John Stephens and of Hermitage Farm (Lot XVII, 83 acres), a Mr George Alexander Pridmore, as recorded in the later tithe survey of 1846 (Fig 72).[2]

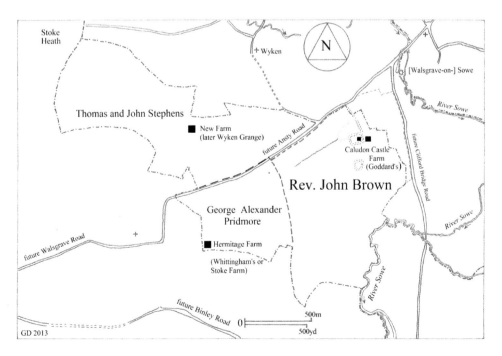

Fig 72 *Plan of the Caludon estate in the second quarter of the nineteenth century showing the tripartite division after the 1822 sale.*

Hermitage Farm was also known either as Whittingham's, after the name of the tenants, or Stoke Farm, owing to its location on the boundary with that parish. A member of this family established a career and a reputation far beyond that which could normally be expected of the seventh child of a Caludon farmer. Charles Whittingham was born in 1767, named after his father, the tenant farmer.[3] His prospects of taking on the family farm were remote and so he was apprenticed to Richard Bird, a printer and bookseller in Coventry. He managed to prosper in the trade and after first working in Birmingham he moved to London and set himself up in business in Dean Street, a world away from his rural upbringing. He invested in new technologies and by the 1820s had become a respected and successful printer, known for the sharpness and evenness of his impressions. Works such as Whittingham's Pocket Novels, Whittingham's French Classics and Whittingham's Cabinet Library adorned the bookshelves of many respectable homes. He never returned to Warwickshire and died in Chiswick in 1840, a wealthy man. He passed the business to his nephew and namesake, Charles Whittingham (1795-1876), who was successful in his own right as a London printer.[4]

In 1815 there were seven years left unexpired of Richard Goddard's lease of Caludon House and Farm. He must have renewed his lease in 1822 for in February 1826 he decided to retire putting up for sale his entire stock of animals and farming implements and machinery:[5]

> The Entire Live and Dead Stock, Farming Implements, Ricks of Corn, and Part of the Household Furniture of Mr William Goddard of Calowden House… comprising 250 well-bred Ewes, Treaves, Stearhogs, Rams, etc., 36 Superior long horned Dairy and Fat Cows, Heifers, and Oxen,16 Stirks, Yearlings and Calves, 2 Bulls, 7 young Cart Horses and Mares, 7 in-pig Sowes and Stores, Corn Rick, Waggons, Carts, Ploughs, Harrows, Scuffle, Winnowing and Haymaking Machines, Land Roll, Horse Gearing, Brewing and Dairy Utensils, and a general Assemblage of modern and useful Household Furniture.

The advertisement drew attention to the fact that the 'Cow Stock are of true Canley breed and the Sheep equal, if not superior, to any flock in this and the adjacent counties.' It is evident that Richard Goddard had maintained the now long-established tradition of prosperous grazier-tenants of Caludon, breeding sheep and cattle for their meat, hides and wool, although he had ploughs and harrows to cultivate a certain proportion of arable. Unfortunately Richard did not enjoy a long retirement for he died within a year, perhaps leaving it too late for a man of seventy after a long life in farming. He had moved to Binley where he was buried in the churchyard on 20 January 1827. Elizabeth Goddard, aged sixty three, 'of Calledon', and probably his wife, predeceased him by four years.[6]

The next tenant at Caludon House, Edward Driver, is first recorded in 1835. It is not known if the Rev. John Brown granted a lease to Edward Driver immediately after Richard Goddard left. Edward was born in Market Harborough, Leics, and gave his age as 33 in the 1841 census, but as 48 in the 1851 census. Even if the higher figure is used to calculate his earlier age, he would only have been 24 years old in 1827 and very young to take on the tenancy without the necessary financial means. He is known, however, to have inherited a considerable sum of money. John

Driver, his father, left £2000 under his will of 1831 to be divided between Edward and Elizabeth, his sister.[8] In 1841 Edward was still a bachelor and lived without any family at Caludon House, supported by two male and two female servants.[9] In the following year, however, on 6 January, Edward married Elizabeth Lees, daughter of a Coleshill farmer, John Lees, at Coleshill church.[10] By the 1851 census Elizabeth Driver had already borne him four sons and one daughter.[11] Edward was recorded as a farmer of 234 acres employing four labourers.

The availability of census information for the 1840s and 1850s coincides with the period of the tithe commutation surveys. The details for Caludon are in fact disappointing, due to the 'peculiar' local tithe arrangements. Essentially Caludon was tithe free, paying only 6s per annum to the Coventry Corporation, a payment that can be traced back to the thirteenth century when the vicar of St Michael's was the recipient.[12] Much of the usual information is, therefore, missing: the individual fields were not surveyed and the Caludon area of the St Michael's parish map is shown as a blank with only landownership boundaries. There are consequently neither field names nor the names of the tenants that held them. It is fortunate, however, that the 1815 sale particulars and map (Figs 68 and 66) to a great degree compensate for this lack of the usually informative tithe data.

According to the 1846 tithe survey the Rev. John Brown owned 'Land in Caludon,' including Caludon House, measuring 212 a 2r 22p (1815, 206a 0r 29p)(Fig 72). Thomas and John Stephens possessed the second largest Caludon farm (New Farm, later inaccurately named Wyken Grange), similarly described and nearly the same size (210a 3r 35p). The third farm of 85 acres belonged to George Pridmore (Hermitage/Stoke). These acreages confirm that the original three lots, as defined in 1815 sale particulars and covering the core of the ancient Caludon estate (park and demesne), had remained intact. There had been no subsequent land sales and exchanges.

John Brown had been disappointed in not being able to purchase the Manor of Caludon in 1822. The Cliffords had retained it despite his protestations, but in 1846 Hugh Charles Clifford, the 7th Baron, sold the Lordship or Manor of Caludon to William, the Earl of Craven and lord of the neighbouring Combe estate, Binley and large parts of Sowe and Wyken (Fig 73).[13] The most tangible benefit to the Cravens was a number of quit or chief rents, but they only amounted to £1 11s 9d. Below the ground there was potential value in coal deposits, but this was never realised and no coal was ever mined in the modern sense near to Caludon House or the former park.

The Rev. John Brown died on 17 August 1850 at Sowe, probably at his brother's house, Walsgrave Hall (Fig 71). A short obituary in the *Gentleman's Magazine* provides the basic facts of his life and career, spent mostly at Trinity College Cambridge.[14] He graduated in 1799 and obtained his M.A. in 1802. His alumni record lists the several positions he held at the college, including Senior Dean and Vice Master.[15] He appears to have served a parish only for a year in 1828 at Bottisham, Cambridgeshire. His obituary provides a fleeting insight into his character, affirming that his memory would be 'long held in reverence, for almost unbounded charity and unostentatious manners.' It is known that he supported a small infant school on Hawkesbury Lane.[16]

Under his will of 17 November 1849 John Brown left the Caludon estate to his two brothers, William Wale Brown and Thomas Brown.[17] The will was proved on 8 January 1851 and within two years William Wale had sold his undivided half of Caludon and land in Wyken, Foleshill and Sowe

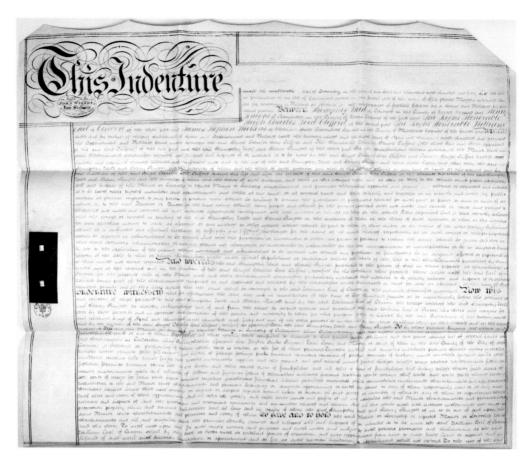

Fig 73 *Deed of sale of the Lordship of Caludon and its manor in 1846 from Lord Clifford to the Earl of Craven*

to his brother, Thomas, Lord of the Manor of Kinwarton, for £1750.[18] On 22 May 1862 Thomas's only daughter, Sarah, married Edward Holland Garrard of Clopton House, Mickleton, at Kinwarton parish church (Fig 71). The wedding was reported in several newspapers, including the description of the bride's attire: 'a rich moiré antique dress trimmed with white lace.' Eight carriages made up the wedding procession and after the ceremony at Kinwarton a peal of bells rang out at Alcester church. The marriage service was performed by the Rev. Samuel Garrard, brother of the groom and the bride was given away by her brother, John Brown.[19] The latter must have inherited other property as Caludon House and farm passed from the Brown to the Garrard family through Sarah and Edward's marriage settlement.[20] Sarah was to hold Caludon for life, followed by her husband, and after their deaths it was to be divided equally between their children.

Before this transfer of ownership, Caludon's tenant, Edward Driver, had left to take up farming in Elmsthorpe in Leicestershire and was replaced by his younger brother, William Driver. The 1861 census records that he was aged 38 and married to Mary Anne, nine years his junior. They had two young children, a son, aged 4, and a daughter, aged 2. Another much older Mary Driver, William's mother (80), had also left Leicestershire and joined the family. One male and three female servants completed the household and there were an additional six labourers and three boys helping to farm the 240 acres.[21] In 1871 William Driver was still tenant of Caludon farm, sharing the house with his wife, daughter of fourteen and his elderly mother, now 90. She was to die at Caludon House in February 1872, 'relict of the late John Driver of Market Harborough.'[22] The son, William H Driver, had been sent away to be educated at Enfield Town Palace School.[23]

By the time of the next census (1881) the Drivers had left Caludon, the last in a long line of farmer-graziers stretching back to the early seventeenth century. In 1891 William was living with his wife, and daughter on 'his own means', served by a cook and two housemaids in Bathampton, Somerset, sharing another characteristic of this lineage – a comfortable level of affluence.

By 1880 Caludon House had been converted into Caludon College, run by Anton[y] Beaumont. He was also master of Binley Church of England School, which had been established by the Earl of Craven in 1839.[24] In 1879, when already at Binley School, he married Elizabeth Hopkins Hawthorne, a resident of Sowe, and by November of 1880 they had moved to Caludon in which month their son, John, was baptized at Binley church.[25] In 1881 the census records Anton[y]'s age as 32, his wife, Elizabeth, younger by six years. Caludon College was a 'gentleman's' boarding school with six resident pupils, in age ranging from 11 to 14, who had come from as far as London and Boston, Lincolnshire.

It is assumed that Anton[y] Beaumont did not cultivate the 232 acres recorded in the 1871 census, but that the farm buildings and land were leased or sub-leased to someone farming elsewhere. An 1880 directory entry for Caludon lists Walter Dan Claridge as farmer at Caludon Farm and his name appears in Caludon entries in directories as late at 1892.[26] Walter D Claridge was in fact a hotel proprietor and victualler, running the Craven Arms in the High Street in Coventry where the census recorded him between 1871 and 1911. This was a large traditional inn offering accommodation, in later directories described as a commercial hotel. Walter's parents were maltsters, his father also a horse dealer, and in 1861, when he was aged 15, the family occupied the Hare and Squirrel in Cow Lane, Coventry. By 1871, remarkably when only 25, he had already taken on the large enterprise of the Craven Arms. Walter tried to revive coach travel, his premises having previously been a coaching inn, but by the late nineteenth century this would only have been a novelty.[27] He was apparently the last person to drive a coach from Coventry to London. It was not unusual for a victualler or innkeeper to rent agricultural land in order to grow the barley essential for brewing beer, and his parents most likely taught him this specialised trade. Caludon Farm was large, however, consisting of well over 200 acres, and it is not known how else he may have cultivated this extensive area. Cattle or sheep might have been reared for their meat to feed his customers and guests. In 1915 Walter moved from the Craven Arms in High Street to its namesake in Binley, rebuilding it within a few years, but by this time he had long left Caludon Farm.

It is not known exactly how long Caludon House itself functioned as a school. The first edition of the Ordnance Survey 1:2500 map (1887) provides the first large-scale plan of Caludon and its fields when the house was possibly still occupied by the Beaumonts (Fig 74). The whole building

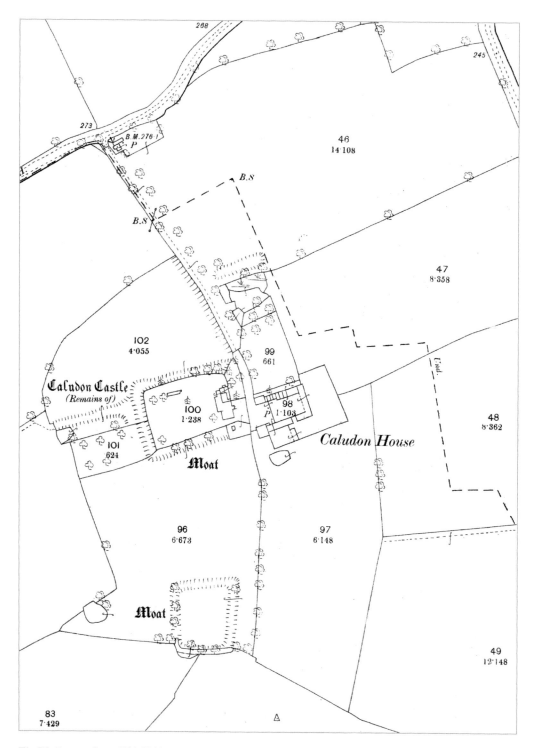

Fig 74 *Extract from OS 1:2500 map 1887*

complex was called Caludon House, consisting of the house itself, situated at the eastern end of the moat, and deep 'U' shaped group of farm buildings lying farther to the east. The access drive from the main road divided the two groups of buildings, which would have been relatively easy to lease separately. The map clearly shows the eastern arm of the moat filled in, partially forming a forecourt to the house. The remainder of the castle platform with its ruined wall to the west of the house has been laid out as a garden with network of paths and a number of trees, including conifers, planted (Fig 75). The site of the former pool to the north can be discerned from the shape of field no 102 (4.055 acres), which still also contained a distinct bank in the south-western corner required to prevent water spilling in this direction. To the south of this east-west dam lay a small orchard (field no 101, 0.624 acres). The main dam on a north-south orientation coincided in part with the farm access road leading to Ansty Road. Immediately below the dam was a disturbed area containing a pit with water and beside it to the north a sausage -shaped dry pit. The presumed earlier medieval moat to the south was drawn by the Ordnance Survey into field no 96 (6.673 acres) and still held water in its southern arm.

By 1891 the Beaumonts and their pupils had left to be replaced by the Aviss family. Llewellyn Aviss, although clearly of Welsh ancestry, had been born in Foleshill and ran a successful cigar making business.[28] In 1862 the tobacconist partnership of Griffiths and Aviss had been dissolved, William Aviss, Llewellyn's father, continuing to trade on his own under the same name.[29] Their retail shop was located in High Street, Coventry, by coincidence close to the Craven Arms, and their manufactory lay a little farther from the centre of the town at 90 Gosford Street.[30] In 1881 Llewellyn, when living in Gosford Terrace, overlooking Gosford Green and now under Sky Blue

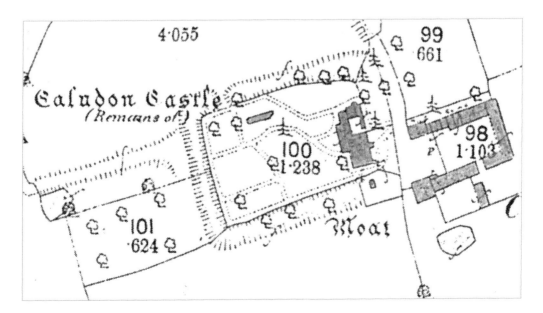

Fig 75 *Detail from another edition of the OS 1:2500 map 1887 showing the garden on the moat platform*

Way, described himself as a 'cigar manufacturer, employing five Men, 6 Boys, 160 Women and Girls'. The Coventry firm, not surprisingly, marketed a cigar called the 'Godiva', but the reason why they also advertised the 'El Caludon' cigar in the early 1890s is now obvious (3d each, 5 for a shilling, 100 for 18 shillings).[31] The firm of Griffiths and Aviss was liquidated in 1906 and their premises at Gosford Street were taken over by the Arno Motor Works, which moved out in 1913.[32] The French firm of Hotchkiss et Cie, displaced by the Great War, set up a machine gun works in 1915 using the old cigar manufactory building, but it also constructed a multi-storey factory fronting Gosford Street.[33] In 1923 the Morris motor company purchased the premises and constructed an engine works on the street frontage next to the Hotchkiss factory. This required a large multi-storey rear extension, resulting in the demolition of Aviss's original manufactory.[34] After the Second World War the buildings were taken over by the Department of Health and Social Security, as it was them known, and the rear extension famously caught fire in June 1964, sending a massive plume of black smoke into the sky over the centre of Coventry. In the early 1990s the surviving buildings were renovated by Coventry University and now form part of its campus.

Llewellyn Aviss appears to have taken some interest in agricultural production despite the fact Walter Claridge listed himself a farmer at Caludon Farm in 1892. In the same year classes for teaching butter and cheese making were organised at the dairy at Caludon House, arranged by a local committee chaired by Aviss in co-operation with the Technical Education Department of County Council.[35] It is, moreover, possible that in his own right he employed a cowman to look after his own stock. The only other entry under Caludon in the 1891 census was for John Lambert, aged 70, who lived in a 'Farm House' on Coventry (Ansty) Road with a dairy maid and laundry maid. This building might have been the small house, called Caludon Lodge, situated at the corner of Caludon Park Avenue and Ansty Road.[36]

In fact Llewellyn had other interests to occupy his time, for he was elected as Liberal councillor for Earl Street Ward in 1894, eventually resigning from Gosford Street Ward in 1903.[37] His occupancy of Caludon House was to prove of short duration, as by 1896 he was living in Stoneleigh Terrace, Queens Road, close to the centre of the city. In 1891, while still at Caludon, his family included his wife, Elisa, and three sons and one daughter, all less than eleven years of age. There were three live-in servants: a cook, a housemaid and groom.

The engraving of the ruins published in Elizabeth Hodge's book (1895) was made towards the end of the Aviss tenancy, confirming that the garden had been laid out for some time with trees already mature (Fig 76).[38] Both this and an earlier photograph of perhaps about 1880 clearly show the intact tracery of both fourteenth-century windows (Fig 77). A more distant view from the west over the castle platform and its garden, drawn in 1897, also provides a rare glimpse of Caludon farmhouse (Fig 78).

It would appear that Caludon House was vacant in 1899. In July the Coventry Church of England Sunday School Association held their annual picnic at Caludon Castle 'by permission of Mr W. Pridmore.' The latter was probably William Frederick Pridmore, a farmer and agricultural valuer, who lived at Wyken House in 1891 and 1901 and may have farmed and managed Caludon on behalf of the owners (Sarah and Edward Garrard) (Fig 71) for a few years after Aviss's

Fig 76 *Engraving of south side of ruined wall, published by Elizabeth Hodges 1895*

Fig 77 *Possibly the earliest photograph of Caludon Castle ruins c.1880-1890?*

departure.[39] It is interesting that appreciation of the site from an antiquarian point of view had already begun, for a talk on its history was delivered to the picnickers by a Mr V.C. Blyth. In 1876 the Warwickshire Field Group had visited Caludon, inspecting the surviving wall, and noticing 'a large octagonal hollow stone…which appears to have been attached to the gatehouse or barbican of the fortifications.'[40] This mysterious stone artefact has subsequently been lost.

By 1901 John Thomas was the new tenant of Caludon House. Continuing the trend established two decades earlier, leases were no longer being granted to farmer-graziers. John was a business man, although one that had failed in previous ventures and was about to be declared bankrupt again. Aged 57 and born in Redditch, he described himself in the 1901 census as a managing director of Tomcox Ltd. His wife, Sarah, (55) was away visiting in Birmingham, whilst at home were his daughters, Sarah (24) and Agnes (22), and two sons, John (20) and Harry (15). John Thomas appeared at the Coventry Bankruptcy Court in June 1902, described as a poultry farmer of Caludon House. The row of small sheds and pens seen to be almost filling the upper moat on the 1906 OS plan may have been the poultry's accommodation (Fig 79). He had already been made bankrupt in 1889 'while in business in London as a commission agent and director of public companies' the

Tomcox and Thomas Sewing Machine Companies mentioned specifically.[41] Thomas claimed that he had taken out between fifty and one hundred patents, including a harness buckle inflator and a bird catcher. More recently before February 1901 he had been a cycle accessories manufacturer and blamed the recent failure of his business on an accident which had incapacitated him for fifteen months. He was visiting Birmingham on 5 February 1901 when a steam tram collided with his cab in Great Lister Street, injuring his spine and breaking six ribs.[42] He was confined to hospital for over a month and was not able to return to Caludon until 10 March 1901. For the injuries sustained, John Thomas took out an action against the Birmingham Tram Company, claiming £6000, but was eventually awarded £750 plus costs. Despite the substantial compensation received this was insufficient to rescue his finances, his trading deficit being over £600. One might wonder why this serial inventor and entrepreneur with a distinct bias towards engineering projects took up poultry farming. Thomas revealed at the bankruptcy hearing that he had some experience as an amateur and that he began to rear poultry after his doctors advised him that he could not return to his normal engineering business. A partner had been found who had advanced £200 but in the end 'the taking up of Caludon House… resulted in a terrible loss.'[43]

Caludon Castle.   Feb 23/97   SJB

Fig 78 *Pen and ink drawing of Caludon Castle ruins and farmhouse by SJB 1897 (initials unidentified)*

163

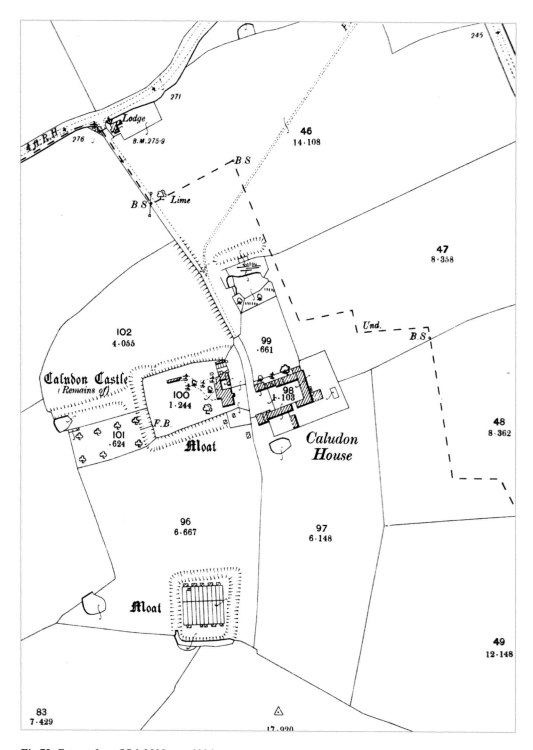

Fig 79 *Extract from OS 1:2500 map 1906*

Fig 80 *The site of Caludon Lodge 2013*

John Thomas's household does not seem to have settled at any one place for any length of time. He had previously lived in Lambeth (civil engineer, 1881) and Newington (manufacturers agent, 1891) and his several children had been born elsewhere in the south-east of England. Whether his frequent moves were to avoid creditors is not known, but when tracked down in the next census (1911), he had left Caludon and was living in Kenilworth, managing director of the Smoke Consuming Company Limited, in which his two grown-up sons, John and Harry, worked as engineering fitters. In these circumstances it is likely that John Thomas was never an active farmer, but only occupied the house and a possible descendant of the Pridmore family, who had purchased part of the estate in 1822 adjacent to Hermitage Farm, cultivated the land itself.

Information on the next occupants of Caludon Farm is contained in reminiscences provided by Harold Green, son of the next tenant and eventual owner, Henry James Green.[44] The family moved from a tiny one-up, one-down cottage opposite the Bull's Head on Binley Road, situated in what was later known as Morton's Yard. According to Harold the year was 1907 when he was aged about eight. This is confirmed by the directory entry for 1908 where Henry James Green is recorded as farmer at Caludon.[45] The family had been forced to move by the loss of their presumably leased farmland to the Royal Show held the one time in Coventry (at Ball Hill) in 1907. With a few cows Henry, the father, had built up a retail milk round, relying on his wife and young son, Harold, to do the milking. Henry had been crippled by an agricultural accident and was forced to take waged work from his father. By 1911 Harry, as he was also known (aged 40), had been married for nineteen years to his wife Elizabeth (also 40), and was sharing Caludon farmhouse with their five sons and three daughters.[46] According to Harold he was eventually to be the eldest of twelve children.[47] Two house servants and a farm assistant made up the remainder of the household, in all thirteen persons. Ten years earlier we find the census recording Henry Green living with his younger and smaller family in Bull's Head Lane, describing himself as a 'farm manager,' but whether this was Stoke Farm is not known.[48] In contrast to all the earlier farmer-graziers, however, Henry was in due course to become owner of Caludon House and its farmland, admittedly much diminished in size from the estate that had been once owned by absentee aristocratic families stretching back to the early seventeenth century.

Fig 81 *Caludon Cottages which housed workers from Caludon Farm, 2013*

In 1904 the Rev. Edward Garrard died in Leamington Spa, husband of the heiress of Caludon, Sarah, neé Brown (Fig 71). He had followed his father and brother into the church, having been ordained in 1869, seven years after marrying Sarah.[49] Sarah moved with her husband to parishes in Derby, Luton, Wickersley, Yorkshire, finally settling at Marston Sicca (Long Marston) where he was appointed rector in 1880, near to his wife's original home in Mickleton (Glos) and his own in Dumbleton (Glos).[50] Sarah had retained ownership of Caludon for life under their marriage agreement and was recorded as 'principal landowner' in 1912.[51] By 1911 she had moved to Weston-super-Mare, where she lived on 'small private means' with her grown-up daughter, Gertrude (48) and son, Edward Brown (43), both unmarried.[52] Sarah died on 13 December 1916, and left personal effects valued at £1,439 5s 2d, a sum far less, though substantial, than the value of the Caludon estate, which would automatically pass to her surviving children.[53] These were three: Gertrude Francis, who had lived with her mother until her death, Edward Brown, a doctor of medicine who had left Weston-super-Mare for Dominica in the Leeward Islands and Hubert Cowper, a schoolmaster and resident of Nelson, British Columbia. They had already collectively decided to sell Caludon, since only nine days after their mother's death the estate was conveyed for the first time in its history to a sitting tenant, in this case, Harry James Green.[54] The purchase price was £10,500 for 233 acres 1 rood and 33 perches of land and for the house called 'Caludon Farm and the cottage or lodge [on Ansty Road corner] and the ruins known as Caludon Castle and two cottages known as Caludon Cottages [adjacent to the lodge previously mentioned].' Although the lodge has been demolished and replaced by a small block of flats bearing the same name, the cottages still survive today (Figs 80 and 81). In 1909 the mineral rights to the western half of the land had been leased to a Glasgow company Merry and Cunningham for sixty years, a dubious transaction considering that Lord Craven had purchased these with the manor of Caludon from the Cliffords in 1846 (see above).

We are fortunate also to have a written memoir left by Lydia, Harold's second oldest sister, describing her time at Caludon Farm.[55] Her account is not easy to reconcile with her brother's for she states that it was from Stoke Farm that the family moved to Caludon, its kitchen and dining room 'recently redecorated' and unlikely to have been part of a tiny cottage. As result of the redecoration Mrs Green was 'not too pleased with the news' that her husband had taken the Caludon tenancy. Lydia was about 11 years of age when they moved, her father not having 'sufficient capital to take such a big step, but the step was taken with a lot of grit and hard work on my parents part.' Although she considered her father to have been a good farmer, meticulous about hygiene, the family did not seem to her to have a great deal of money. Harry Green kept a herd of around fifty cows, five cart horses, a mare for the trap and two ponies

Fig 82 *The north side of Caludon's ruined wall with all the window tracery intact 1936*

Fig 83 *Postcard of the ruins from north side showing a boundary hedge and crenellated garden wall or hedge immediately behind c.1930s. The orchard lies to the right of the photograph*

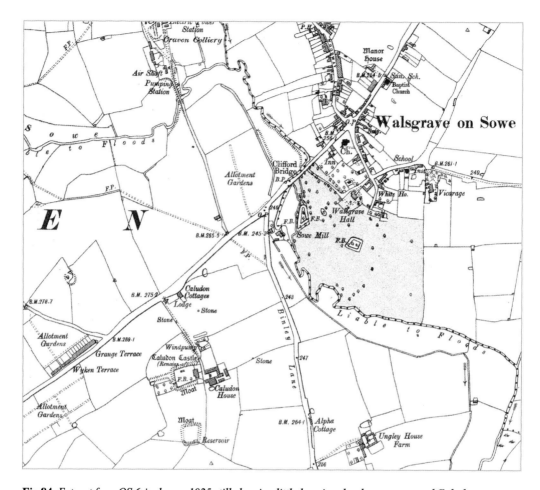

Fig 84 *Extract from OS 6-inch map 1925 still showing little housing development around Caludon.*

for the milk float. Milk was produced for sale in the local area, transported on the milk float. His customers included Wyken and Walsgrave residents as well as bulk purchasers such as the Coventry Workhouse on London Road, confirmed by Harry as having a delivery twice a day, morning and night.[56] Soon after settling in to Caludon, the milk round was sold to Harry Case, their farm hand.

Despite their lack of cash the Green family regarded themselves as the 'better sort', ambitious and aspiring, and Harry had a reputation as being the unofficial 'Squire of Caludon'. Lydia's eldest sister, Florence, married Tom Treharn, who owned an aluminium foundry. As the family fortunes improved, Harry could afford to buy Stoke Farm (from whence they had left for Caludon) followed by Caludon Castle Farm in 1917, the agreed price of £10,500 being a significant amount of money. It appears that Harry raised sufficient capital for this purchase by selling a third farm, Neales, named after the Green's tenants. It is not known when and how this had been acquired.

Harry Green's reputation as the 'Squire' rests on his considerable social presence in the area. He was a magistrate for the county of Warwick in 1928 and was involved in the local community, acting as church warden.[57] All but one of his sons also became magistrates, reflecting the family's hard-won status. A church fete was held annually in the castle grounds.

The ruins of Caludon Castle served as a picturesque backdrop to the Greens' back garden. This was where Lydia recalls conducting most of her courtship with a local boy before her marriage in 1920. The garden was already well established by the late nineteenth century with paths laid out and trees planted (Fig 76). It appears that it was enclosed partly by a low crenellated wall of presumably recent construction and partly by a hedge (Figs 82 and 83).

The farm was slow to join the twentieth century with electric lighting installed in the 1920s, run by an unreliable generator, though still more convenient than oil lamps and candles. Farm practices remained un-mechanised and labour intensive, the cows being walked from market at Coventry and Rugby.

A local man who remembered the Green family at Caludon was Alec Flynn, who was born in newly built houses (1909) on Ansty Road at the beginning of the First World War in 1914.[58] They were known as Wyken Terrace and Grange Terrace and most still stand on the town-side of the junction of Ansty Road with Wyken Croft next to the Wyken Working Men's Club (Fig 84). This long history of Caludon, told primarily from written sources, had at long last encountered living memory. His house diagonally faced the castle just a few hundred yards distant across open fields. When the publisher interviewed him at his home in 2008, Alec recalled that the roads then were practically deserted.

"If you were lucky when we were kids there might have been a horse and cart coming by who might give you a ha'penny for opening the (turnpike) gate." The scene has since changed beyond recognition with the quiet country lane turned into a busy dual carriageway to the M6 motorway and housing blocking the view not only towards to the castle, but in all directions.

Caludon Farm and its owners were a significant presence in Alec's childhood. For instance, during May Day celebrations the Greens erected a flagpole in front of the castle for the local children to use and he spent much of his time as a boy playing by the ruins of what he and his friends thought of as 'our Castle'. Alec, who sadly passed away in 2009, said that he 'felt privileged' to live opposite a 'real' castle.

"We used to think that it was wonderful, smashing, the Castle. We were ignorant, we never had history books or facilities like that. You only went on what you had heard. We heard that there was a tunnel which went and cut across by Binley church to some old cottages there. It went to Stoneleigh and then to Kenilworth."

His terrace of cottages provided the only working class housing in the area, and in fact the only other house he remembered was Caludon Farmhouse. Interestingly, Alec recalled this being a 'horrible' grey, which suggests that it was cement rendered or coated in dull or weathered lime wash. An eighteenth-century farm house would normally have been constructed in brick in this part of Warwickshire and the appearance described suggests that it had been constructed out of older material that had needed to be rendered or lime washed, perhaps from the demolished material of the castle itself. Moreover, it is possible that much of it was a previous building dating from the castle period (see below).

Alec was also adamant that there was a 'windmill' in the farm complex. It had about five wooden slatted sails and stood next to a pond, round and deep, as one entered the farm site. Beyond were the castle, the house, the stables and the cow sheds. He remembered that the windmill was connected to a water tank and that it had been used to irrigate local fields. Rather than this being a conventional timber windmill for grinding corn, however, it is likely that the sails were erected on a pylon-type structure and drove a water pump. Fortunately Derek Priest remembers 'an iron windmill' beside the pond surrounded by trees and bushes, which he reckoned pumped water out of a spring to the farmhouse.[59] The location is significant as it is where water emerged immediately

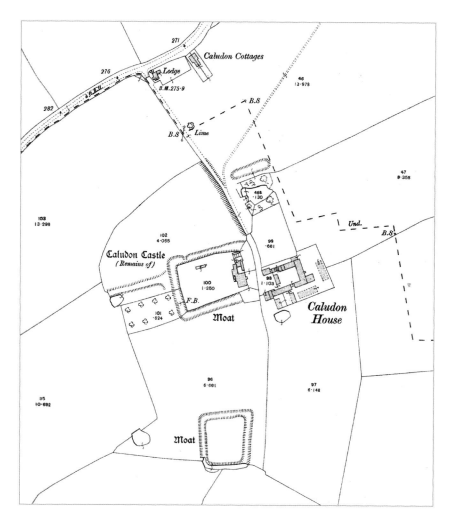

Fig 85 *Extract from OS 1:2500 map 1913*

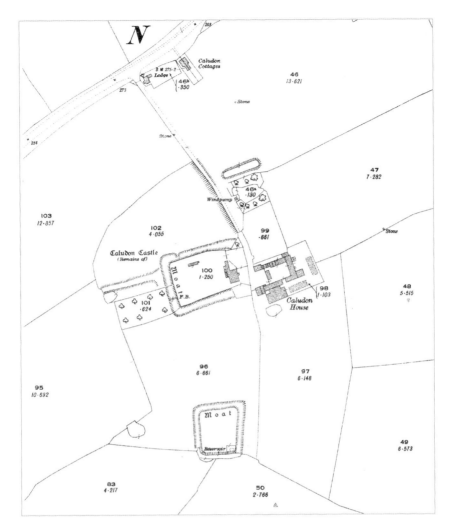

Fig 86 *Extract from OS 1:2500 map 1925*

below the former pool dam flowing eastwards as a small stream to join the Sowe. A water-filled pit can be seen on all early Ordnance Survey plans at this point and was possibly dug to form a small pond to intercept the flow (Figs 74, 79 and 85). The water at this low level needed to be pumped into a higher tank so that it could be conveniently used for irrigation and perhaps for other uses associated with the farm buildings.

The early large-scale 6-inch (1:10,560) and 25-inch (1:2500) scale Ordnance survey maps not only recorded such minutiae of the local farming practices, but eventually reflected the great changes that were wrought upon it in the twentieth century. The castle had long stood in the hinterland of a major English city, but no-one who had lived through earlier centuries could have imagined that Coventry, with its soaring spires visible in the distant west, would eventually advance so far during the century as to envelope the Caludon estate. Not satisfied with consuming Caludon,

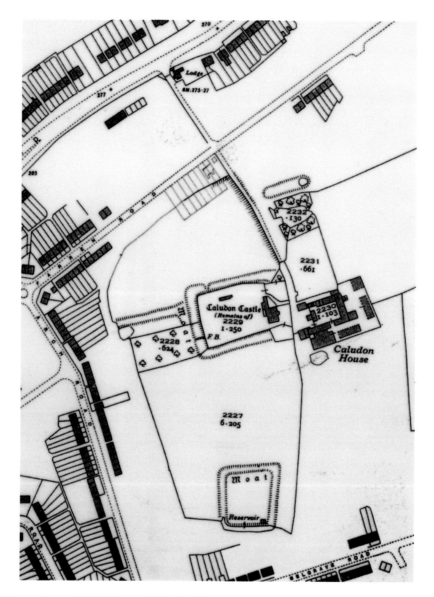

Fig 87 *Extract from OS 1:2500 map 1938 with Caludon now surrounded by new housing development*

the momentum, interrupted by the Second World War, carried the expanding wave farther outwards to absorb most of the fields of Sowe village, now Walsgrave-on-Sowe. At first the pace was slow and there was little or no change to the appearance of the Caludon area before the First World War (Figs 79 and 85). In the 1880s the edge of the city was still effectively at Gosford Green, except for two suburban islands at Stoke Green and Upper Stoke. By the outbreak of the Great War these outlying areas had become attached to the built-up area, but there was still a mile of open fields between them and Caludon. The terrace of houses built on the north side of Ansty Road in which the young Alec Flynn lived, was the only intrusion into a largely unaltered rural landscape (Figs 84 and 86). The phenomenal success of Coventry as an industrial city, manufacturing motor cycles, cars and machine tools was most clearly evident in the inter-war period. As a consequence, the mile of open countryside between Caludon Farm and built-up Coventry was swallowed up by the construction of many new streets, characteristically straight or slightly curved and predominantly residential. Most of the growth took place in the 1930s, the street network advancing in a salient along the Ansty Road. By 1939 the edge of the city had reached Caludon, Arch Road its new physical boundary, but any further progress was halted by the outbreak of the Second World War (Fig 87). Farren Road had been built up at its western end, but beyond Arch Road much of it was no more than dirt strip following the approved future line. A start had also been made on Belgrave Road to the south. The only unchanged view was eastward towards the fields of Sowe and Hungerley Farm.

In the late 1930s Harry Green made considerably more money through selling land for development than from farming and milk sales. He could not have anticipated the growth of Coventry when he purchased Caludon in 1917, but he was able to take advantage of the position of his farm as Coventry marched remorselessly towards Caludon. On 1 January 1937 he sold much of the western half of his land to Caludon Castle Estates Ltd (93.56 acres) for £21,000 (about £1m at today's prices).[60] He had already disposed of a block of land on the corner of Ansty Road and the newly laid out Hipswell Highway, Farren Road (west end), Oldham Avenue and Hocking Road (Fig 4). Roads to be developed by Caludon Castle Estates on this larger and irregularly shaped block of land included Arch Road, Hyde Road, Edyth Road, the western end of Belgrave Road and the northern ends of St Ives and St Austell Roads. It is possible that the photograph in Fig 88 was taken about this time when the garden about the ruins was still reasonably well tended.

Shortly afterwards Harry Green entered into an agreement with the Caludon Castle estate to sell the remainder of the farm (the eastern half), but this coincided with Coventry City Council's decision to create a public park centred on the castle remains and the two moats. Dedicating a public open space focused on a historical and archaeological site was enlightened thinking for the age, but the Council's action must have been helped by the new legal status of the castle ruins, its moat and adjacent dry pond site. In 1922 they were scheduled as ancient monuments by the Ministry of Works.[61]

A roughly square area of land, measuring 20.45 acres, was delineated within the remaining Caludon farmland focused on the castle moat. A link along the ancient medieval dam to Farren Road was added to provide the public entrance (Fig 4). The land was sold jointly by Harry Green and Caludon Castle Estates Ltd to the City Council on 28 January 1939, 'for the purposes of a public park or recreation ground,' the purchase price being £5000 (about £250,000 at today's prices).[62] The residual land encircling the park on the north, east and south was later developed for housing by the laying out of the east end of Farren Road, Bodmin Road and the east end of Belgrave Road,

When Harry Green sold the core of the historic estate to the Council in 1939 he was no longer resident at Caludon, having acquired Quarry House in Lutterworth Road, on the then south-eastern fringe of Nuneaton.[63] Harry lived at Quarry House until he died on 5 January 1958, aged 87.[64]

It appears that Harry had retired in about 1938 and found new tenants, a Mr and Mrs Bedding, who lived at Caludon Farm from 1938 to 1941.[65] After it was sold in January 1939 their landlords became Coventry Corporation. The outbreak of the war halted plans to convert the farm into a municipal park. With the policy of using all available land for food production, Caludon was converted into a pig farm with Mr Bedding acting as 'keeper', cooking the swill and feeding it to the pigs. Mrs Bedding remembered the night of the Blitz on 14 November 1940: 'We watched the flares being dropped by the Germans, till we were glad to get down one of the cellars.' The devastation being wrought on the centre of Coventry was clearly visible from Caludon fields, but fortunately there were no significant industrial targets in the vicinity to attract concentrated German bombing. Nevertheless, owing to poor bomb aiming and jettisoning of the payloads, hardly any area of Coventry escaped destruction and consequent injury or death.

> Injuries were recorded along Ansty Road. No. 50, No. 222, No. 251, No. 253, No. 256, No. 333. One person from Caludon Farm detained in Chadshunt Hall Auxiliary Hospital, Kineton. At 276 Ansty Road, married couple, Maurice William Lovell and Ethel Mary Lovell, died as a result of enemy action at their home.[66]

Although the war had brought a halt to civilian house building, the war effort and the strategic importance of Coventry as an industrial centre combined to bring in a huge influx of workers into the city to work in the factories. There was insufficient housing available, particularly as a result of the Blitz, and hostels, very similar in appearance and layout to army camps, were constructed on open land all around the fringes of the city. They were built under the control of the National Service Hostels Corporation formed in 1941 and two hostel sites were laid out in the vicinity of Caludon Farm. One was located on the east side of Clifford Bridge Road, a few hundred yards due east of the farm, and the other on the west side of the same road and south of the not yet completed Belgrave Road.[67] These hostels were opened in April 1943 and had a capacity of 840 workers.[68] Their sites are now part of the car parks fronting Walsgrave Hospital and the Westmorland Road estate respectively.

It is not known who lived at Caludon Farm during the remainder of the war to witness these hostels consuming more 'greenfield' sites, contributing to the eventual complete encirclement of the surviving farm land. This took place in the 1950s and 60s with the completion of the residential streets, Farren Road and Belgrave Road, and, in complete contrast, the development of Bodmin Road as an industrial estate. The intended conversion of Caludon Farm into a park, reduced to a rump of 20 acres (less than a tenth of its size in 1822), had been reprieved by the war and other more pressing priorities of post-war reconstruction. Aerial photographs, taken by under-employed RAF pilots in 1946, provide a revealing snap-shot of the area before the expansion of the city once more got under way (Fig 89).[69]

The castle moat can clearly be seen but, unlike its modern bare appearance, the ruins were surrounded by a number of ornamental trees which had been planted as part of the garden for the farmhouse. The ruins cast a long shadow across the site of the pool, the two windows showing as

Fig 88 *View of the garden and south side of ruined wall 1930*

bright slashes. There appears to be a thick dense hedge encircling the interior of the moat acting as a garden boundary. The farmhouse at the east end of the moat is distinguishable by its double pitched roof and its single-pitched extension. It is overwhelmed in scale by the large complex of farm buildings standing farther to the east. The dam that retained the former fish pond on the west side of the moat is clearly visible forming the north boundary of a rectangular orchard. The south moat can be picked out by a square circuit of trees and shrubs growing within it, little different from today.

The photograph shows how very nearly Caludon was engulfed by new housing in the late 1930s (Fig 89). The farm was literally being outflanked on both sides by the advancing edge of the city when it was brought to sudden halt by the war. As a consequence Caludon Farm was temporarily petrified into a half-urban and half-rural environment. Neither Farren Road nor Belgrave Road were finished, but ahead of the 'enemy lines' the war time worker's hostels have left their distinct imprint in the open fields. Most of the area between the farm buildings and Clifford Bridge Road was ploughed, except for a narrow strip of allotments stretching southwards from the rear of Farren Road along the park access road. The remainder of the farmland was under grass, presumably used as pasture, but a field immediately to the south of the farm buildings was laid out as a football field and a narrow strip of allotments ran along the rear of Arch Road. One of the most striking features of one of the photographs is a line of bomb craters just to the south of Hungerley Farm, but no bombs appear to have been dropped onto the Caludon fields.

After the war Gill Jones, a local resident, recalls that she and her friends would 'explore the ruins of the castle.'[70] She remembers that: "In those days (the 1940s) there was no water in the moat and

Fig 89 *RAF vertical aerial photograph over Caludon showing one football pitch and the fields to the east ploughed for crops, 15 January 1946*

it was possible to get under the ruins. There were grilles that had been broken up and it was possible to walk three or four yards under the Castle."[71] At this time it appears that the tracery in the windows of the castle ruins still survived (Fig 88). Caludon Farm was still just operating and was occupied by the Pullet twins from whom Gill would purchase eggs and the castle ruins were kept as a farm garden. Its land had shrunken further, however, for by 1949 an aerial photograph shows the field between the moats had been converted by the Council into another football field (Fig 90). This explains the employment of Mr Prescott, the 'Parky,' remembered by Gill Jones as someone 'you never crossed'.[72] She also recalled the allotments that were reached 'from a path going down a hill

Fig 90 *RAF vertical aerial photograph over Caludon with another football pitch laid out 10 May 1946; the site of the future industrial estate in Bodmin Road is still under arable*

alongside a spinney and walking over a wooden bridge.'[73] The spinney had grown in the pit immediately below the former pool dam, mentioned above, and the footbridge crossed the small outflow stream that at that time ran eastwards. This open grassed area is now devoid of any feature, the pit filled in and the stream culverted.

Another local resident, John Burge, who lived at Arch Road, remembers that in the 1950s: "There were cattle grazing in the rear of Farren Road, and there were farm buildings and a big Dutch Barn."[74] He too took his chances in trying to raid the gardens: "It was a challenge...when the apples and plums were ripening...and many boys were chased out." The sloping sides of the dried up moat provided hours of fun as John and his friends raced up and down the bank; "Many boys fell off and had minor injuries." (Fig 91). It is clear from these reminiscences that in the 1950s the miniscule Caludon Farm was still functioning in some way within its physically constrained environment.

Bob Nash adds further details on the park in the post-war era.[75] Summarising his words, there were two sets of swings at the rear of a corrugated iron 'Dutch' barn for younger and older children and the farm buildings were used by the Council for storing equipment. At this time the east side of the park, separated by a fence, was still used for growing crops. The area between the main moat and Farren Road was an area of rough pasture called 'Pig Field' and was used by local residents to build two bonfires for Bonfire Night, which brought the community together.

Electoral registers record who lived at Caludon Farm in its last two decades.[76]

1945	No voters registered	
1946	Mary and Alexander Brown	Caludon Castle Farm
	Vera D Cartwright	
1947	Mary, Alexander and James Brown	Caludon Castle Farm
	Alfred E and Donald E H Knight	
1948	Mary Alexander and James Brown	Caludon Castle Farm
1949	No voters registered	
1950-1	Thomas E Lake and Sylvia E Lake	Flat Caludon Castle Farm
1953-4	Thomas E and Sylvia Lake	No 1 Flat
	Frederick T and Hannah A Upton	No 2 Flat
1955-7	Thomas E and Sylvia E Lake	No 1 Flat
	Donald H Wild	No 1 Flat
	Frederick T and Hannah A Upton	No 2 Flat
1958	Frederick T and Hannah A Upton	No 1 Flat
	Brian D Fox and Hazel I Fox	No 2 Flat
1959-60	Ernest and Mabel A Insley	Flat 1
	John and Sheila M Wilson	Flat 2
1964	Mabel A Insley	Flat 1
	John, Sheila and Derek Wilson	Flat 2
1965-6	John, Sheila and Derek Wilson	Flat 2
1967	no record of Caludon Farm	

It appears that as in the late 1940s the farm house was divided into two separate dwellings, the main double-roofed house, later designated Flat 1, and the smaller north wing, Flat 2. According to Brian Fox, between 1955 and 1958 the house was shared between the Uptons, Flat 2 and Brian Fox and his wife, Hazel, Flat 2. The electoral roll, however, has the Fox's registered for one year only in 1958. Mr Upton worked for the Parks Department as a driver. Brian Fox drew a plan of the house, which reveals some curious features (Fig 92). The Uptons did not occupy the ground floor, but lived on the first floor and presumably the attic storey. The ground floor contained three horse stalls and a tack room, an unusual arrangement for a farmhouse, these functions usually contained in a separate stable block. The remainder of the ground floor had a 'tea room used by workers' with a cooking range and another room whose use is unknown, as it was boarded up. Unless the stable and tack room were installed at a later stage after the abandonment of part of the farmhouse, there is a possibility that the building began its life as the stable block to the demolished Caludon Castle

Fig 91 *Photo of local boys on their bicycles in front of Caludon Castle c.1956; from left to right: Colin Dunstan, David Hillier, Malcolm Taylor, Andrew Hillier, Paul Copsey and Alan Huxtable. Photo by Dr Bob Nash*

(pre 1748). Stable blocks often contained accommodation for grooms on an upper floor and it would not have been difficult to re-use such a building, concentrating the living space on the first floor and in a new attic storey, created by constructing a new double pile roof in place of a tall single pile span. More accommodation was provided by the smaller range attached on the north side, but it is not known if this had been an earlier building. When Brian Fox lived in this part, it consisted of a living room and kitchen on either side of the stairs rising from a small entrance vestibule. On the first floor there was a bedroom above the living room and another bedroom with a bathroom over the kitchen. There was a separate pantry at the rear (west side) and a serviceable cellar, location unknown. When Harry James Green completed his census return in 1911 he listed twelve rooms, which would have included the kitchen, but not rooms such as bathrooms and service rooms. Six rooms have been accounted for on Fig 92, leaving six to be fitted into the first floor and attic of the larger part of the house. In Brian Fox's time the 'Dutch barn', a corrugated iron structure, and another brick barn were still standing, but the other farm buildings had been reduced to 'a pile of bricks and rubble'. Part of the south arm of the 'U' layout had already been demolished by June 1953 and the remainder, except for the 'Dutch' barn and the so called 'Cromwell's barn' (probably eighteenth century in date), by June 1959.[77] In March 1962 only 'Cromwell's barn' was still standing (Fig 93).[78]

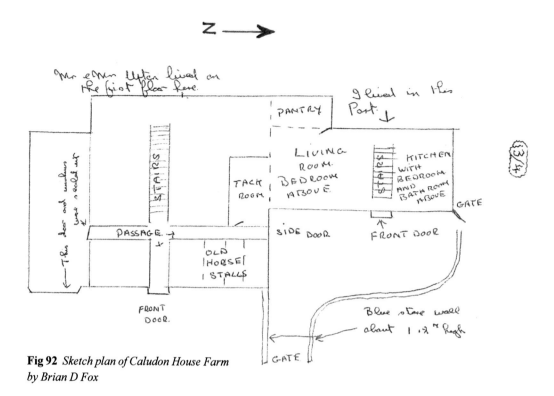

Fig 92 *Sketch plan of Caludon House Farm by Brian D Fox*

By the 1960s the city had been rebuilt and the economy was growing sufficiently strongly for the Council to implement fully its pre-war plan for the park. Tradition has it that the farmhouse was demolished in 1964, but the Victoria County History states that in this year it was in a poor state of repair and awaiting demolition.[79] A colour photograph taken about this time just catches the house on the extreme left (Fig 94). According to the electoral roll it was still standing in 1966, the Wilsons continuing to occupy Flat 1 of the farmhouse (see above). This however contradicts the evidence from a 1962 aerial photograph that shows only Flat 1 standing, the large part of the farmhouse.[80] It is possible that the electoral roll is not accurate in failing to record their move into Flat 2. If it was not updated annually then it cannot be taken literally that the remainder of the farmhouse was demolished some time in late 1966 or early 1967 when it finally disappears from the electoral roll.

After the Council demolished the farmhouse it set about integrating all its twenty acres. The former arable fields, not cultivated for some time, were divided between the new park and land set aside for an industrial estate based on Bodmin Road. It was decided to level all the rough ground that lay to the west north and east of the main moat, but unfortunately this operation also removed the mediaeval fish pond dam and remains of the orchard enclosure adjacent to it. The garden features on the moat platform also disappeared. The site of the former medieval fish pond was too extensive to fill in, although the pit and on the east side of the dam was filled in with the loss of its trees. It is a pity that the greater awareness today of historic landscapes that have been incorporated into municipal parks had not yet emerged in the late 1960s and early 1970s.

Fig 93 *The last remaining farm building at Caludon, locally named 'Cromwell's Barn', in the mid 1960s*

Fig 94 *View of the castle ruin and a glimpse of Caludon Farmhouse*

Fig 95 *The new Caludon Castle School*

About this time, Billy Butlin, the owner of the famous holiday camps, provided funding for a changing room complex to be built on the site of the recently demolished farm buildings. This survived until the mid-1990s when a vehicle was deliberately driven into the building, necessitating its demolition.

The park, reduced by a coincidence to the same size as the deer enclosure (*Franchehay*) given in the 1279-80 survey, was only a small fragment, although the most important, of the original medieval park and demesne (see Chapter 1). Fortunately the Caludon name was allowed to carry on as part of its former estate by the establishment of Caludon Castle School a few hundred yards to the south. The site corresponds with the River Sowe river meadow originally called *Lake Meadow*, taken into the medieval park and first mentioned in 1250 (Fig 19). Caludon Castle School was one of the first secondary schools to be built by the City Council after the Second World War and was opened in 1954 with places for 1,150 boy pupils. Its location reflects the rapid growth of the city in the Caludon area both before and after the Second World War. As a result of the educational reforms the school was converted into a mixed comprehensive. In 2008 the new school was opened after being completely rebuilt at a cost of £24 million and became an Academy in 2013 (Fig 95). The inclusion of the history of Caludon Castle and its manor in the school curriculum for the first time in 2010 was a significant step for the school to make, introducing local history and archaeology into the classroom. This, it is hoped, will instil an appreciation of the historic value of the original Caludon Castle site and 800 years of its history as a manor.

Additional statutory protection was given to the standing ruins by their listing as a building of architectural and historic interest on 5 February 1955. The ruined wall of the great chamber block was given the highest grade (I) in recognition of its importance. The ruins continued to attract artists who had long recognised its aesthetic and antiquarian value (Fig 96). The medieval pool bed had

Fig 96 *Pen and ink of Caludon Castle ruin with a rare glimpse of the farmhouse on the left hand side c.1950s*

Fig 97 *The former dam from the original pool bed, which now carries the park access road 2013*

Fig 98 *Oblique aerial photograph of Caludon Park and immediate area 2001; the moat platform of the upper moat is clearly visible, the moat itself overgrown with trees.*

been scheduled from 1922 along with the main moat, but on 4 Jan 1996 the pool site was descheduled (Fig 97). In compensation, however, the earlier south moat was scheduled on 7 February 2000 in recognition of its intrinsic worth as a medieval moat and its likely connection with the main castle site. The aerial photograph of the park was taken in the following year (Fig 98).

One of the authors, George Demidowicz, when heading the Conservation and Archaeology Team at Coventry City Council, had become aware of the deterioration of the castle wall as a result of vandalism and the effect of weather. In 2004 about £30,000 was spent by Coventry City Council on repairing the ruins, removing vegetation and graffiti and consolidating the important protective capping. Local people will remember the scaffolding that was erected in order to carry out this work, but are probably less aware of the defensive measures that were needed to prevent the nightly attack on the wall. Intruders prised open the corrugated metal sheeting to climb the scaffolding, new stonework repairs were dismantled and ladders removed and thrown into neighbouring gardens. The situation became critical, the contract approaching the point of abandonment, but the project was saved by the instigation of night patrols, high corrugated sheeting, tarred at all the joints to prevent intrusion. We wryly called the events - the 'Second Siege of Caludon', not aware at the time that no Civil War attack had ever taken place. It cannot be renamed the 'First Siege', however, in view of the new information that has come to light on the attack by Anne Berkeley in about 1545-8, attempting to remove her tenants (see Chapter 3).

On a more positive note there are many local people who care about Caludon Castle and its park. A local group, the Friends of Caludon Park, has been established to encourage the improvement of the park. The establishment of the Caludon Society, the vision of this book's publisher, John Clarke OBE, will do much to continue this renewed sense of appreciation, promoting, protecting and preserving the unique history of Caludon. The Council prepared a Management Plan covering the period 2011-2012 and raised about £150,000, which was spent on an

Fig 99 *The new plaque in the park depicting the history of Caludon Castle and its lords 2013*

extension of the play area, a new grass screed car park and the resurfacing of the access drive across the dam (completed June 2013). The Friends of Caludon Park contributed £50,000 as a result of their successful Lottery bid to the 'Changing Spaces' fund (part of the 'Big Lottery Fund'), which in 2012 paid for an interpretation board on the history of Caludon Castle, already incorporating the new findings from this book (Fig 99) and new gates at Farren Road and Belgrave Road (Fig 100).

Fig 100 *The new park gates at the Farren Road entrance 2013*

Last but not least, John Clarke, as chairman of the Caludon Society, stands out for his major contribution in raising the profile of Caludon Castle. His long-held passion for its history since childhood is well known, but he has also translated this enthusiasm and energy into action by publishing this book, which he first started 45 years ago. It is to be hoped that it will serve as the first definitive history of Caludon for many years to come.

Chapter 7 – NOTES

1   Clifford, II/6/3d; Clifford W (L) 1/7
2   Warwick RO, St Michaels Tithe Apportionment, 1846; Coventry City Council, Historic Environment Record
3   Dictionary of National Biography, Charles Whittingham (1767-1840)
4   ibid., Charles Whittingham (1795-1876)
5   *Coventry Herald*, 17, 24 February 1826
6   Binley Parish Registers; Sowe parish Registers
7   *Topographical Dictionary of England*, Vol 1, (1835) 983
8   Cambridgeshire Record Office, Huntingdon, papers relating to Drivers Trust, 1832/256
9   1841 Census
10 Coleshill Parish Registers
11 1851 Census
12 1815 Sale Particulars relating to Callowden Farm, Clifford, W (L) 1/7; this payment has its origins in the thirteenth century so that tithes could be collected locally to support the chapel.
13 Warwick RO, CR2582/20/1-3
14 *Gentleman's Magazine*, Vol 189 (Oct 1850) 448;
15 Cambridge University Alumni, 1795-1850, website
16 *Directory of Warwickshire*, 1850
17 SBTRO ER/91/4; ER5/27
18 ibid.
19 *Worcester Chronicle*, 28 May 1862; *Morning Post*, 28 May 1862; *Worcester Journal* 31 May 1862.
20 Birmingham Central Library, Archives, 193323; Coventry City Council deed no 1174, Abstract of Title reciting pre-nuptial agreement of 20 May 1862 and settlement of 23 Nov 1866.
21 1861 Census; only 24 acres recorded against Caludon House, most likely an error.
22 *Leicester Chronicle*, 10 Feb 1872
23 1871 Census
24 *Kelly's Directory of Warwickshire*, (1880); VCH Warwick, Vol 8, 300
25 Binley Parish Registers
26 op. cit, Kelly's Directory (1880); *Kelly's Directory of Warwickshire*, (1892)
27 Census, 1851, 1861, 1871, 1881, 1891, 1901, 1911. 'Real Ale History of Pubs in Coventry Area, The Craven Arms, High Street, Coventry,' ancestry.com website
28 1891 census; *Coventry Times*, 1 Oct 1879, advertisement
29 *London Gazette*, 14 June 1862
30 OS plans 1:500 scale, 2nd edition, 1905, OS 1:2500 scale, 1904; Coventry Directory, (1874-5). 31 (William Aviss at 90 Gosford Street)
31 *Gloucester Citizen*, advertisements, April, May, June, December 1893, October, November, December 1894,
32 TNA BT 34/1618/63229; Grace's Guide to British Industrial History, website for Arno Motor Co
33 Grace's Guide to British Industrial History, website for Hotchkiss; CA, PA 787/8/1-14, PA1508/14/4
34 Grace's Guide to British Industrial History, website for Morris
35 *Coventry Evening Telegraph*, 22 April 1892
36 OS 1st edition 1:2500 scale plan
37 *Coventry Evening Telegraph*, 2 Nov 1894, 17 Jan 1903
38 op. cit., Hodges
39 Coventry Evening Telegraph, 25 July 1899; 1891 and 1901 Census, Wyken; Wyken House was situated in the area of the present Wordsworth and Coleridge Roads
40 Leamington Spa Courier, 12 Aug 1876
41 Coventry Evening Telegraph, 16 June 1902
42 ibid; 4 June 1902, 9, 10 Aug 1901
43 *Coventry Evening Telegraph*, 16 June 1902
44 Reminiscences of Harold Green, 1899-1971 Farmer, Coventry University Open Collections, Curve Resource website, Richardson Transcripts, no CT10 (subsequently Harold Green)
45 Kelly's Directory of Warwickshire, 1908
46 1911 Census
47 op. cit., Harold Green; this statement contradicts his sister, Lydia's, memoirs, who stated that there were six sons and three daughters; see n. 55 below.
48 1901 Census
49 *Derby Mercury*, 2 June 1669
50 *Bath Chronicle and Weekly Gazette*, 26 Feb, 1880; *Gloucester Citizen*, 4 Oct, 1904; Census 1871, 1881
51 *Kelly's Directory of Warwickshire*, 1912; op. cit., Coventry City Council Deed no 1174, Abstract of Title 1937
52 1911 Census
53 National Probate Calendar, 1858-1966, ancestry.com website
54 op. cit., Coventry CC deed no 1174
55 Lydia Mary Skelton, 'Caludon Farm in the Parish of Wyken,' private collection.
56 op. cit., Harold Green
57 *Directory for Warwickshire*, 1928
58 The Young Boy Who Grew Up In The Shadow of 'Our Castle' - an interview with Alec Flynn conducted by John Clarke.
59 'Interview with Derek Priest of Hermitage Road with Bob Nash,' private collection

Chapter 7 – NOTES

60 op. cit., Coventry CC, deed no 1174

61 ibid., letter from HM Office of Works to H. J Green, 6 Feb 1932

62 op. cit., Coventry CC deed no 1174

63 Quarry House was located on the south side of Lutterworth Road east of the junction with Golf Drive and Bulkington Lane. It survived until the early 1970s.

64 *London Gazette*, 11 Nov 1958

65 Private collection, letter from Mrs L Bedding to Mr E N Woodbridge, 29 November 1980

66 Trevor Harkin, *Coventry 14th/15th November 1940 Casualties, Awards and Accounts (2011)*, 95

67 OS maps, scale 1,2500, 1952; 1:10,560, 1955

68 Kenneth Richardson, *Twentieth-century Coventry*, (1972) 93-4, 222; Virtual Museum Willenhall, Coventry, website – Clifford Bridge Road Hostel

69 English Heritage, the National Monuments Record, 3C/TUD/UK10PART2 20 Dec '45:F/12//90SQDN (A3), frame 5143; RAF3G/TUD/UK12/28, frame 5206, 15 Jan 1946.

70 'Recollections of the Park' Gill Jones recalled to Bob Nash, (2008) typescript, private collection.

71 Probably an exaggeration, as the thickness of the wall being described is about two metres.

72 English Heritage, National Monuments Record, RAF/541/256, 10 May 1949, frame 256; op. cit., Gill Jones

73 Bob Nash recalls the same 'crude wooden bridge over which you went to the allotments'. 'Recollections of Caludon Park by Bob Nash, Chair of Friends of Caludon Park,' private collection.

74 John Burge, 'My Memories of Caludon Park' (2008), private collection

75 op. cit., Bob Nash, 'Recollections'

76 Electoral Register, Walsgrave Ward, no 3 District and Oc District, Ansty Road, Wyken East Ward, District Oc, Ansty Rd

77 English Heritage, National Monuments Record, RAF/5OP/225, 9 June 1953, frame 0039; RAF/58/2947, 17 June 1959, frame 0398, F22

78 English Heritage, National Monuments Record, RAF/543/1698, 15 March 1962, frames 0050-51, F 21

79 VCH, Warwick, Vol 8, 122

80 op. cit., note 74

C H A P T E R   8

Caludon Castle
~ the Buildings

aludon Castle, as recounted in previous chapters, has enjoyed a long and eventful history. It is a frustrating fact, however, that this well-chronicled story took place in buildings that have vanished from sight except for a single standing remnant. This forlorn wall is insufficient to reconstruct the appearance of the whole castle, although it does provide evidence for the architecture of the building in its immediate vicinity (Figs 101 and 102). There is fortunately a moat, well preserved, which at least helps define the wider extent of buildings on the platform, but only in this so called 'defended' area – many more lay beyond the moat (Fig 103). For some local manor houses or mansions which have entirely disappeared, there are at least plans, drawings and paintings, but for Caludon there are none.[1] In fact the earliest known illustration of Caludon dates from about 1800, when it was no more than the wall we see today, albeit with the tracery in the two windows still intact (Figs 61, 62 and 63). The assumed decline and decay of the fabric that took place in the seventeenth and early eighteenth century, and its demolition before 1748, predated the interest in 'romantic' or picturesque ruins that arose during the latter half of the eighteenth century.

The standing wall was interpreted over a century ago as belonging to a medieval hall range, with an undercroft on the ground floor and a hall situated above (Figs 104 and 105). Without evidence to the contrary this would seem to be a reasonable interpretation. Richard Morris, the country's leading expert on medieval architecture, has examined early photographs that show the tracery intact and has dated the upper windows to the 'mature Decorated' period (1320-1350). He describes them as consisting of:[2]

> Two lights with trefoil-cusped archlets and a quatrefoil ogee reticulation unit in the head. A plain transom without archlets is set below the halfway point of the lights, suggesting that the larger area of the lights above it was glazed, with the head; below the transom the window was presumably grilled and shuttered.

The two smaller windows below in the undercroft is described as consisting of

> Two short lights divided by a plain transom, the lights with trefoil-cusped archlets and a squashed trefoil in the head.

189

Fig 101 *The ruined wall of the great chamber block from the south 2013*

Good examples of a 'hall and undercroft' locally are St Marys Guildhall, Coventry (complete, c. 1350) and the Great Hall at Kenilworth (ruinous, 1373-1380).

An intriguing feature is the chimney built into the thickness of the wall between the two windows. Its opening is not at chamber level, as would be expected, but within the undercroft, where it has had to be consolidated in recent times with brickwork. Undercrofts were normally used for storage, with relatively small windows to maintain low temperatures and aid security. It would be unusual for them to be heated. This fact, therefore, casts doubt on the interpretation of the ground storey as a storage area, particularly since its windows were also elaborately traceried and quite large in size. It is more likely, therefore, that the ground floor was used for accommodation rather than storage. With the window sills now level with the ground, more akin to doorways, the original floor level lies buried below an accumulation of rubble and soil.

New evidence on the plan of the buildings came to light as a result of the first geophysical survey carried out on the moat platform in 1985 (Fig 106). Myk Flitcroft carried out an electrical resistivity survey as part of his BA dissertation.[3] For the first time foundations of buildings, other than the surviving wall, were revealed, their location concentrated on the west side of the moat. The wall formed part of a building, which he called Complex 1, orientated east-west, but attached on its

Fig 102 *The ruined wall from the north taken from within the moat 2011; the scars of the three buttresses between the windows are clearly visible*

Fig 103 *One of the best preserved parts of the moat on the southern side 2013*

southern side was another large building (Complex 2), orientated north-south, which included a small square structure in its south-eastern corner, interpreted as a porch (Complex 3). Flitcroft also identified another building immediately to the east of Complex1, which was divided into two by a wall that continued farther eastwards and abruptly stopped (Complex 4). He interpreted an area of high resistance near the edge of the moat as part of a curtain wall that he envisaged entirely surrounded the castle along the inside of the moat, but a subsequent geophysical survey has demonstrated this was part of a circular footpath laid out when the moat platform formed a garden to Caludon Farm (see below).

Flitcroft was the first to interpret the surviving wall as part of a chamber rather than a hall range, assigning the latter to the building attached on its south side together with its porch (Complexes 2 and 3).[4] The reasoning behind this conclusion lies in the standard layout of a medieval hall, in which the 'lower end' contained the draughty entrance with its screens passage, separating the hall from the service buildings such as the kitchen. The opposite ('upper') end of the hall, the location of the Lord's table, usually led directly to the family chambers.

In view of advances in geophysical survey that had taken place since 1985, it was considered worthwhile to commission another survey in 2008. This was carried out in June 2008 by Northamptonshire Archaeology under the direction of Ian Fisher.[5] The results of the electrical resistivity were remarkable for the clarity of the plan that was revealed (Fig 107). The broad form of the buildings in the 1985 survey was confirmed, but the sharpness of the image produced was in great contrast to the earlier blurred outlines of walls. It is clear that over a large area of the moat the walls lie relatively close to the surface to have been detected by the resistivity meter. Furthermore much of the demolition rubble must have been cleared off the platform, as any significant spread of material left where it fell would have hidden the walls below from the detection by the meter or interfered with the readings. Demolition rubble does not usually travel far in the age of horse-drawn carts and manual labour. The site of the buildings was cleared, but apparently the rubble was only moved to the edge of the moat where it was tipped into the eastern arm of the moat, a convenient 'skip'. As a consequence, this area has much archaeological potential as an underground 'storeroom' of the former upstanding remains of the castle buildings. It is hoped that in due course the site can be excavated.

A resistivity survey was also carried out on the south moat platform. An irregular shaped area of high resistance was detected but the cause cannot be satisfactorily explained.

A magnetometer survey was also carried out at both moats, the machine sensitive to the presence of iron. It clearly picked out the line of a path that once circulated around the perimeter of the moat, but recently buried. It also found concentrations at the east end of the platform in the area of the farm buildings and may indicate the site of cellars full of rubble and debris. No meaningful results were found on the south moat.

Fig 104 *Drawing by Myk Flytcroft of the north elevation of the ruined castle wall emphasising the scars of the three missing buttresses 1986*

Fig 105 *Drawing of south elevation of the ruined wall by Myk Flitcroft 1986*

The plan of the buildings found in each survey is closely comparable (Figs 106 and 107):

```
1985...........................................2008
Complex 1 ...............................building D (western three-quarters)
Complex 2 ...............................building A
Complex 3 ...............................building C
Complex 4 ...............................building D (eastern quarter, composed of two compartments)
```

In both surveys a major wall was found running eastwards dividing the eastern end of D into two and continuing onwards to finish abruptly. The position of this wall is more clearly seen in the later survey as corresponding with the whole of the south side of the remainder of building D, although of varying thickness. Without archaeological excavation it is difficult to determine any phasing of the buildings. Was building A constructed before building B? Was the porch (building C) built as the same time as the building A? The wall that divides the east end of D may have been constructed first and D second, but equally the sequence could be reversed. These unanswered questions beg for a series of carefully-placed archaeological trenches to be dug.

The walls of building A show clear signs of buttresses (Fig 107), which would have been required to support the principal trusses of a roof. There were also buttresses on the porch and on building D west. The north face of the standing wall has three vertical scars between the windows indicating where buttresses have subsequently been removed. The 2008 survey also detected the south wall of A, but also picked up a wall continuing south from the porch and another continuing the line of south wall westwards, both ending abruptly. A stub of a wall in building A may indicate the position of the screen that helped keep drafts out of the main hall.

The sharper image produced by the 2008 survey has not altered the earlier interpretation of the plan. Most of D is regarded as belonging to the chamber range and all of A with its porch C to the hall. The chamber range had at least four windows, as visible in the wall today, and there is room for at least another window bay westwards. With a buttress on the west wall there must have been two windows lighting this end and another two on either side of the buttress on the south wall (Fig 107). The generous windows with their tracery on the ground storey would not be inconsistent with the use of this level as another series of private apartments, rather than as an undercroft for storage.

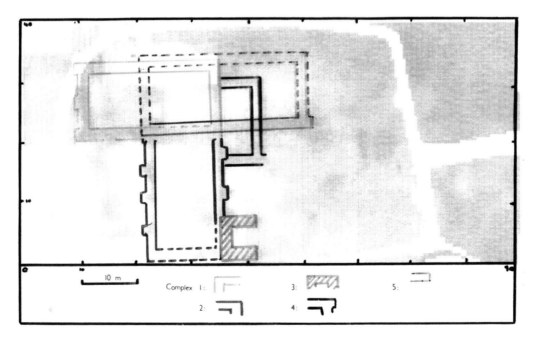

Fig 106 *Plan of resistivity survey by Myk Flitcroft 1986*

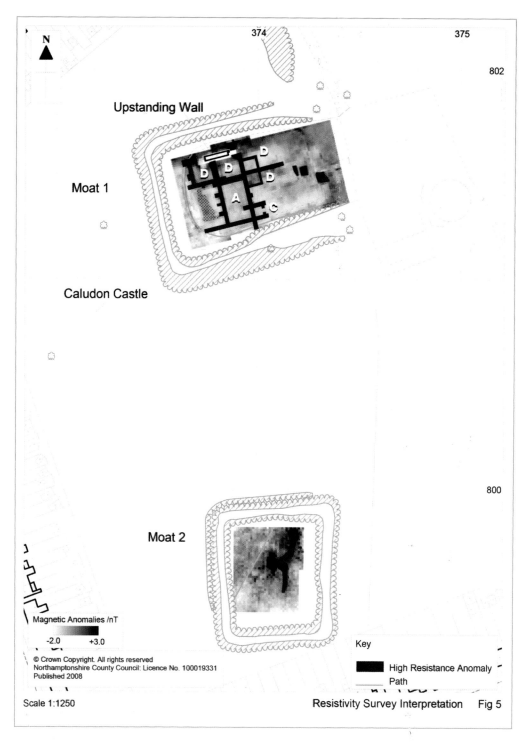

Fig 107 *Plan of resistivity survey by Northamptonshire Archaeology 2008*

The existence of a chapel at Caludon is well documented and its conventional position in a medieval manor house was close or attached to the private chambers for the convenience of the lord and family. With windows on the west elevation, the likely location of the chapel was at the opposite east end and the wall that divides the east end of D into two compartments may have been its south limit. The loss of its other walls, if in this position, cannot be explained. The chapel may have been located on the ground floor, as has been interpreted in the 3-D reconstruction, but some manorial chapels were confined to an upper storey with the ground storey used for other purposes.

The windows in the hall, placed between the buttresses, would have numbered at least two on the east and four on west wall. There may have been a window on the south side of the porch belonging to the service range. The interception by the south compartment of building D (east) of the northernmost bay of the hall's east elevation suggests that D may have been constructed later, blocking this window and resulting in the demolition of the possible chapel, but it cannot be certain. D might, in fact, have predated the hall and chapel. With the porch on the south side of the hall, it would be normal to find attached to this end service rooms and buildings such as the kitchen, buttery (originally a barrel store) and pantry. The site is confined with the edge of the moat close by, but there is sufficient room, as indicated by the truncated walls, for such rooms or buildings to be located immediately to the south and west.

The remainder of the platform, between a half and a third of the east end, provided room for more buildings which may have been ranged with their 'back' to the moat around an outer courtyard, entered by a gatehouse from a bridge across the eastern arm of the moat. They have left no trace in the ground detectable by the resistivity survey, and, as service buildings, they may have been less substantially built, perhaps timber framed, with low stone plinths. There is a possibility that some were constructed of stone, but that their foundations were subsequently entirely robbed out and back-filled with soil.

The two concentrations of high readings at the east end of the moat probably relate to the foundations of the later Caludon Farm and its filled-in cellars.

The two geophysical surveys have significantly added to our knowledge of the layout and appearance of Caludon Castle, but there is yet much unknown. Nevertheless the plan revealed is sufficiently certain to have been used as the starting point for 3-D bird's-eye reconstructions (Figs 26, 29 and 30). These have required a good deal of thought, the consideration of parallels elsewhere in the country and no little speculation, but the exercise has been worthwhile as most people interested in the history of Caludon Castle ask what the buildings looked like. Their actual appearance may not have exactly resembled these skilfully drawn reconstructions, but they provide an impression of the appearance of Caludon before it was drastically altered at the end of the sixteenth century.

In the remainder of this chapter the relevant evidence will be gathered together to establish the main building phases of Caludon Castle. These are summarised in Fig 108 for guidance, but a more complicated phasing, not easy to represent cartographically, is described below. Phase A relates to the earliest period on the south moat site, Phase B to the castle on the present (north) moat and Phase C to the farmhouse built later on the same moat platform

Phase A1 **soon after 1217**

Stephen de Segrave, Lord of Caludon, constructs a hunting lodge and manor farm to serve his park and demesne land and surrounds it with a fashionable moat. It lies on the north slope of the 'Caludon hill' overlooking a shallow valley whose stream flows eastwards into the Sowe, later dammed to make a fish pond. The buildings could include a hall, agricultural buildings such as a barn, and accommodation for the demesne workers. It is not known whether any of these were built of the stone rather than timber-frame.

Phase A2 **before 1239**

Stephen de Segrave constructs a chapel on the same half-acre moated site, possibly also using stone.[6]

Phase B1 **1305-1350s**

John de Segrave is granted a licence by Edward I to crenellate his house at Caludon in 1305.[7] Such a licence should not be seen literally as permission to build a castle and was often sought by the lord to confirm his status while usefully providing revenue to the royal treasury. Nevertheless the licence to crenellate has been interpreted as reflecting a major change at Caludon involving the abandonment of the first moated site and the construction of a larger one-acre moat, beside the existing fish pond. Work may have begun before 1305 on digging the moat and the construction of a new manor house complex. It is possible that the hall (Fig 107 building A) was constructed first with some service buildings and a modest solar (private chamber) block, the latter replaced between 1320 and 1350 with an extensive two storey-chamber range, of which only a fragment of the north wall survives today (Fig 107 building D (west)). Apart from the major earthwork of the moat, only modest expressions of fortification may have been used on the buildings themselves such as crenellated parapets. There is no evidence at Caludon of curtain walls and towers. Other examples are Baddesley Clinton, Warks, and Haddon Hall, Derbyshire. The gate house, appearance unknown, could also have been embellished with pseudo architectural features of a castle entrance, even though its principal purpose was to control entry rather than repel attackers. It is a cause for debate that it incorporated a drawbridge. The passage across the moat was most probably provided by a permanent timber or stone bridge. All this was sufficient, however, to describe Caludon in 1325 as a *fortalice*, a fortlet or fortified manor house.[8]

Phase B2 **1380s**

William Bagot, ward of the young Sir John Mowbray and his brother, Thomas, despoils (asset-strips) the Caludon estate, including the carrying away of a building situated within the moat and another two beyond the bridge.[9] The case against William Bagot confirms that buildings had been constructed outside the moat, perhaps opposite the bridge in the position of the later Caludon farm buildings.

Phase B3 **1390s-1500 Gradual decline.**

The Mowbrays do not use Caludon as a principal residence and it is left in the hands of administrators or leased out. It is unlikely that any major investment in buildings takes place.

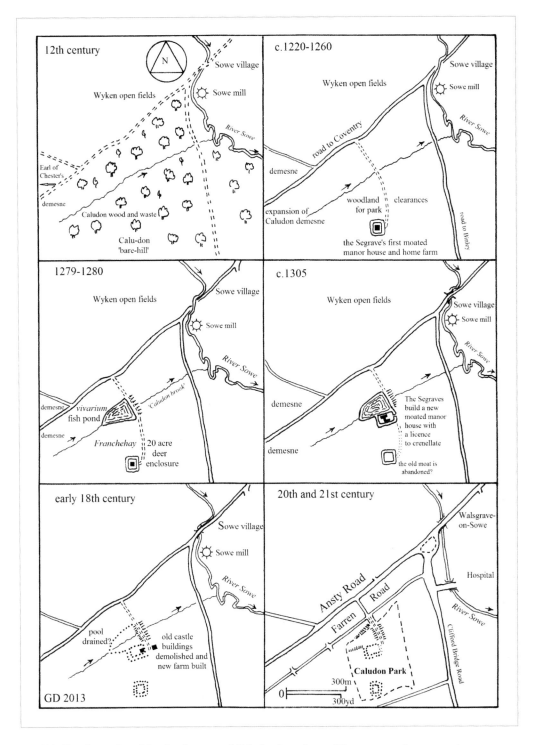

Fig 108 *Six-phase plan of the development of Caludon from the twelfth century to the present day*

Phase B4 Before 1514 Renewal and refurbishment

Thomas Try is granted a lease of Caludon in 1514 by Maurice Berkeley and his mother, Isabel.[10] Thomas was a kinsman and trusted servant, and the lease was a reward for his having previously at great cost 'built and edified many houses on the site of the manor.' Unfortunately we do not know exactly what this work entailed, but it is likely that after many years of neglect Try made the castle habitable and more comfortable. The work may also have involved renewing or rebuilding some of the service buildings.

Phase B5 1579-1590s Caludon castle reconstructed

By the 1570s Caludon had become a favourite residence of Henry Berkeley and Katherine, his wife, and between 1579 and 1580 a major phase of refurbishment and reconstruction began at Caludon lasting perhaps six or seven years, the last three of which the Berkeleys spent at John Hales' house at Whitefriars in Coventry. Buildings both within and out of the moat were affected, including the porters lodge, 'the building towards the great poole on the northwest part of Callowdon house', the brewing house and stables. Many of the old roofs are taken down and so far altered that the whole house is said to have been 'moulded and made new.'[11] The fourteenth century manor house was probably regarded as old-fashioned at this time, particularly the hall as a principal living space.

The classically-inspired architecture of the Renaissance is also in vogue. Masonry chimneys with elaborate patterned brickwork and large mullioned windows, often in projecting bays, pour light into the new and refurbished mansions of the aristocracy. At Caludon the hall range possibly undergoes a radical alteration by inserting a floor to create a new first storey. Smaller, more flexibly-used rooms can partition the new floors, including an attic storey in the former roof space. None of these above-ground alterations would necessarily show in the earlier foundations found in the geophysical surveys (Figs 106 and 107). The chamber block was also altered, possibly in this phase or later, as one of the earliest views of the surviving wall shows the windows blocked with masonry on the exterior, rendered and lime-washed (Fig 61). This action helps preserve the tracery in the window, but the purpose of the work is not known. Locally, Kenilworth castle retains both the earlier medieval ranges (e.g., the hall) and the Renaissance chamber block, constructed by Robert Dudley in 1575 for the visit of Queen Elizabeth I. The latter may have inspired the Berkeleys to modernise Caludon.

Between 1597 and 1599 a prayer retreat and banqueting house are erected for Elizabeth Berkeley, wife of Thomas, and daughter-in-law of Henry Berkeley. The positioning of the banqueting house on the north side of the pool provides the opportunity for both drama and entertainment in allowing arrival by boat, in the same way that guests at Kenilworth castle were rowed across the Great Mere to enjoy their feasts at the Pleasaunce (a banqueting hall).

Phase B6 1590s-1613 The golden age.

Caludon reaches its zenith in the last decades of the Berkeley ownership of Caludon. It is probably the first time in the history of the castle that its lords treat it as one of their principal, if not favourite, seats. As a consequence, the buildings are now at their most impressive architecturally, laid out on their most extensive plan, lavishly appointed and decorated and probably maintained to the highest standard. The accounts of the period fill in much detail that has been frustratingly lacking, but the rooms and buildings can only be listed. There is no contemporary survey of the castle, for example, that would help in reconstructing the arrangement of the rooms and the layout of the buildings.

We now know that there was a 'great chamber' in the chamber range, most likely the one lit by the surviving windows.[12] Other rooms probably located here were 'my lord's chamber,' 'my lady's chamber' and possibly 'my lord's study' and Master Berkeley's study. There was also a 'Clarke's chamber', an armoury and schoolhouse, location unknown. The hall was still in existence hung with an Arras tapestry, but it may have been a reduced version of the earlier medieval room, as suggested above. Several service and out buildings were mentioned as they needed repair: the lodge, kitchen, larder, brew house, backhouse, pigeon house, laundry house, dairy house, granary, tallow house and candle house, straw house, and slaughter house. A new park lodge was constructed in 1604 and the bridge across the moat was repaired with stone and timber in 1605. There was also a great garden, perhaps situated on the western side of the moat, an upper garden and a hop yard.

Phase B7 1620s to 1730s The last long decline.
By the time that the Berkeleys sell the Caludon estate in 1632 to the Morgan family, it has been in tenants' hands for at least a decade. The leaseholders were unlikely to have had the resources to maintain the house and fill it with a large household of family and servants, as in Berkeley days. The Morgans, followed by the Prestons and Cliffords, never live at Caludon and the buildings gradually decline, albeit tenanted by prosperous farmer-graziers. In the 1660s and 1670s there are at least twenty rooms of which eight are probably unused. In 1668 the banqueting house is listed in a survey of the estate, along with the 'manor house', which suggests that it was still standing at this time.[13] Unfortunately, the plan of Caludon House, as it is more frequently called in its later years, cannot be reconstructed from the rooms listed in the two probate inventories of 1670 and 1680.[14]

Phase B8 1730-1748 Demolition.
The century of decline takes its toll and Caludon House is demolished by the Cliffords or their agents, who have already taken down another of their Warwickshire mansions, Weston Hall in Weston-under-Wetherley. A fragment of the medieval chamber range is left standing, for perhaps picturesque reasons, and the remaining demolition rubble is swept into the eastern arm of the moat.

Phase C1 1730-1748
A more modest farmhouse replaces the ancient complex (Fig 109). There is a possibility that the former castle stable block was adapted and modified to serve as the new house, hence its location at the east end of the moated platform. Other new farm buildings are constructed farther to the east on the site of earlier buildings. It is not known when the narrower and lower north wing on the house is built.

Phase C2 1748-1966

Caludon House or Farm continues to operate mostly as an agricultural enterprise with little change to the buildings, except for the construction in the twentieth century of a corrugated iron 'Dutch' barn. The land, mostly built over the 1930s, is reduced to only 20 acres and purchased by the City Council in 1939 to create a park, a plan not immediately implemented as a result of the outbreak of the war. The farm house is occupied by a succession of council tenants until 1966 and some of the farm buildings are demolished in the 1950s. The farmhouse consists of a taller and wider two and a half storey building under a double pitched roof and a narrower and lower north wing. In the late 1950s the former contains a stable, a tack room and at least two unused rooms on the ground floor, and two floors of living accommodation on the first floor and in the attic storey. The north extension has a living room and kitchen on the ground floor and a two bedrooms and bathroom on the first floor. There are also cellars.

Phase C3 1966-7 Demolition.

The Council implements its pre-war plan of creating a municipal park and demolishes the farmhouse and remaining farm buildings. The cellars are probably filled with demolition rubble of potential archaeological interest, as some could date to the castle phases.

Fig 109 *Photograph of Caludon Farmhouse from the north (n.d.) (source unknown)*

Chapter 8 – NOTES

1 New House, belonging to the Hales family, stood at the junction of Radford Road and Sadler Road in Coventry and was demolished in 1930 but has a very fine drawing of the front elevation. Likewise there is a view of Weston Hall, in Weston-under-Wetherley, the other Clifford house in Warwickshire, demolished before 1830; op. cit, Tyack (1994) 269; *The Story of Whitefriars*, published by Leisure Services, Coventry City Council (n.d.)

2 Richard Morris, personal correspondence

3 M E Flitcroft, 'A Historical and Archaeological Survey of Caludon Castle, Coventry,' dissertation submitted for the degree of B. A. (Hons) Archaeology, University of Durham (January 1986); Myk was later to be appointed as an assistant archaeologist at the Herbert Art Gallery and Museum,

4 op. cit., Flitcroft, 20,

5 op. cit Ian Fisher; The survey and report were jointly funded by Coventry City Council and John Clarke, OBE

6 *Calendar of Papal Registers relating to Great Britain and Ireland*, Vol 1: 1198-1304, (1893) 184

7 Clifford, W(E) 1/3

8 *Calendar of Inquisitions post Mortem*, Edw II, Vol VI, (1910) no 699, 429

9 *Calendar of Inquisitions Miscellaneous*, 1377-1388, Vol IV, (1957) no 299, 169

10 Smyth Vol 2, 201; Clifford W (E) 1/4, 1528; Inquisition post mortem of Isabel Berkeley

11 Smyth Vol 2, 362

12 Berkeley, GBB 107, fiche 1478/167, GBB 108, fiche 1478/171-80

13 WRO CR1097/87

14 TNA Prob 4/3443 (1670); Lichfield R O, Richard Hayward inventory 7 April 1680

APPENDIX

Caludon and the Legend of St George

In this new history of Caludon Castle several myths have been dispelled, most notably that of its destruction in the Civil War. The many new facts that have been uncovered serve as a more than adequate counterbalance to the unsubstantiated claims and interpretations that have clouded many previous accounts of Caludon and its 800 years of recorded history. It would also be appropriate, therefore, to consign once and for all another myth - that of St George and Caludon - to the box named 'Fiction'. It may seem unnecessary to remind the reader that St George, a soldier, possibly born in Cappadocia, Turkey, or Lydda in Palestine, and martyred in the persecutions of the emperors Diocletian and Maximilian in the year 303, had no connection with Caludon.[1] But so strong has the myth taken root since the medieval English crusaders returned home inspired in their battles by the rapidly growing myth and popularity of St George that even recent local newspaper articles and numerous websites treat the story uncritically, even as fact. This despite the clear assertion in the 1969 Coventry volume of the *Victoria County History* that, 'The story easiest to reject is that the house [Caludon] was the birthplace of St. George.'[2]

It can be stated, therefore, without any doubt, or fear of future evidence coming to light, that St George was neither born at Caludon nor did he return there to die. All other parts of the Caludon version of the story, a later elaboration, are equally fictitious: the naming of his father as Albert, giving him the title of Lord of Caludon in King Arthur's time - and his mother's death in giving birth to George. After being kidnapped by a witch and brought up by her as a fearless knight, George apparently left England for many adventures abroad, returning when he heard that a dragon was terrorising Coventry, his lair a cavern hidden under Hill Top! George managed to slay the dragon but eventually died from the wounds sustained in the combat and was taken to Caludon, where he died.

What is of interest is how an early fourth-century martyr, transposed to England, becoming its patron saint in the reign of Edward II (1327-1377) and obtaining a suit of medieval armour in the process, came to be specifically connected with Caludon Castle. The saint was already a figure of veneration and cult worship in many parts of medieval Europe and Asia Minor. The kernel of the story appeared capable of being fantastically elaborated and given a local flavour. The importance of late medieval Coventry probably played a significant role. Mummers or travelling actors would have been attracted to the bustling town and one of their favourite performances involved the

Fig 110 *St George and the Dragon – commemorating a local performance of the legend rather than any historical fact*

exploits of St George. A script adapted to the locality would clearly have been even more popular. Coventry was nationally known for its medieval cycle of 'mystery' or sacred plays, giving ample opportunity to weave in the legend of St George, his feast day (23 April) an important early date in the festival calendar.[3] Many of the guilds owned processional carts, which were brought out on such days from the 'pageant houses' where they were kept, the vehicles used as stages for performances. The Shearman and Taylor's guild had a chapel adjacent to Gosford Gate dedicated to St George, finally demolished in 1822 after having been used for many years as living accommodation.

The local story of St George as briefly summarised above was given its final shape in the publication of *The Seven Champions of Christendome* by Richard Johnson (fl. 1592-1622).[4] It was published in two parts in 1596 and 1597, the first part dedicated to Lord Thomas Howard, the 1st Earl of Suffolk, hero of victory over the Spanish Armada and the raid on Cadiz (1597). He was nephew of Katherine Howard, wife of Henry Berkeley, whose colourful and extravagant life has been described in Chapters 3 and 4. Caludon Castle was at its epicentre, a destination for troupes of actors, singers and musicians in constant demand to entertain the Berkeleys and their guests. Calling on the already well-established and extensive Coventry repertoire of sacred and mythical stories, it is possible the St George legend was given an extra local dimension when it was enacted at Caludon, perhaps staged by or witnessed by Richard Johnson. The performance may have delighted the Berkeleys and perhaps their Howard relatives, who encouraged and supported its subsequent publication.

Appendix 1 – NOTES

1 Michael Walsh, *A New Dictionary of Saints East and West,* (2007) 224

2 VCH Warwick, Vol 8, 121

3 VCH Warwick, Vol 8, 211-215

4 Dictionary of National Biography

Bibliography

List of Abbreviations

Berkeley	Berkeley Castle Archive at Gloucester County Record Office
BL	British Library
Clifford	Clifford Archive, Ugbrooke House, Devon
Coventry RO	Coventry Record Office or Archives, now part the History Centre in the Herbert Art Gallery and Museum
Lichfield RO	Lichfield Joint Record Office
SBTRO	Stratford Birthplace Trust Record Office
TNA	The National Archives
Warwick RO	Warwick County Record Office

Primary Sources

There are two principal repositories of archival sources for Caludon.

1. The Clifford Archive, Ugbrooke Park, Devon. This contains the family and estate papers and was provisionally calendared by the Royal Commission in 1976: Report on the Family and Estate Papers of Lord Clifford of Chudleigh held at Ugbrooke Park, Chudleigh, Devon, Royal Commission on Historical Manuscripts, Great Britain, Typescript, 78 pages.

On the sale of Caludon to the Morgans in 1631 the Berkeleys passed on their deeds and related material, dating back to the Segrave period (13th century). These were fortunately transferred to the Prestons and finally the Clifford family (c.1685), where they have remained ever since.

The material is being re-catalogued and these new references have been used where available. The archive also contains material on the other former Clifford Warwickshire estates, such as Sowe, Foleshill, Wyken and Weston-under-Wetherley.

2. The Berkeley Archive

There is a massive archive of material lodged at Berkeley Castle, for which a printed catalogue has been produced for the medieval period:

A Catalogue of the Medieval Muniments at Berkeley Castle, edited by Bridget Wells-Furby, (in two volumes), Bristol and Gloucester Archaeological Society, Vols 17 and 18 (2004).

This catalogue contains relatively little Caludon material for reasons outlined above. It appears, however, that only Caludon property deeds and related material was removed following the sale of the Caludon manor in 1631, but estate papers such as rentals and accounts remained undisturbed. This material along with the rest of the post-medieval archive is being comprehensively catalogued by David Smith, the Berkeley Castle archivist, and much has already been microfiched or microfilmed and made available at Gloucester Record Office. In addition, the cataloguing work now appears on A2A (Access to Archives), with extremely useful commentaries and administrative histories of the principal families. The archive is identified on A2A as BCM (Berkeley Castle Muniments).

Other material relating to Caludon is scattered and much smaller in extent, and can be found at the National Archives, Kew, London and in local collections at the former Coventry Archives, now the History Centre at the Herbert, at Warwick Record Office, Stratford Birthplace Trust Record Office and the Archives Department of Birmingham Reference Library. The Coventry Archive has relatively little material specific to Caludon Castle and manor, a fact that has inhibited the writing of a definitive history. Its holdings on Caludon are biased to more recent centuries and is particularly useful for the twentieth century and the role of Coventry City Council. Caludon is hidden away in generic sources such as land tax assessments and electoral rolls.

Newspaper sources on Caludon have been made much easier to find as a result of the recent scanning of local papers and their availability on dedicated websites, e.g., the British Newspaper Archive and the British Library version. Information on owners and tenants has also been notoriously difficult to track down, but the task is now aided by a mass of on-line genealogical material, particularly the site, ancestry.co.uk. The census data has enriched the history of Caludon House in the nineteenth and early twentieth centuries.

There is still a huge quantity of archival material that is not yet available on computer and will not be for a long time, if ever. A search on-line is, therefore, insufficient on its own. The Clifford archive, which has significantly contributed to this new history of Caludon, does not reside on the web. It is also worth noting that much historical material that has been published on the web is unreliable, misleading and strewn with error and myth. It is there to catch the unwary and the Caludon sites are no exception.

Printed Sources

Arkell, Tom with Alcock, Nat (eds.), *Warwickshire Hearth Tax Returns: Michaelmas 1670*, Dugdale Society Vol XLIII (2010)

Barraclough, Geoffrey (ed.) *Charters of the Anglo Norman Earls of Chester, c.1071-1237*, The Record Society of Lancashire and Cheshire, Vol 126 (1988)

Calendar of Charter Rolls, 1341-1417, Vol 5 (1916)

Calendar of Close Rolls, Edward II, 1323-1327, Vol IV (1898)

Calendar of Close Rolls, Henry IV, 1402-1405, Vol II (1929)

Calendar of Close Rolls, Henry IV, 1405-1409, Vol III (1931)

Calendar of Close Rolls, Henry VI, 1422-1429, Vol I (1933)

Calendar of Close Rolls, Henry VI, 1429-1435, Vol II (1933)

Calendar of Proceedings of the Committee for the Advance of Money: Part 1 1642-45, (1888)

Calendar of Fine Rolls, Henry IV 1399-1405, Vol XII (1931)

Calendar of Inquisitions Miscellaneous, 1377-1388, Vol I (1957)

Calendar of Inquisitions Miscellaneous, 1392-1399, Vol VI (1963)

Calendar of Inquisitions post Mortem, Edward II, Vol VI, (1910)

Calendar of Inquisitions post Mortem, 39-43 Edward III, Vol XII (1938)

Calendar of Inquisitions post Mortem, Henry IV, 1399-1405, Vol XVIII (1987)

Calendar of Papal Registers relating to Great Britain and Ireland, Vol 1: 1198-1304, (1893)

Calendar of Patent Rolls, Edward I, 1281-1292, (1893)

Calendar of Patent Rolls, Edward I, 1301-1307, (1898)

Calendar of Patent Rolls, Henry IV AD 1399-1401, Vol I (1903)

Calendar of Patent Rolls, Henry IV AD 1405-1409, Vol III (1907)

Calendar of Patent Rolls, Philip and Mary 4 & 5, 1557-8, (1939) 267

Carter W. F. and Barnard E. A. B., *The Records of King Edward School Birmingham, Vol III,* (1933) Dugdale Society Vol XII

Estcourt, Rev Edgar and Payne, John (eds.), *The English Catholic Nonjurors of 1715,* [1885]

Fosbroke, Thomas Dudley, *Berkeley Manuscripts Abstracts and Extracts,* (1821)

House of Commons Journal, 1648-1652, Vol 6 (1802)

Maclean, Sir John (ed), *The Lives of the Berkeleys. Lords of the Honour, Castle and Manor of Berkeley in the County of Gloucester from 1086 to 1618 by John Smyth of Nibley,* (published 1883 in three volumes)

Letters & Papers, Foreign and Domestic, Henry VIII, Vol 7

Letters & Papers, Foreign and Domestic, Henry VIII, Vol 9

Names of Catholics, Nonjurors and others, who refused to take the oath to his late King George, (printed 1745, reprinted 1862)

The New England Historical and Genealogical Register, Vol 8, (1924)

Parsons, Rev Daniel (ed), T*he diary of Sir Henry Slingsby,* (1836)

The Register of Edward the Black Prince, England 1351-1365, Vol 4 (1933)

John, Trevor (ed.), *The Warwickshire Hundred Rolls of 12879-80, Stoneleigh and Kineton Hundreds,* (1992)

Smith, J. P. (ed), *Lancashire Registers III Northern Part*, Catholic Record Society Vol XX, (1916)

Stokes, Ethel and Wellstood, Frederick C. (eds.), *Warwickshire Feet of Fines (1345-1509)*, vol III, Dugdale Society, Vol 18 (1943)

Articles

The Builder, 4 Aug 1883

Broadway, Jan, 'John Smyth of Nibley: A Jacobean Man-of-Business and his service to the Berkeley Family', *Midland History*, Vol 24, (1999)

Broadway Jan, 'Unreliable Witness; Sir William Dugdale and the Perils of Autobiography,' in *William Dugdale, Historian 1605-1686*, edited by Christopher Dyer and Catherine Richardson (2009)

Carpenter, Christine, 'Sir Thomas Malory and Fifteenth Century Local Politics', *Bulletin of Institute of Historical Research*, 53 (1980)

Coulson, Charles, 'Hierarchism in Conventual Crenellation', *Medieval Archaeology*, Vol 16 (1982)

Curie, Christopher, 'Fishponds as Garden Features, c 1550-1750', *Garden History*, Vol 18, No. 1 (spring 1990)

Cust, Richard, 'Catholicism, Antiquarianism and Gentry Honour: the Writings of Sir Thomas Shirley', *Midland History*, Vol XXIII, (1998)

Cust, Richard, 'William Dugdale and the Honour Politics of Stuart Warwickshire,' in *William Dugdale, Historian 1605-1686*, edited by Christopher Dyer and Catherine Richardson (2009)

Greenfield, Peter A, 'Entertainments of Henry, Lord Berkeley, 1593-4 and 1600-1605', *Records of Early English Drama*, Vol 8, no 1 (1983) 12-24

Kerry, Anthony (ed), 'The Responsa Scholorum of the English College, Rome', *Catholic Record Society*, Vol 55,(1963)

Whitteridge, Gweneth, 'The identity of Sir Thomas Malory, Knight Prisoner', *Review of English Studies*, Vol 24, 95 (1973)

Books

Archibald, Elizabeth and Edwards, A. S. G. (eds.), *A Companion to Malory* (1996);

A W & C Barsby, *Manorial Law*, (1996

Baugh. A. C., 'Documenting Sir Thomas Malory,' *Speculum*, Vol 8 (1933)

Besterling, Charles Starle; *William Preston of Newcastle-upon-Tyne, England: and Philadelphia, Pennsylvania, and allied families*, (1934)

Brooks, Harold F. (ed), *A Midsummer Night's Dream*, Arden Shakespeare (1979)

Burke, John, A genealogical and heraldic history of the extinct and dormant baronetcies of England, Ireland and Scotland, (1841)

Burke, John, *A genealogical and heraldic history of the commoners of Great Britain and Ireland*, (1834)

Carpenter, Christine, *Locality and Polity: A Study of Warwickshire Landed Society 1401-1449*, (1992)

Chambers, E. K., *English Literature at the Close of the Middle Ages*, (1945)

Colville, Frederick, *The Worthies of Warwickshire – who lived between 1500 and 1800*, (1869)

Coss, Peter, *Lordship, knighthood and locality, A study in English society C.1180-C.1280*, (1991)

Crisp, Frederick Arthur (ed), *Sepulchral Memorials of Bobbingworth, Essex, with genealogical notes and pedigrees*, (1888)

Demidowicz, George, *A History of the Bluecoat School and Lych Gate Cottages, Coventry*, (2000)

Dugdale, William, *The Antiquities of Warwickshire*, (1730 edition)

Field, P. J. C., *The Life and Times of Sir Thomas Malory*, (1993);

Furness, Horace Howard (ed), *A Midsummer Night's Dream, A New Variorum Edition*, (1895)

Gelling, Margaret, *Place-Names in the Landscape*, (1984)

Goddard, Richard, *Lordship and Medieval Urbanisation: Coventry 1043-1355*, (2004)

Gover, J. E. B and Mawer, A. (eds.), *The Place-Names of Warwickshire*, (1936)

Helen Hackett, *Shakespeare and Elizabeth A Meeting of Two Myths*, (2009)

Hodges, Elizabeth, *Some Ancient English Homes and their Associations Personal, Archaeological and Historic*, (1895)

Hughes, Ann, Politics, *Society and Civil War in Warwickshire*, 1620-1660, Cambridge, (1987)

Mitcheson, J. C., *The Warwickshire Coalfield, in Birmingham and its Regional Setting A Scientific Survey,* (1950)

Nicolson, Joseph, *The History and Antiquities of the Counties of Westmoreland and Cumberland, Vol 1* (1777)

Nichols, John, *Bibliotheca Topographica Britannica*, Vol 8; (1780)

Phillimore, W. P. W. and Carter, W. F., *Some Account of the Family of Middlemore,* (1901)

Rackham, Oliver, *The History of the Countryside,* (2000)

Reader, William, *Description of St Michael's Church Coventry, with the inscriptions, etc.,* (1830)

Richardson, Kenneth, *Twentieth-century Coventry,* (1972)

Riddy, Felicity, *Sir Thomas Malory,* (1987)

Serjeantson, R. M., *Chapels of Kingsthorpe and Upton,* (1904)

Geoffrey Tyack, *Warwickshire Country Houses,* (1994)

Shirley, E. P., *Stemmata Shirleiana,* (1873)

Soden, Iain, *Ranulf Blondeville, The First English Hero,* (2009)

Topographical Dictionary of England, Vol 1, (1835)

Victoria County History of Warwick, Coventry and Warwick, Vol 8, (1969)

Vincent, Nicholas, *Peter des Roches: An Alien in English Politics,* 1205-1236 (1996)

Wiles, David, *Shakespeare's Almanack: A Midsummer Night's Dream, Marriage and the Elizabethan Calendar,* (1993)

Woodhouse, Frederick, *The Churches of Coventry,* (1909).

Unpublished Reports / Memoirs

Flitcroft, M. E., 'A Historical and Archaeological Survey of Caludon Castle, Coventry', dissertation submitted for the degree of B. A. (Hons) Archaeology, University of Durham, (January 1986)

Fisher, Ian, *Archaeological geophysical survey at Caludon Castle, Coventry, West Midlands*, Northamptonshire Archaeology, (June 2008)

Harold Green, 1899-1971, Farmer, Coventry University Open Collections, Curve Resource web-site, Richardson Transcripts, no CT10

Lydia Mary Skelton, 'Caludon Farm in the Parish of Wyken'

Index

Abbot of Combe (Coombe) 63, 65
Alcester church 156
America 119
Ansty 10
Ansty Road, Coventry 35, 54, 135, 147, 153, 159, 160, 166, 169, 172-74,
Arch Road, Coventry 173, 175, 177
Archbishop of Canterbury 51, 52, 53
Archbishop of Cologne 25
Archbishop of York 50
Arundell, Hon Eleanor Mary 132
Ash, Joseph 135
Ashton, Somerset 64
Astley, Warwickshire 84
Astwell, Northamptonshire 88
Atherstone 52
Attoxhall Road, Coventry 14
d'Aubigny, Roger 37
Augustine Green 70
Aula, Richard de, *see* Hall, Richard
Aviss, Llewellyn 159, 160
Aviss, William 159
d'Avranches, Hugh, Earl of Chester 11, 12
d'Avranches, Richard, Earl of Chester 12
Axminster, Devon 146, 148
Ayr castle 25
Bablake 64
Baginton 41
Bagot, William 41, 45-46, 48
Bagshawe, Francis 116
Balistarius, Philip, crossbowman 37
Ball Hill, Coventry 165

Bannockburn 59
Barbican, London 85
Baron, Peter 37
Barras Heath, Coventry 42
Bathampton, Somerset 157
Bayley Lane, Coventry 9
Bayning, Paul, Viscount
Bayning of Sudbury, Suffolk 92
Beaumont, Anton(y) 157
Beaumont, John 157
Bedford, Lord 107
Bedfordshire 20
Bedminster, Somerset 64
Bedworth 127
Belgrave Road, Coventry 13, 14, 18, 173-75, 185
Bell Green Road, Coventry 143
Bellamy, William 115
Benfoy, Mary *see* Mary Jeacocks
Berkeley Castle 59, 68, 69, 74, 85, 86, 92

Berkeley family:
Berkeley, Anne (daughter of John Fiennes, Lord Dacre) 61, 62
Berkeley, Anne (daughter of Maurice V and Isabel) 60, 64
Berkeley, Anne (Savage) (m. Thomas Berkeley VI) 60, 69, 70, 71, 73
Berkeley, Elizabeth (Carey) (m. Thomas Berkeley VII) 60, 78-80, 83, 85, 86, 90, 91, 92
Berkeley, Elizabeth *see* Elizabeth West

Berkeley, Elizabeth *see* Elizabeth Stanhope
Berkeley, Ferdinando 60, 76
Berkeley, Frances (Francis) 60, 76, 88
Berkeley, George 60, 91
Berkeley, Lord Henry 60, 71, 73-78, 81, 83, 84-91, 95-98, 100, 102-107, 109
Berkeley, Isabel (Mowbray) (m. James Berkeley) 56, 60, 61, 62
Berkeley, Isabel (Mead) (m. Maurice Berkeley V) 60, 63, 64, 65, 81
Berkeley, Isabel (Mead), funeral of 64-65
Berkeley, James (m. Isabel Mowbray) 56, 59, 60, 61
Berkeley, James 59, 60
Berkeley, James (son of Maurice V and Isabel) 60, 64
Berkeley, Jane 60, 76
Berkeley, Jane (Townsend) (m. Lord Henry Berkeley) *see* Jane Stanhope
Berkeley, Joan, (Willoughby) *see* Strangeways
Berkeley, Katherine (died in infancy) 60, 61
Berkeley, Lady Katherine 60, 72, 74-76, 78, 80-89, 95-96, 98, 100, 102, 105, 107
Berkeley, Lady Katherine, funeral of 83, 98, 107
Berkeley, Mary (wife of Maurice VI) *see* Mary Hastings
Berkeley, Mary (daughter of Lord Henry) 60, 76

Berkeley, Maurice de (granted Berkeley castle in 1189) 59
Berkeley, Maurice (fought against Edward II and the Despencers) 59
Berkeley, Maurice (d. in 1361) 59
Berkeley, Maurice (V) 60, 62, 63, 64
Berkeley, Maurice (VI) 60, 64, 65, 66, 67, 68
Berkeley, Theophila 60, 85, 86
Berkeley, Thomas de (captured in 1314) 59
Berkeley, Thomas (tried for the murder of King Edward II) 59
Berkeley, Thomas (d. 1417) 59
Berkeley, Thomas (b. 1470) 60, 61
Berkeley, Thomas (V) 60, 64, 67, 68
Berkeley, Thomas (VI) 60, 68, 69, 73
Berkeley, Thomas (VII) (Son of Lord Henry) 60, 76, 77, 78-86, 96, 97, 105, 106
Berkeley, Lord William (d. 1492) 56, 60, 61, 62, 63, 73

Berkeley, Sir William of Stoke Gifford 60, 65
Berkeley, Katherine, daughter of Sir William of Stoke Gifford 60, 65

Berkshire 112
Berkswell 74
Berwick 26
Bigod, Hugh, Earl of Norfolk 26

Binley Bridge 65
Binley, Coventry 10, 16, 70, 84, 154, 155
Binley church 119, 135, 157, 169
Binley Church of England School 157
Binley, manor of 37
Binley Road, Coventry 165
Bird, Richard 154
Birmingham 154, 162, 163
Birmingham Tram Company 163
Bishop of Rome 72
Bishop Street, Coventry 86
Black Death 45
Blondeville, Ranulf de, Earl of Chester 12, 13, 14, 30, 39
Blount, Elizabeth see Elizabeth Clifford
Blyth, V.C. 162
Bodmin Road, 173, 174, 180
Boleyn, Anne 60, 80
Boleyn, Mary 79, 80
Bolingbroke, Henry (King Henry IV) 45-50, 59
Bolingbroke, John de 30
Boroughbridge, Battle of 37
Boston, Lincolnshire 157
Bosworth 62
Bottisham, Cambridgeshire 150
Bottolph (Bottle) Bridge 88
Bourchier, Eleanor see Eleanor Stafford
Bradgate, Leicestershire 74
Brailes 112
Braveheart 26
Brentford 45
Brinklow 9, 22
Bristol 21, 64, 70, 148
Brittany 20, 21
Broadgate 37
Brotherton, Lady Margaret, Duchess of Norfolk 15, 30, 31, 49, 50
Brotherton, Thomas, 1st Earl of Norfolk 15, 30, 42
Broughton, John 54
Brown, Edward 166
Brown, John (brother of Sarah Garrard) 156
Brown, Rev John 146, 149, 150, 153, 154, 155
Brown, Sarah, see Sarah Garrard
Brown, Sarah see

Sarah Wale
Brown, Thomas 149, 150, 155, 156
Brown, William 149
Bruce, Robert 26
Brymore, Somerset 114
Buckinghamshire 20
Bucknam, Edward 74
Bull's Head, Coventry 165
Bull's Head Lane, Coventry 166
Burbage 139
Burge, John 177
Burgh, Hubert de 20,
Burton, Staffordshire 21
Burton, William 88
Butlin, Billy 182
Caen 50
Caernarfon castle 9,
Calais 43, 44, 47, 50, 51

Caludon see Calladowne, Calledon, Calledown, Calloughdon, Calloughdowne, Callowden, Callowdon, Caloudon, Caloughdan, Caloughdoun, Caloughdon, Calowden, Calowdon, Caludown, Caludun, Caluedon, Calughdon, Calwdon, Kalwedon,

Caludon House, see Calloughdon Manor House, Callowdon House, Caledon House, Calladownehouse, Callowdonhouse, Calidon House, Calowden House 86, 153-57, 159-60, 162-63, 166, 180, 153-55

Callowdon Wood(s) see Caludon wood

Caludon Farm see Callodon Farm(e) Callowdon Farm(e), Callodine Farm, Callowden Farm(e), Caludon Castle Farm, 135-137, 139, 143, 145, 146, 147, 149, 150, 155-157, 160, 165, 166, 167, 168, 169, 173, 174, 175, 176, 177, 178, 181

Caludon Castle Estates Ltd 173
Caludon Castle School 21, 182

Caludon College 157
Caludon Cottages 166
Caludon Farm residents 1945-1967:
Alexander Brown, James Brown, Mary Brown, Vera D Cartwright, Brian D Fox, Hazel I Fox, Ernest Insley, Mabel A Insley, Alfred E Knight, Donald E H Knight, Sylvia Lake, Thomas E Lake, Frederick T Upton, Hannah A Upton, Donald H Wild, Derek Wilson, John Wilson, Sheila M Wilson,

Caludon Lodge 160, 165
Caludon, Manor of;
Ashmoore, Ashmore, Ashmore Meadow, Assemore, Asshemour, (see Long Ashmore, Millers Ashmoore and Little and Great Ash Moor) 35, 37, 45, 84, 91, 99, 122, 135
Banqueting house 78, 84, 99, 122, 123
Bynley 45
Caludon Wood 16, 17, 18, 24,
Crabtree feylde, Crabtree field, Crabtree Meadow 84, 122, 135, 146
Deadmore, Dedemoor 41, 84
Field 146
Fishpond 122
Gardens 122
Great Court 122
Greate Parke, Great Park 122, 134
Henleye 45
Hungerlowe, Hungerlie Meadow 54, 99
Lakemede, Lake Medowe, Lake Meadowe, Lake Meadow 37, 45, 84, 86, 91, 99, 122, 134, 182
Lawne Parke 135
Le Cowelesewe 54
Little and Great Ash Moor 143
Little Court 122
Little Close 122
Litle Feyld, Littelfeld, Little Field, 35, 45, 84

Litle parke, Little Park 122, 134
Littelstobyfelde, Little Stubbyfield, Little Stubble Field, the Stubble field 146
Long Ashmore 122
Mannor house 122, 134
Michelfeyld, Michelfield; Michel Field, Middelfield, Midelmede 35, 45, 46, 84
Mildnis 37
Millers Ashmoore 35
Motte 122
New Close, alias le Slaughterhouse Close, Slaughterhouse Close, The Slaughter House Close 84, 99, 122, 134,
Newhewen, Newhaven, Newhewn 41, 42, 54, 84, 122, 135
Moneriddingge, le 35
Oxe Close 54
Oxonfeld 54
Partridge Meadow 146
Parvus Campus 35
Pertridge feyldes, Pattridge field, Partridge Fields 84, 122, 135
Platbrigge, Platebrigge 37, 46
Stoake hooke, alias Caldwell, Stokehoke 84, 99
Sowebrigge 46
Sowe Wast(e), alias Morgayn's Waste 84
Stubbyfeyldes, Stubyfield, Stublefeild, Stublefield Grove, Stubblefield (Great and Little) 45, 84, 122, 134, 135, 146
The wood yard 122
Woodcock Close 135

Caludon Park: see Callidowne Park, Calloughdon Park, Caludon Park Avenue, Coventry 160
Caludon Society 185
Caludon Wood 16, 17, 18, 24, 117

Cambridge University 150
Cambridgeshire 24
Canley, Coventry 154
Canterbury castle 20, 25
Cardinal Poole 72

Carey, Elizabeth *see* Elizabeth Berkeley
Carey, George, Lord Hunsdon 79
Case, Harry 168
Castle Rising, Norfolk 74
Chadshunt Hall Auxiliary Hospital, Kineton 174
Chambers, E.K. 52
Charles I, King 112, 114, 115
Charles II, King 115, 131, 133
Cheilesmore *see* Cheylesmore, Coventry
Chellesmore, *see* Cheylesmore, Coventry
Chepstow 44
Cheshire 43
Cheylesmore 10, 37, 49, 69
Cheylesmore manor 19, 49
Chilvers Coton 84
Chipping Campden 86
Chiswick 154
Christchurch College, Oxford 111
Christian IV, King of Denmark 104, 106
Chudleigh, Devon 119
Claridge, Walter Dan 157, 160
Clifford Bridge Road, Coventry 153, 174-75
Clifford estate 16, 27

Clifford family:
Clifford, Anne 131-34, 136
Clifford, Anthony of Borscombe 131
Cifford, Charles, 6th Baron 132, 142
Clifford, Elizabeth 132, 136
Clifford, Lord Hugh (d. 1730) 110, 119, 132
Clifford, Hugh, 2nd Baron 131, 132, 133, 136
Clifford, Hugh, 3rd Baron 132, 136
Clifford, Hugh, 4th Baron 132, 136, 137, 141
Clifford, Hugh, 5th Baron 132, 141
Clifford, Hugh Charles, 7th Baron 132, 142
Clifford, Sir Lewis 131
Clifford, Sir Thomas, 1st Baron 132, 133
Clifford, Thomas (b. 1687) 132, 136

Clopton House, Mickleton 156, 166
Clynton, Thomas de 49
Codnor, Derbyshire 76
Coke, Sir Robert 85
Colchester castle 20
Coleshill 52
Colne, manor of 40
Cologne, Archbishop of 25
Combe 21, 155
Combe Abbey 52, 53, 120
Connecticut 119
Constantinople 39
Conway castle (Conwy) 9, 49
Cooke, Edward 116
Coombe, *see* Combe
Coombe Abbey, *see* Combe Abbey
Coombefields Farm 120
Courtney, Sir Piers 131
Coventry Bankruptcy Court 162
Coventry Blitz 174
Coventry Church of England Sunday School Association 160
Coventry City Council 173, 184
Coventry Corporation 83, 155, 174
Coventry, manor of 10, 11
Coventry Registry Office 37
Coventry, Walter de; *see* Walter of
Coventry, Walter of 16, 17, 18, 21
Coventry Workhouse 168
Cow Lane, Coventry 157
Cowper, Edward 76, 83
Cowper, Hubert 166
Cranford, Lady Elizabeth of 91
Cranford, Middlesex 90, 92
Craven Arms, High Street, Coventry 157, 159
Craven Arms, Binley 157
Craven family 149
Crick, Northamptonshire 41
Cromwell, Thomas 71
Cromwell's Barn 179, 181
Cubbington 135
Culcheth, Thomas 118
Cumberland 28
Dacre, Lord, *see* John Fiennes
Dedemoor, *see* Deedmore
Dean Street, London 154
Deedmore 42

Denmark 106
Denys, Sir William 66
Derby 76, 166
Derby Fair 104
Derbyshire 25, 76
Despencers, Earls of Winchester, 28, 37, 59
Devon 16, 27, 119, 131, 134, 141, 143, 146
Dog Lane, Coventry 37
Domesday Book 10
Dominica 166
Dorchester Way, Coventry 54
Dover castle 20
Dowland, John 104-106
Drapers Chapel 81, 83
Draycote 42
Draycote Water 54
Driver, Edward 154, 156
Driver, Elizabeth 155
Driver, John 154
Driver, Mary 157
Driver, Mary Anne 156
Driver, William 156, 157
Driver, William H 157
Dudley, Robert, Earl of Leicester 75, 76
Duke of;
Buckingham 51-53,
Burgundy 51
Gloucester 51
Lancaster 42, 45, 49
Norfolk 36, 42, 45, 50, 51, 52, 53, 55, 62, 63, 75
Northumberland 85
Suffolk 51, 55
York 61, 131
Dumbarton castle 25
Dumbleton 166
Dutch Barn 177, 179
Earl of;
Arundel 36, 42-44
Chester 10, 11, 12-14, 16-19, 30
Craven 155-57
Essex 112
Gloucester 43, 43, 44
Huntingdon 69
Lancaster 37
Leicester 23, 75, 76
Lichfield 137
Mercia 10
Moray 44
Norfolk 15, 30
Northampton 60, 85, 90
Nottingham 36, 40, 49, 50
Oxford 42

Pembroke 20, 42, 61
Shrewsbury 56
Surrey 67, 68, 72
Warwick 21, 26, 43, 41, 43, 44
Westmorland 49, 50
Winchester 37
Earl of Derby's Players 107
Earl Street, Coventry 37, 82, 160
Earle Street, *see* Earl Street
East Anglia 44, 51, 55
Edgefield, Peter de 37
Edyth Road, Coventry 173
Edmund, King of Sicily 23
Edward, the Black Prince 35
Edward, Duke of York 54, 55
Edward I, King 9, 15, 24, 25, 26, 27, 28, 30, 39
Edward II, King 15, 28, 30, 37, 59
Edward III, King 37, 59
Edward IV, King 56, 61, 62, 64
Edward V, King 62
Edward VI, King 72, 73
Edward, Prince 21, 24
Egiffeeld, Peter de; *see* Peter de Edgefield
El Caludon cigar 160
Elizabeth I, Queen 71, 74, 76, 79
Elmsthorpe, Leicestershire 156
Eltham Palace 40
Emperor of the Holy Roman Empire 44
Enfield Town Palace School 157
Epworth 37
Essex 20
Eton 133
Ettington 88
Europe 39, 44, 47, 51, 55, 141
Eustace, son of King Stephen 12
Exhall 10, 25, 84, 135, 143
Farren Road, Coventry 40, 173-75, 177-78, 185
Fennys, Constance 109
Fermor, Henry 110, 115, 117
Fermor, Jane 110, 112-114, 116, 117, 136
Fermor, Sir Richard 112
Fermor, Ursula 117
Fiennes, Anne *see* Anne Berkeley

Fiennes, John, Lord Dacre, 61
First World War 169, 172
FitzAlan, Elizabeth 36, 42
FitzHardings 59
Fitzjames, Sir John 66
fitz Miles, Philip 18
fitz Richard, Walter 18
Flanders 118, 119
Fleet Street, London 40,
Flodden 68
Flodden, Battle of 66
Flynn, Alec 169-70 173
Foleshill, Coventry 10, 84, 135, 143, 155, 159
Foleshill, manor of 37
Framlington castle, Suffolk 50
France 40, 136
Frankfurt 44
Frankton 139
Friends of Caludon Park 185
Free Grammar School, Coventry 86
Frodsham, Cheshire 69
Furness, Lancashire 112, 113, 114, 115
Garrard, Edward Holland 149, 156, 160, 166
Garrard, Samuel 149, 156
Garrard, Sarah 149, 156, 166
Gascony 21, 25, 55
Gaveston, Piers 28
Germany 47
Gernon, Ranulf de, Earl of Chester 12
Gibbard, Timothy 117, 118, 119, 120, 121, 122, 126
Gibbert, Timothy; Gibberts, Tymothy, see Timothy Gibbard
Gibbard, William 119
Gibson, Mel 26
Glasgow 166
Gloucester 74, 112
Gloucestershire 64, 65, 67, 68, 70, 73, 91
Goddard, Benjamin 135, 139
Goddard, Elizabeth (m. Thomas Goddard) 135, 140
Goddard, Elizabeth (d. of Thomas and Elizabeth Goddard) 135, 140
Goddard, Elizabeth (m. William Goddard) 135
Goddard, James 135, 140
Goddard, John 135, 140
Goddard, Richard 10

Goddard, Thomas 135, 137, 139, 140
Goddard, Thomas (Son of Thomas and Elizabeth Goddard) 135, 139, 140
Goddard, William 135, 140, 141, 143
Godgifu, see Godiva 10
Godiva 10
Godiva cigar 160
Gosford Green, Coventry 46, 47, 48, 159, 172
Gosford Street, Coventry 96, 159, 160
Grange Terrace 169
Great chamber 72, 88
Great hall 29, 103
Great hall, Kenilworth Castle 30
Great House 9
Great Lister Street, Birmingham 163
Great Palace Yard, Coventry 82
Great War 160, 172
Green, Elizabeth 165
Green, Florence (see Florence Treharn)
Green, Harold 165, 167
Green, Henry James (Harry) 165-168, 173
Green, Lydia 167-169
Gregory, Arthur 84
Grendon, Warwickshire 149
Griff 91
Griffiths and Aviss tobacconists 159, 160
Groby, Leicestershire 74
Gryffyn, see Podmore and Gryffyn
Hales, John 76
Hall, John 44
Hall, Richard 17
Hampton, Geoffrey, Mayor of Coventry 48
Hare and Squirrel, Cow Lane, Coventry 157
Harold, King 10
Harper, Harpur, Mary see Mary Shirley
Harry Rose Road, Coventry 14
Hartshill, Nuneaton, 149
Hastings, Sussex 10
Hastings, George, Earl of Huntingdon 69
Hastings, Mary 60, 69

Haward, see Richard Hayward
Hawcoat, Cumbria 113
Haweness, Bedfordshire 48
Hawkesbury 91
Hawkesbury Lane, Coventry 155
Haye, John de la 24
Hayward, John 127, 134
Hayward, Richard 117, 118, 121, 126, 127
Hayward, Richard junior 126, 127
Henley mill 24, 42, 54, 135
Henley Road, Coventry 143
Henrietta, Princess, of France 112
Henry I, King 12
Henry II, King 13
Henry III, King 14, 20, 21, 23
Henry IV, King, see Henry Bolingbroke
Henry IV, King of France 112
Henry V, King 50
Henry VI, King 50, 53-54, 55
Henry VII, King 62, 64
Henry VIII, King 65-67, 69, 71, 72
Henry, Lord Hunsdon 78, 79, 106
Herbert, Mary 61
Herbert, William, Earl of Pembroke 61
Herbert, William, 2nd Marquis (Marquess) of Powis 110, 119
Hermitage Farm (Stoke Farm) (Whittingham's Farm) 143, 153-155, 165, 166, 167, 168
Hertford castle 20
Hertfordshire 20
Heyford, Northamptonshire 92, 109, 115
High Street, Coventry 157, 159
Hipswell Highway, Coventry 173
Hochens, John 54
Hocking Road, Coventry 173
Holland, Dr Philemon 86
Hollar, Wenceslaus 82, 83
Holy Land 24, 55
Holy Trinity church, Coventry 64
Hopkin, Sampson 82, 83
Hopkins Hawthorne, Elizabeth 157
Hornsey 43

Horton, Thomas 69
Horton, Ann(e) see Ann(e) Try
Howard, Henry, Earl of Surrey 72
Howard, Katherine, see Lady Katherine Berkeley
Howard, Thomas, 4th Duke of Norfolk 75
Hungerley Farm 54, 173, 175
Huntingdonshire 40, 88,
Hyde Road, Coventry 173
Ingjaldsson, Olaf 37
Inner Temple, London 111
Ireland 26, 43, 51
Isabella, Queen of France 30
Isle of Ely 24
Isle of Man 25
James I, King 74, 111, 113
James II, King 131, 133
Jeacocks, Abraham 135
Jeacocks, Ann 135
Jeacocks, Elizabeth 135
Jeacocks, Joshua 134, 135
Jeacocks, Judith 135
Jeacocks, Mary 135
Jeacocks, Thomas 135
John of Gaunt 41, 45,
John, King of England 14,
John, Prince; see King John
Jones, Gill 175, 176
Jorse, William 48
Katherine, the Lady Peyto 52
Kenilworth 74, 75, 76, 107, 165, 169
Kenilworth castle 20, 28, 75, 76
Kentish Town 70
Kevelioc, Hugh, Earl of Chester, 12, 13
Kineton 63
Kineton Hundred 111
King's Head Inn, Coventry 143
Kings Langley Palace 40
Kingsley (Kingeley), John 49, 50
Kingswood Forest, south Gloucestershire 65
Kinwarton 150
Kinwarton parish church 156
Knight, Mr, steward and agent for Lord Clifford 146, 148
Knightlow Hundred 91
Kyngton, see Kineton
Lambeth 165
Lancashire 112, 113

Lancaster, Henry of 40
Lancaster, Thomas of 28
Langleys, Lords of Wyken 22, 23
Leamington Spa 166
Lee, George, the 2nd Earl of Lichfield 132, 137
Lee, Lady Anne 132, 137
Leek, John 48
Lees, Elizabeth see Elizabeth Driver
Lees, John 155
Leeward Islands 166
Leicester 14, 23
Leicester Forest 74
Leicestershire 14, 19, 20, 25, 27, 44, 45, 52, 156, 157
Lentons Lane, Coventry 143
Leofric, Earl of Mercia 10
Lewes 44
Lewes, Battle of 23
Liegrus 13, 14
Ligon, William 76
Lincoln 13
Lincolnshire 20, 23, 44, 51
Lindal Close, Battle of 113
Lisle, Thomas, Bishop of Ely 40
Lisle family 75, 76
Llanfihangel-Llantarnam, Monmouthshire 111
Llewellyn, Elisa 160
London 40, 43, 44, 45, 49, 64, 65, 73, 74, 78, 85, 86, 90, 92, 102, 111, 112, 154, 157, 162, 168
London Road, Coventry 168
Longfellow Road, Coventry 135
Long Marston 166
Lord Bedford 107
Lord Chamberlain's Men 79
Lord Dudley 107
Lords of Wyken, see Langleys 22-23
Lordship of Carlow 43
Lordship of the Manor of Caludon 39
Louis IX, King of France 21, 23
Louis XII, King of France 66
Louviers 50
Lovell, Ethel Mary 174
Lovell, Maurice William 174
Luke of Caludon 22
Luton 166
Lygon, Thomas 86, 88

Magdalen College, Oxford 76
Malory, Thomas 51-54
Maney, Sir John 113
Mangotsfield 73
Mareschal / Marchall, William, see Marshall
Margate 42
Market Harborough, Leicestershire 154, 157
Marquis of Dorset 65
Marshal, Richard, Earl of Pembroke 20
Marshall, William 13, 14, 16, 48
Marshalsea Prison 53
Marston Jabet, Warwickshire 84
Marston Sicca, see Long Marston
Mary, Queen of England 71, 72, 73
Mary, Queen of Scots 75
Maryburgh, Ireland 110, 118
Maud, Empress 12
Mauney, Sir Walter 31
Mayor of Coventry 65
Mead, Isabel (m. Maurice Berkeley V) see Isabel Berkeley
Mead, Philip 64
Melton Mowbray, Leicestershire 44
Mercia, Earl of, see Leofric
Merry and Cunningham Co, Glasgow 166
Meschines, Ranulf de, Earl of Chester 12,
Mickleton, Gloucestershire 166
Middlesex 90
Midsummer Night's Dream, A 78, 79, 80
Milan 47
Molyneux, Caryll, 3rd Viscount Molyneux of Maryburgh 118
Moyneux, Mary see Mary Preston
Monks, Hugh 52
Monks, Joan 52
Monks Kirby 52
Montague, Audrey 39
Montague, Edward 39
Montalt, Cecily 30
Montalt, Roger 30
Monte Alto, Robert de see Roger Montalt

Montfort, Simon de, Earl of Leicester 23, 26
Morgan / Preston estates trustees: 113 see John Carew Esquire, Knight, Anthony Niccols Esquire, Alexander Pym, Francis Rous Esquire, Sir Benjamin Rudyard, Oliver St John Esquire

Morgan family:
Morgan, Anthony 110, 111
Morgan, Bridget (m. Anthony Morgan c. 1597) 110, 111
Morgan, Bridget (daughter of Thomas Morgan) 110, 112
Morgan, Francis (d. 1558) 109, 110
Morgan, Francis (d. 1672) 118
Morgan, Jane see Jane Fermor
Morgan, Jane 110,111, 113-117
Morgan, Mary see Mary Saunders
Morgan, Mary (d. unmarried) 110, 112, 114, 115
Morgan, Thomas (d. 1603) 109
Morgan, Thomas (d. 1643) 92, 110-115
Morgan, Sir William of Tredegar 111

Morris, Richard 189
Morton's Yard 165

Mowbray family:
Moubray, John de see John de Mowbray
Mowbray, Anne (child heiress d. aged circa nine) 56
Mowbray, Elizabeth see Elizabeth Segrave
Mowbray, Elizabeth, Duchess of Norfolk, see Elizabeth Talbot
Mowbray, Isabel see Isabel Berkeley
Mowbray, John see John de Mowbray I
Mowbray, John de I 37
Mowbray, John de II 37
Mowbray, Sir John III 15, 31, 35-37, 39, 40,
Mowbray, John de IV 37, 40, 41
Mowbray, John V 50, 56, 61

Mowbray, John VI, 51, 53, 54, 55
Mowbray, John VII, Fourth Duke of Norfolk 55, 56, 61, 62, 63
Mowbray, Roger de 37
Mowbray, Thomas I, Earl of Nottingham 36, 39, 40, 41, 42-49
Mowbray, Thomas II 48, 49-50

Mowbray Park, Bedfordshire 48
Munich 141
Naples 85
Nash, Bob 177, 179
Nashe, Thomas 80
National Service Hostels Corporation 174
Nelson, British Columbia 166
Nevell, Agnes 54
Nevell, Jolina 54
Nevell, Robert 54
Neville, Ralph, Duke of Northumberland 50
New Farm (later Wyken Grange) 143, 153, 155
New Haven, Connecticut 119
Newbold Revel, Monks Kirby 52
Newbury, Battle of 112
Newcastle 26
Newcastle-under-Lyme 21
Newgate Prison 53
Newington 165
Norfolk 55, 74
Norham castle, Northumberland 14
Norman Conquest 45, 131
Normandy 14
North Wales 9, 43
Northampton, Battle of 55
Northamptonshire 20, 25 109, 111, 114 ,115, 119
Northumberland 14
Nottingham castle 28
Nottinghamshire 48
Odiham castle 20
Oldham Avenue, Coventry 173
Oxford 23, 76, 78 111, 112
Oxfordshire 115
Paris 85
Percy family 49
Perth 26
Pig Field (in 20th century park) 178

Plessy, Christiana 15, 26, 28
Plessy, Hugh de 26
Plessy, John de, Earl of Warwick, 26
Podmore and Gryffyn, yeomen of Warwickshire 53
Poitou 21
Pole, William de la, Duke of Suffolk 51
Pons 21
Pope Alexander IV 23
Pope Clement VI 39
Pope Gregory 72
Pope Julius II 65
Pope Paul II 61
Potters Green(e) 143, 146, 148
Pratt, Elizabeth 88

Preston family:
Preston, Anne *see* Anne Clifford
Preston, Francis 110, 118
Preston, Jane *see* Jane Morgan
Preston, John 111
Preston, Sir John Jnr 116, 118
Preston, Mary 110, 118, 119
Preston, Sir Thomas 118, 131, 132
Preston Patrick, Cumbria 110, 112, 113
Pridmore, George Alexander 153, 155
Pridmore, William Frederick 160
Priest, Derek 170
Pym, John Esq 113, 114, 116
Pym, Alexander 113, 114, 116
Pym Charles 114
Pym, Katherine 114
Queen's College, Cambridge 111
Queen's Players 107
Queens Road, Coventry 160
Radcot Bridge, Oxfordshire 43, 45
Ranulf of Stivichall 18
Redditch 162
Rempston, Thomas 48
Richard I, King 13
Richard II, King 40-49, 59
Richard III , King 56, 62
Richard, Duke of York 56, 61, 62
Richard Lee Primary School, Coventry 16
Riffane, William 48, 49
Ringers of Sowe (church) 107

River Sowe 14, 16, 17, 24, 171, 182
River Trent 25
Roches, Peter des 20
Rochester castle 20
Rockingham castle 23
Rome 31, 71, 85, 88, 131
Rooms at Caludon: 120 hall, wardrobe, darye, cellars, dynring room, servantes chamber, room next that chamber, long chamber, maides chamber, green chamber, wooll chamber, corne chamber
Rouen 50
Round Hill, Essex 112
Rugby 179
Sacheverell, Sir Richard 67, 68
Saunders, Sir Edward 109, 110
Saunders, Mary 109, 110
Sauvey castle, Leicestershire 14, 20
Savage, Anne (m. Thomas Berkeley VI) *see* Anne Berkeley
Savage, John 69
Savey, John 53, 54
Scotland 25, 26, 28, 29
Scrope, Richard, Archbishop of York 50
Seagrave, Leicestershire 14, 19, 25
Second World War 160, 172-73, 182
Segrave, Alesia de 15, 30
Segrave, Alice *see* Alesia
Segrave, Elizabeth de *see* Elizabeth Mowbray 15, 31 35, 36, 39
Segrave, Gilbert de 15, 21, 23
Segrave, John de I 15, 26-30
Segrave, John de II 15, 30, 31
Segrave, John de III 15, 30, 35
Segrave, Matilda de 15, 25, 26
Segrave, Nicholas de, d. 1295 15, 21-26
Segrave, Nicholas de, d.1325 15, 25
Segrave, Sir Stephen de 12, 14-18, 20, 21, 39
Segrave, Stephen de 29

Segrave manors;
Bretby, 25, 27
Chacombe 25

Cold Overton 25
Cotes-in-the-Elms 25
Diseworth 25
Rosliston 25
Seagrave 14, 19, 25
Sileby 25
Staunton 25

Shakespeare, William 47
Sheldon, William 111
Sheriff of Warwickshire 51
Shilton 10
Shirley, Frances, *see* Frances Berkeley
Shirley, George 60, 88
Shirley, Henry 88
Shirley, Henry (II) 88
Shirley, Mary 60, 88
Shirley, Sir Thomas 60, 88
Sieges of Caen, Louviers and Rouen 50
Skille, John 63
Skinners Farm, Potters Green 148
Sky Blue Way, Coventry 159
Slingsby, Sir Henry 113
Smithfield, London 44
Smoke Consuming Company Ltd 165
Smyth, John 62-65, 67, 68, 69, 71, 73, 74, 76, 78, 80, 81, 83, 95, 96, 90, 91, 95, 100-103, 105
Somerset 31, 64, 114, 157
Somerton, county Oxford 112
South Wales 44, 62
Southwick, Hampshire 51
Sowe *see* Walsgrave-on-Sowe
Sowe bridge 37
Sowe church, Coventry *see* (Walsgrave-on-Sowe) church
Sowe river, Coventry 37, 45, 171, 172, 182
Sowe, manor of 37
Sowe mill, Coventry 24, 84, 135
Spanne, *see* Spon End
Spon End, Coventry 17
Spon Street, Coventry 37
Sprotton, Thomas 52
Spyne, Guy 45
St Andrews chapel 83
St Augustine Friars church, London 64
St Austell Road, Coventry 173
St Ives Road, Coventry 173

St John's church, Coventry 64
St Mary the Virgin church 86
St Mary's cathedral priory, Coventry 64, 65
St Mary's hall, Coventry 65
St Michael's church, Coventry 20, 39, 81, 82, 83, 86, 89, 135, 155
St Paul's cathedral 46

Staff and servants at Caludon 100-102, *see* John Wheeler, John Prowting, Hugh Fowler, John Creswell, John Freeman, John Watson, Humfrey Ellis, Robert Kinge, Thomas Pinkerman, Ralph Heath, Roger Segar, Richard Cole, John Borlson, Barnaby Knott, Thomas Stratton, John Burnell, Ralph Heath, Roger Segar, Richard Cole

Stafford, Eleanor, Duchess of Norfolk 51, 52
Stafford, Humphrey, Duke of Buckingham 51, 52, 53
Stafford, Humphrey, of Southwick, Hants 51
Stafford, John, Archbishop of Canterbury 51, 52, 53
Staffordshire 21
Stamford Bridge, Lincolnshire 23
Stanhope, Elizabeth, 60, 91
Stanhope, Jane 60, 85
Stanhope, John, 1st Baron
Stanhope of Harrington 60, 85
Stanhope, Sir Michael 60, 85
Stanley, William 62
Staunton Harold, Leicestershire 88
Stephen, King 12
Stephens, John 153, 155
Stephens, Thomas 153, 155
Sting 106
Stirling 26
Stirling castle 26
Stivichall, Coventry *see* Styvechale
Stoke, Coventry 10, 17, 37, 54, 143
Stoke Farm (Whittingham's Farm) *see* Hermitage Farm
Stoke Field, Coventry 16, 17, 18

Stoke Gifford, Gloucestershire 65

Stoke Green, Coventry 172

Stoke Heath, Coventry 42

Stoke House, Coventry 16, 143

Stoke, Robert 24

Stoke, Robert de 24

Stoke, Robert of 18

Stoke, Saer de 18

Stoneleigh 21, 169

Stoneleigh Terrace, Queens Road, Coventry 160

Strange, Elizabeth le 36, 40, 42

Strange, Lord John le 36, 40

Strangeways, Joan, (Willoughby) (Berkeley) 60, 61, 63

Stretton-under-Fosse 120

Styvechale, Coventry 54, 84

Suffolk 55, 91, 92

Sullivan Road, Coventry 42

Sussex 44

Sutor, Gregor 37

Sybertoft, Northamptonshire 52

Talbot family:

Talbot, Elizabeth, 56, 62

Talbot, Sir Gilbert, the First Earl of Shrewsbury 56

Talbot, Sir Humphrey 56, 63

Tamworth 91

Tetbury 86

Tewkesbury, Battle of 55

Thomas, Agnes 162

Thomas, Harry 162

Thomas, John 162, 163, 165

Thomas, John junior 162

Thomas, Sarah 162

Thomas, Sarah junior 162

Thomas of Lancaster 28

Thornbury, Gloucestershire 64, 65

Thurlaston 22, 54

Tickenham, Somerset 64

Tirwin, *see* Sieges

Tomcox and Thomas Sewing Machines Companies 162, 163

Tournai 66, 67

Tower of London 53, 56, 62

Townsend, Jane 85

Townsend, Sir Roger 85

Towton 55

Tre, Thomas *see* Thomas Try

Treharn, Tom 168

Treharn, Florence 168

Trinity College, Cambridge 76, 146, 150

Try, Ann(e) 69, 71

Try, Gerrard 70

Try, Thomas 64, 67-71

Trye, Thomas *see* Thomas Try

Tusmore 115

Ugbrooke, Devon 27, 131, 133, 134, 143

Under Levens Hall, Westmorland 112

Upper Stoke, Coventry 172

Venice 48, 85

Vere, Robert de, Earl of Oxford 42, 43

Wake, Blanche 40

Wale, Sarah 149

Wale, William 149, 150, 155

Wale Brown, William 146, 148, 149, 155

Wales 23, 25, 26, 51

Wallace, William, *see* Braveheart 26

Walsgrave Hall, Coventry 149, 150, 155

Walsgrave Hospital, Coventry 174

Walsgrave-on-Sowe 16, 22, 46, 105, 135, 143, 146, 149, 150, 155, 157, 168, 172

(Walsgrave-on-) Sowe church 76, 135

Walsgrave Road, Coventry 19, 20

Walsgrove-upon-Sowe *see* Sowe

Wappenbury 109, 112, 133

Warrewyk, *see* Warwick

Warwick 30, 35, 86

Warwickshire 11, 20, 25, 29, 30, 44, 45, 48, 51, 52, 53, 54, 111, 112, 114, 115, 119, 126

Warwickshire Field Group 162

Wash Common 112

Watten 118

West, Elizabeth 60, 61

West, Reginald, Lord de la Warr 61

Westminster 62

Westminster Abbey 56

Westmorland 112

Westmorland Road, Coventry 174

Weston Hall Farm *see* Weston-under-Wetherley Hall

Weston-super-Mare 166

Weston-under-Wetherley 109, 111, 112

Weston-under-Wetherley Hall, Weston Hall 136

White Ship, the 12,

Whitefriars, *see* Fleet Street, London

Whitefriars Monastery 77, 80

Whittingham, Charles 154

Whittingham's Farm (Stoke Farm) *see* Hermitage Farm

Wickersley 166

Willenhall 135

William, Earl of Craven, 155, 156

William II, King, *see* William Rufus

William the Atheling 12

William the Conqueror 10

William Rufus 11

'William Waste All' *see* Lord William Berkeley

Willoughby family:

Willoughby, Edward 63

Willoughby, Joan (m. William Berkeley) *see* Strangeways

Willoughby, Sir John 63

Willoughby, Richard 63

Willoughby, Sir William 61

Wilmott, Mr, solicitor 148

Windsor 20, 133

Windsor castle 23, 45, 46

Willenhall 135

Winnal, *see* Willenhall

Wolston 41

Wood, Cyprian 83

Wootton Wawen 111

Worcester 23

workmen paid at Caludon 96-98 – *see* Thomas Astin, Henry Buswell, Thomas Cheyney, William Coxe, Robert Eliot, William Howe, Humfrey Kindon, Thomas Newcom, John Sarge(n)son, Robert Seabridge, Thomas Truelove

Wraxall, Somerset 64

Wright, Francis 91

Wright, John 67

Wyatt, Sir Thomas 73

Wyken 10, 16, 19, 22, 23, 29 37, 45, 54, 84, 135, 143, 155, 168, 169

Wyken Croft 169

Wyken Grange 155

Wyken House 160

Wyken Mill 22

Wyken Terrace 169

Wyken Working Men's Club 169

Yate, Gloucestershire 70, 73, 74, 88

York 37

Yorkshire 44, 166

Zouche, Sir John 76